A
Complete
AutoCAD®
Databook

A Complete AutoCAD® Databook

A. E. Hill and R. D. Pilkington

[signatures of the authors]

Prentice Hall

New York London Toronto Sydney Tokyo Singapore

First published 1990 by
Prentice Hall International (UK) Ltd
66 Wood Lane End, Hemel Hempstead
Hertfordshire HP2 4RG
A division of
Simon & Schuster International Group

Typeset in Times 10 on 12pt by Columns of Reading

Printed and bound in Great Britain by Dotesios Printers Ltd, Trowbridge, Wiltshire.

Library of Congress Cataloging-in-Publication Data

Hill, A. E.
    A complete AutoCAD® databook / by A.E. Hill & R.D. Pilkington.
      p. cm.
    Includes bibliographical references.
    ISBN 0–13–054024–2 : $45.00
      1. AutoCAD® (Computer program)   I. Pilkington, R. D.   II. Title.
T385.H544   1989
620'.00425'02855369—dc20
                                       90–6845
                                           CIP

British Library Cataloguing in Publication Data

Hill, A. E.
    A complete AutoCAD® databook.
    1. Microcomputer systems. Software packages: AutoCAD®
    I. Title II. Pilkington, R. D. (Richard D.)
    005.369

    ISBN 0–13–054024–2

---

1 2 3 4 5   94 93 92 91 90

This book is designed to provide information about AutoCAD. Every effort has been made to
make this book as complete and as accurate as possible but no warranty or fitness is implied.

The information is provided on an 'as is' basis. The authors and publishers shall have neither
liability nor responsibility to any person or entity with respect to any loss or damages arising
from the information contained in this book.

Contents

Preface

Objectives

A Complete AutoCAD Databook describes all the major features of the latest release of the industry standard draughting and design package. It is an integrated text that will appeal both to the absolute beginner with no computer experience and to the experienced AutoCAD user.

The scope of the book covers all aspects of AutoCAD usage – from the initial set-up, through the creation of simple two-dimensional line drawings to the most complex three-dimensional aspects of the package. The reader is led through this progression in an ordered, step-by-step manner. The readable style and no-nonsense approach differentiates this book from other publications in this field.

We have had many years of experience with AutoCAD from its earliest release and have set up one of the first AutoCAD Authorised Training Centres in the United Kingdom at the University of Salford. This centre was subsequently chosen by the Department of Trade and Industry as one of only six in the country to be responsible for the training of further education lecturers, themselves responsible for setting up CAD training centres nation-wide.

We have designed and taught many AutoCAD courses orientated to specific industrial requirements and to specific groups from overseas under the auspices of the United Nations.

The many industrialists and educationalists attending our courses have frequently commented on the lack of a clear, concise, easy-to-use learning guide – hence this book.

Features

A speciality of this text is that descriptions of related commands are grouped together – this permits the reader to master all aspects of a particular area of AutoCAD with ease.

The format of commands and responses is presented on the page to resemble as closely as possible the appearance of the text presented on the command line. This prepares the reader for the range of responses that may be expected when issuing a command.

Over 200 original imaginative drawings, sketches and designs in both 2D and 3D enhance and illustrate the use of AutoCAD commands and features described within the text. All the drawings were produced and plotted using AutoCAD Release 10 running on an IBM compatible '386 PC interfacing with a Calcomp 104X A1 plotter.

Fully worked examples covering simple and advanced drawing techniques are distributed throughout the text. In addition, the Appendices contain tried and tested worked tutorials plus valuable additional information on the operation of the Disk Operating System (DOS), the AutoCAD environment and the database package dBASE III+.

The construction of complex 3D designs using the advanced features of the package is covered in depth. A clear and concise explanation of the user co-ordinate system (UCS) and the surface mesh commands – fundamental to successful 3D drawing – is given and drawing tips are supplied. The structured series of worked examples in Appendix 6 is designed to help the reader to 'think in 3D' – without such assistance the transition between 2D and 3D thinking can prove to be a major barrier.

The important subject of data transfer between AutoCAD and dBASE III+ is fully explained and a worked tutorial example incorporates proven dBASE programs which may be typed in and tried.

Other advanced features covered include the generation of user-specified shapes, line types and hatch patterns, writing screen and tablet menus tailored to your own requirements and the use of script files to generate free-running presentation programmes.

The book lends itself to being used for the preparation of student-centred work sheets – as most further education courses are now being structured – with the hard-pressed lecturers being able to incorporate the clear explanations and the worked tutorials within their own material.

Supplementary Disk

As a supplement to the tutorials given in the Appendices, a 5¼-inch floppy disk (IBM PC/AT format) is available containing the following:

1. Free-running AutoCAD presentations illustrating the steps in the construction of all the 2D and 3D drawing tutorials of Appendices 5 and 6. The 3D examples are drawn 'live' under the control of a script file to give a step-by-step build-up culminating in the finished drawing. Each construction step is introduced by an explanatory slide on screen.
2. Copies of the completed tutorial drawings from Appendices 5 and 6

together with the master drawing (including all the blocks) used in the AutoCAD-dBASE transfer tutorial given in Appendix 8.
3. The full suite of dBASE III+ programs detailed in Appendix 8.

Ordering details can be found at the back of the book, on p. 324.

Acknowledgements

We are very grateful to our friend and colleague Dr R. D. Tomlinson for his help in the preparation of the explanatory section on dBASE III and for writing the dBASE III programs in Appendix 8. We also wish to thank Professor D. G. Armour, Chairman of the Department of Electronic and Electrical Engineering at the University of Salford, for his support and encouragement. Finally, thanks are due to the numerous participants on our courses who have provided comments and feedback which have been invaluable in the preparation of this book.

1 · Hardware requirements: specifying an AutoCAD PC installation

Choosing the component bits of an AutoCAD system involves making decisions on five different units:

1. Computer and keyboard.
2. VDU/Monitor and graphics board.
3. Mouse/digitiser.
4. Printer.
5. Plotter.

1.1 The Computer

This will probably be an IBM or IBM-compatible personal computer (PC) (Figure 1.1). A typical hardware configuration could be as follows:

- 640 kbyte RAM: This figure gives the size of the working memory of the computer. The larger the memory the fewer the references that must be made to the hard disk and therefore the faster the system. AutoCAD requires a minimum of 640 kbytes of RAM.

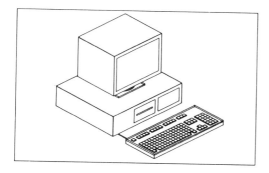

Figure 1.1 A basic computer system

- Hard disk, 10 Mbyte or larger: The hard disk stores not only the CAD software but in most cases also holds the completed drawings. A simple diagram may take up a few thousand bytes but a complicated drawing could be over a megabyte in size, so a large capacity hard disk is an advantage.
- Maths co-processor: This is an extra 'chip' which fits into the computer to speed up the calculations which are performed every time a new shape is drawn or a drawing is expanded or contracted or viewed from a different angle. The addition of such a chip can increase the speed, typically by a factor of 3. AutoCAD *requires* the co-processor to be fitted before it will operate.

The overall operating speed is limited by the rate at which the computer can do calculations. This in turn depends on the type of microprocessor chip at the heart of the machine. As time goes by machines become faster and faster. The original IBM-type machines used a processor called the 8086 but this has been overtaken by the 80286 and the 80386 and still faster processors will soon be available. A '386 machine will run CAD at least five times faster than the old machines so, as usual, 'you pay your money and you take your choice!' Future versions of AutoCAD may not be usable with 8086 machines.

1.2 The Visual Display Unit (VDU) or Monitor

The choice of a VDU is almost as important as the choice of a computer. The VDU's performance has a dramatic effect on the presentation of a drawing and on the ease with which that drawing can be produced.

VDUs come in a variety of sizes but the largest is not necessarily the best for your particular usage. Very broadly the choice of size can be summed up as follows:

14 inch	minimum	(for general desk-top use).
20 inch	professional	(for the drawing office).
26 inch	demonstration	(for teaching or board room).

A less obvious choice is between mono and colour. The VDU may operate in mono or colour or either. Mono systems may be of a higher resolution than colour for a given price but a colour system will usually be preferred.

The VDU must be driven by a graphics board inside the computer. This is an electronic circuit mounted on a board which plugs into one of the sockets inside the computer. The board and the VDU *must* be compatible both with each other *and* with AutoCAD. It is the combination of VDU and graphics board which determines the colours and resolution of the system.

There are very many manufacturers of graphics boards and VDUs, but virtually all units conform to one of the following standards:

	Colour	Resolution
Hercules	Mono only	720 × 348
IBM Colour Graphics Adaptor (CGA)	Colour/mono	640 × 200
IBM Enhanced Graphics Adaptor (EGA)	Colour/mono	640 × 350
IBM Video Graphics Adaptor (VGA)	Colour/mono	680 × 480

The cost of high-resolution colour apparatus is high and increases rapidly with the size of the VDU.

1.3 Mice and Digitisers

Although AutoCAD will allow you to input all your drawing data from the keyboard, this is a very unsatisfactory process. It is far better to be able to move the cross wires on the VDU screen by making corresponding movements with a mouse rather than by tapping the relevant keys on the keyboard.

A mouse is simply a small hand-held device which, when moved around on a suitable flat surface, sends signals to the computer which are used to position the screen cross wires (Figure 1.2). Some mice require a special optical surface to move on, others will work on any desk top. In addition, every mouse will carry at least one push button. This is used to 'pick' objects on the screen after the cross wires are in position. More versatile mice may have several additional buttons, the exact function of which can be controlled by AutoCAD's software. AutoCAD also allows you to set the function of these extra buttons to your own requirements.

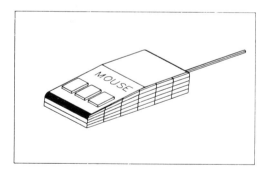

Figure 1.2 A mouse

Mice are generally inexpensive and reliable.

At first sight a digitiser seems to do the same job as a mouse but at many times the cost. It consists of a flat base-plate and a mouse-type pointer, called a puck, which may be single- or multi-button. It may be used for pointing and

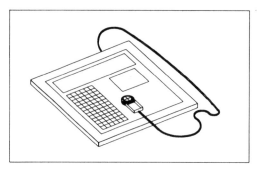

Figure 1.3 A digitiser

picking exactly as a mouse (Figure 1.3). In place of the puck some digitisers offer an alternative pen-type pointing device.

The important 'extra' that you get with a digitiser is that you can use it to give commands. A special overlay or template may be placed on the digitiser tablet which can be divided up into over a hundred small printed areas, each one representing a command or a special shape to be used in the drawing (Figure 1.4). You can then pick a command or a shape by pointing to the relevant area and pressing the pick button. This template, together with a disk of bonus programs, will be sent to you when you register your AutoCAD package.

AutoCAD allows you to design your own template and to tailor the corresponding software to accommodate the shapes and commands most useful to you. Even unique shapes which you have devised yourself can be handled in this way.

A digitiser is also essential if you wish to trace an irregular sketch for insertion into an AutoCAD drawing. The digitiser tablet can be calibrated so that the scale and orientation of the sketch are automatically accommodated.

1.4 Printers and Plotters

While digitisers and mice are input devices, printers and plotters handle output. Although both can be used to record text or drawings on paper ('hard copy devices' in the jargon) they operate quite differently from each other.

A dot matrix printer (Figure 1.5) forms its image by passing a head across the paper a line at a time. The head carries a matrix of 9 or more steel pins which can be moved in and out very rapidly under control of the computer to print a dot pattern on the paper through a typewriter-style ribbon. The process is very rapid and the resultant quality can be quite good – particularly if several head passes are made for each line. Most results are in monochrome, although expensive models using multi-stripe coloured ribbons are available.

The benefits of such a printer are:

1. Relatively cheap.

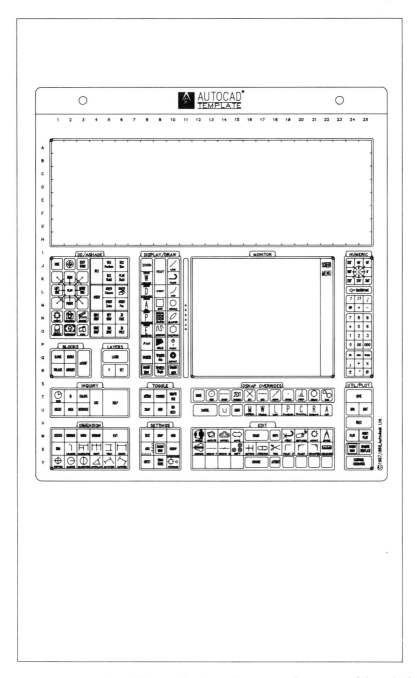

Figure 1.4 The AutoCAD standard template menu (courtesy of Autodesk Ltd)

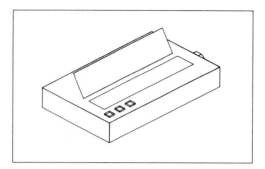

Figure 1.5 A dot matrix printer

2. Rapid printing of drawings irrespective of complexity.
3. The same printer can be used for printing documents (for instance from your word processor package).

Laser and ink-jet printers are now available which give a higher quality than dot matrix printers and which are faster in operation, although they can be considerably more expensive.

A plotter works on a principle which is entirely different from that of a printer. It consists of a pen which can be driven in both X- and Y-directions by stepping motors to trace out each element of the drawing (Figure 1.6). The computer sends data to the plotter telling it about start and end points of lines and whether the pen should be raised or lowered. It can also request a pen change to give a line a different colour or width. The drawing is built up by each object being drawn sequentially rather than by the raster-scan principle used by the printers.

Alternatively, the pen can be driven in the X-direction only and the paper can be moved in the Y-direction. The latter set-up is more usual for large plotters. A stepping motor is able to move the pen or paper in precise steps or increments. The size of one step determines the accuracy of the plotter and is typically a small fraction of a millimetre.

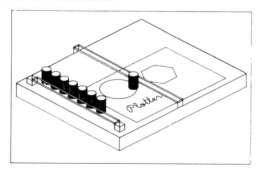

Figure 1.6 A multi pen plotter

In operation the plotter must first decide, or be told, where the origin or reference point of the drawing is. From then on it 'knows' where it is simply by counting the number of steps taken in both the *X*- and *Y*-directions. (If you nudge it and spoil its count it can become totally confused!)

Although a plotter can be expensive it has the following powerful advantages:

1. It produces professional quality drawings on a range of paper sizes (typically A4–A0).
2. Multiple pen operation is available on most plotters (typically 4–12 pens) to produce coloured drawings.
3. Special-ink pens can be used e.g. for transparent foils.

Many installations will use both a printer and a plotter – the printer to produce rapid working sketches etc. and the plotter to produce the final drawing.

2 · Running AutoCAD for the first time

2.1 Installation

AutoCAD is delivered to you on a number of floppy disks and the first task is to install the files onto your hard disk. The organisation of the files and directories on the hard disk is very much a matter of individual preferences and requirements, so it is not possible to be too specific. However, most systems will be set up something like that shown in Figure 2.1 with a system directory, called ACAD, and a number of subsidiary directories for holding the resultant drawing files and various other files which AutoCAD generates. If it is assumed that you have this structure already installed on your disk (see Appendix 1 for information about the disk operating system (DOS) and setting up directories) then you can proceed with the installation.

Place each of the floppies in turn into the floppy drive and copy their entire contents into the system directory:

    COPY A:*.* C:\ACAD

This will certainly give you a workable system although you may find that you

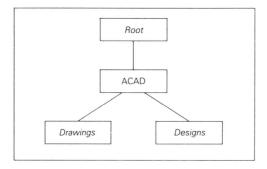

Figure 2.1 A typical directory structure

have files in your system directory that you do not really need. For instance, the driver files which enable you to configure AutoCAD to work with your own particular plotter, mouse etc., will probably not be used very often and may be used from the floppy. Similarly, you may prefer to keep the bonus disk and sample drawings material in a separate sub-directory. On the other hand, there will be some files which are not transferred onto the hard disk. Some less frequently used files are held in sub-directories on the floppies and these will not automatically be transferred by the above process. Have a look on the floppies to make a note of any such files in case you need them at a later date.

2.1.1 Don't Forget the Dongle

Depending on your country of operation, Autodesk may supply a hardware lock device, often called a dongle, which must be installed before you try to run the package. Failure to do this, or removal of the dongle while AutoCAD is running, will prevent the package from working. The dongle is plugged into the parallel printer port at the back of the computer (prior to Release 10 the dongle plugged into the serial port). If you wish to use the printer as well then this can be plugged into the back of the dongle – but you may find that the printer must be switched on before AutoCAD accepts the dongle.

2.2 Getting started

Assuming that you are in the system directory, where all the AutoCAD files are kept, or that you are in a suitable sub-directory, then to start AutoCAD running simply type ACAD at the DOS prompt:

    C› ACAD

The machine will then look for the file ACAD.EXE and this and other system files will be loaded automatically.

    If the system has previously been configured then, after a short delay, the AutoCAD main menu will be displayed. If the package has not been run previously then you will automatically be switched to the configuration routine.

2.2.1 Automatic Start-up from a batch file

Although the simple command ACAD described above may always be used to start up AutoCAD, it is more convenient to issue this command from within a batch file (see Appendix 1 for information on DOS batch files). The advantage of a batch file is that a number of commands may be issued automatically whenever the file is run. Thus, in addition to issuing the ACAD start-up command you can also include commands to SET (Appendix 1) a number of environment variables which allow AutoCAD to operate more efficiently. See Appendix 2 for a fuller explanation of AutoCAD's environment variables.

The batch file should also be used to specify the working directory and appropriate path.

EXAMPLE

An example of a typical batch file which will specify a working directory called MYFILES, a SUPPORT directory containing text fonts, menus etc. and which will set various environment variables to suitable values before running AutoCAD is given below:

PATH=C:\ACAD;\MYFILES;\	– opens a path from ACAD to MYFILES
CD\ACAD\MYFILES	– changes directory to MYFILES
SET ACADFREERAM=28	– reserves 28k of working storage area
SET LISPHEAP=42000	– reserves 42k of RAM for AutoLISP
SET LISPSTACK=2500	– reserves 2.5k of RAM for AutoLISP
SET ACAD=C:\ACAD\SUPPORT	– informs AutoCAD of SUPPORT directory
ACAD	– runs AutoCAD
CD\	– returns user to root directory

2.2.2 Hardware Configuration

AutoCAD is a large software package which may be run on a wide variety of machines with a bewildering choice of plotters, printers and digitisers. Before you can use the package it must be set up or 'configured' to work with your particular set of hardware.

In this case the package will request information on the type of VDU and graphics system in the computer, the type of plotter and whether a digitiser or mouse is to be used.

In some cases the configuration program will ask other related questions, such as whether you will be using one or two VDUs (one for the drawing and one to display the commands), which screen colours you would like etc. If in doubt about the answers to these particular questions it is probably best to accept the 'default' response which is always shown in brackets ‹›.

When configuration is complete a new file called ACAD.CFG will be written to the disk and this file will carry all the configuration data which you have just supplied. Next time you start up AutoCAD this file will be read and AutoCAD will assume that the configuration requirements are unchanged. You will thus be allowed to proceed to the main menu without being asked to configure the system.

2.2.3 The Main Menu

This is the starting point for most AutoCAD operations.

     0. Exit AutoCAD
     1. Begin a NEW drawing
     2. Edit an EXISTING drawing
     3. Plot a drawing
     4. Printer plot a drawing

     5. Configure AutoCAD
     6. File utilities
     7. Compile shape/font description file
     8. Convert old drawing file

  Enter Selection:

The **Enter Selection:** prompt is asking you to choose one of the tasks by number.

Tasks 1–4 are the most commonly used, being concerned with all aspects of drawing and plotting. Task 1 is for starting a brand new drawing. Task 2 is used to load an existing drawing from disk and to display it on screen where it may be viewed and additions or deletions made where necessary. Tasks 3 and 4 cover the tasks of making a permanent paper record of the drawing on a plotter or on a printer.

Task 5 allows you to re-configure AutoCAD (for example if you wished to use a different plotter or digitizer) without leaving the package. Task 6 is a file-handling utility allowing you to list, copy, delete or re-name files on the disk. Task 7 is used when designing special symbols or lettering fonts while Task 8 allows you to work with old AutoCAD drawings produced under earlier versions of the package.

2.3 Starting a New Drawing

To start a completely new drawing from the main menu simply type 1 followed by the 'return' or 'enter' key.

Enter Selection: 1 (Press the Return key.)

All drawings must have a title and AutoCAD will respond with a prompt for the name of the drawing. Supply a suitable name

Enter NAME of drawing: TEST (Press the Return key.)

The screen will clear while the drawing editor – the piece of software which controls all drawing operations – is loaded. After a few moments the screen is set up ready for drawing (Figure 2.2), with a screen menu down the right-hand side of the display and a command line at the bottom. The last items to appear are the cross wires which may be moved by either the digitiser or the mouse or alternatively by the arrow keys on the number pad on the right of the keyboard.

2.3.1 Coordinates

At the top of the screen you will see a pair of coordinates. These represent the position of the cross wires. As you move the cross wires these co-ordinates should change. If they do not, try pressing function key F6. This should turn the coordinates ON. If they still do not work, check your configuration and consult your mouse or digitiser manual. Some people find the continually changing co-ordinate display distracting. In this case the display may be disabled by pressing function key F6, after which the coordinates will change only when a point is selected.

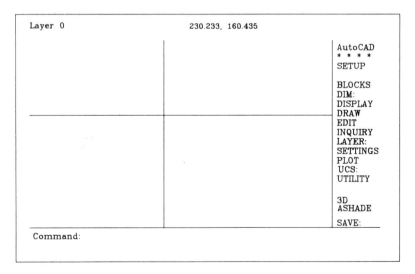

Figure 2.2 The graphics screen

2.3.2 Drawing UNITS

The coordinates at the top of the screen will show you which drawing units are specified in your prototype drawing. These can easily be changed to one of the alternative systems.

There are five different systems of drawing units. If you call up UNITS from one of the menus, or if you simply type the command UNITS, the following menu is displayed:

Systems of units:	(Examples)
1. Scientific	1.55E+01
2. Decimal	15.50
3. Engineering	1'–3.50"
4. Architectural	1'–3 1/2"
5. Fractional	15 1/2

Enter choice, 1 to 5

You have a totally free choice. Just because you are an engineer does not mean that you have to choose option 3! The alternative units are there for your convenience. When in doubt, option 2 – the simple decimal system – is probably the best.

After choosing the required system of units AutoCAD proceeds to the Angle menu:

Systems of angle measure:	(Examples)
1. Decimal degrees	45.0000
2. Degrees/minutes/seconds	45d0'0"
3. Grads	50.0000g
4. Radians	0.7854r
5. Surveyor's units	N 45d0'0" E

Enter choice, 1 to 5 ‹default›:

AutoCAD normally measures angles in degrees, taking positive angles to be measured anticlockwise from a horizontal reference (Figure 2.3). As with most of AutoCAD's units you can change all this if you wish – but it is probably better to stick with the usual notation.

The whole subject of drawing units causes unnecessary concern. Whichever system of units you choose, your drawing will always be to scale. The decimal numbers of system 2, for instance, can be thought of as millimetres or miles.

When you come to plot out your finished drawing, you will have the chance to tell the plotter either to plot it to an exact scale, say 1 millimetre on the paper = 5 drawing units, or simply to plot the complete drawing to some convenient size which will fit comfortably on the page.

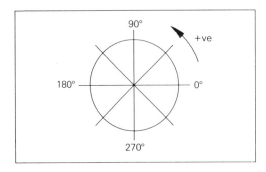

Figure 2.3 Angle conventions

2.3.3 Drawing LIMITS

People get the wrong idea about drawing limits. The name rather implies that these are limits to a drawing which can never be crossed. In fact, the idea of drawing limits is to *aid* you in laying out a drawing if it must conform to a particular size.

AutoCAD assumes that all drawings will be constructed *full size* – it is therefore useful to set the limits of the drawing to a value slightly larger than the outside dimensions of the object(s) to be drawn.

EXAMPLE

For example, if your drawing extremities are 200 mm by 100 mm, then you may find it helpful to set the system of units to decimal, the bottom left-hand limits to 0,0 and the top right-limits to 240,180.

> **Command:** LIMITS
> **ON/OFF/‹Lower left corner›‹0.00,0.00›:**
> **Upper right corner ‹400,300›:** 240,180

An ON response will set the system variable LIMCHECK (see section 2.3.7) to ON and this will warn you if you subsequently transgress the limits.

After changing the limits it should be noted that the screen will still be set to the original limits (see the coordinates – top right); to change the screen to the new limits use the ZOOM All command.

2.3.4 The UCS Icon

At the bottom left corner of the screen you will see a crossed arrows symbol (Figure 2.4). This is called the UCS (user coordinate system) icon and is used primarily when constructing 3D drawings. See Chapter 12.

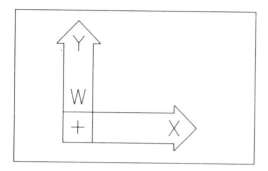

Figure 2.4 The UCS icon

Users may at first find this to be distracting, in which case the icon may be removed from the screen by the command UCSICON followed by OFF.

2.3.5 Function Keys

Many of the function keys act as toggle switches (on/off) for some of AutoCAD's most useful functions. These include the following:

F6	Coordinates on/off.
F7	Grid on/off.
F8	Ortho on/off.
F9	Snap on/off.
F10	Tablet on/off.

In addition, if your system is configured for a single VDU performing both text and graphics functions, then function key F1 acts as a toggle between the two modes.

Some of the function key commands are duplicated by control (Ctrl) keys. These are activated by holding down the Ctrl key together with the corresponding letter key.

Ctrl B	Snap on/off (see Section 3.2.1).
Ctrl C	Cancel (see Section 2.4.1).
Ctrl D	Coordinate control (see Section 2.3.1).

Ctrl E	Isoplane left/top/right (see Section 11.1).
Ctrl G	Grid on/off (see Section 3.2.3).
Ctrl O	Ortho on/off (see Section 3.2.2).
Ctrl Q	Print echo.
Ctrl T	Tablet on/off (see Section 3.5.1).

2.3.6 The Prototype Drawing

When you start a new drawing using Task 1 the drawing area will be clear, but you are in fact already using an existing drawing called ACAD.DWG. This is the *prototype drawing* supplied with the package. Although it looks blank the prototype drawing contains all the preset values and parameters which AutoCAD needs in order to operate. It can be thought of as a framework upon which your new drawing will be built.

If the prototype drawing is absent then the package will complain and return you to the main menu. You can get round the problem by responding with an = sign after your drawing name:

Enter Selection: 1
Enter NAME of drawing: TEST=   (return)

This will get you started by setting all the parameters to their default value. These values are stored as *system variables* (see Section 2.3.7). However, the problem will recur and you should at some stage recover ACAD.DWG via main menu Task 1 simply by entering the following:

Enter Selection: 1
Enter NAME of drawing: ACAD=
(Press the Return key to start a new drawing called ACAD)

Command: END
(This saves the new drawing called ACAD with the default parameter settings and returns you to the main menu)

You can use any drawing as the prototype simply by re-naming it ACAD, by saving it as ACAD or by citing it as the prototype when you start a new drawing:

Enter Selection: 1
Enter NAME of drawing: TEST=MYPROTO   (return)

This will cite the existing drawing called, say, MYPROTO, as the prototype for the new drawing TEST so that TEST is built on top of MYPROTO. If MYPROTO incorporates a feature such as a company logo or a draughtsman's name, then this will be incorporated into the new drawing automatically.

2.3.7 System Variables and the SETVAR Command

The drawing parameters which are contained in the prototype drawing are known collectively as *system variables*. Appendix 4 gives a full list of all AutoCAD's system variables for reference. They control just about everything within the drawing from its overall size down to the way the smallest point is represented. There are over 150 of these system variables – this is why the prototype drawing system is so useful. Without this you would have to set all these variables manually. As it is you can be happily unaware of the existence of the vast majority of these parameters and their function. However, as you become more adept at using AutoCAD you will need to be able to access and change the system variables within a drawing. This may be done using the SETVAR command.

Command: SETVAR
Variable name or ?:

If you respond with a ? you will be presented with the full list of all the system variables and their current values (but no explanation of what each one does – see Appendix 4). Locate the one you want, repeat the SETVAR command and supply the system variable name. AutoCAD will then respond with the current value of this variable and allow you to change it. When you save the drawing the new value will be recorded so that, when the drawing is later retrieved, the variable will remain set to the new value.

2.4 Giving Commands

You may give an AutoCAD command in any one of the following ways:

1. *From the keyboard.* The command will be echoed below the drawing area on the *command line*. The command is executed by pressing the Return key or the space bar – either immediately or after some secondary information has been typed in.

> *Note:* AutoCAD is unusual in that the space bar acts as a Return
> key – except when inputting text.
> The last command issued may be repeated simply by pressing the Return key
> or the space bar.

2. *Through the screen menu.* If the digitiser or mouse is moved beyond the extreme right of the drawing it can be used to highlight items on the screen menu. Pressing the 'pick' button causes the highlighted command to be executed. Alternatively, the screen menu area may be accessed from the keyboard by first pressing the 0/Ins key on the numeric keypad.

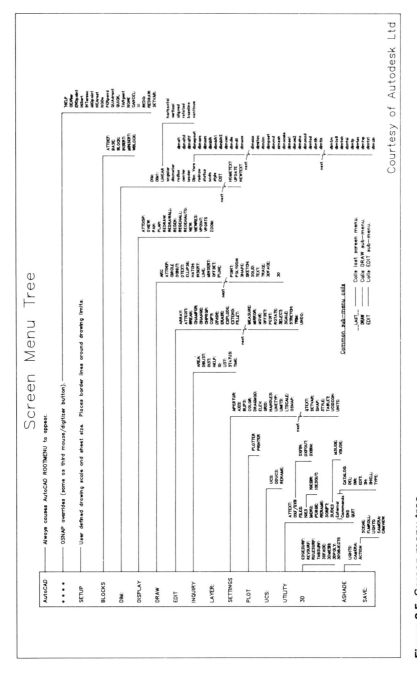

Figure 2.5 Screen menu tree

Because there is room only for a few commands to appear on the screen at any given time they are arranged into a 'tree' structure as shown in Figure 2.5. Similar types of command are grouped together on one branch of the tree. Thus all drawing commands are grouped together, as are edit commands, display commands, utility commands etc. All menus have the word AUTOCAD as the first item and *selecting this will always return you to the root or outermost menu of the tree.*

3. *Through a pull down menu.* If the digitiser/mouse points to the top of the screen then a menu bar appears – picking one of these menu items reveals a pull down menu on screen from which the desired command can be selected.

> *Note:* There is no way to access the pull down menus other than by a mouse or digitiser.

The standard pull down menu structure can be seen in Figure 2.6.

It is possible to mix command entries from the keyboard and from the menus – i.e. you can pick the main command from one of the menus and enter secondary information from the keyboard. It is useful to have some familiarity with the menu tree even if you normally enter commands from the keyboard because it gives a useful insight into the way the package is structured.

4. *Through a tablet menu.* If a digitiser is used instead of a mouse it is possible to assign areas on the digitiser surface to act as input pads for selected commands. An overlay/template placed on the digitiser tablet can then be used and the various commands picked as required. This is particularly useful when specialised symbols are to be used – a custom-designed overlay can give quick access to these non-standard shapes.

Screen, pull down and tablet menus can be purpose-designed to suit the individual user (see Chapter 15).

2.4.1 Getting Out of a Command

If you give a wrong command or if you find that AutoCAD has assumed that you wish to stay with an old command then you will need some way of getting out of it. The universal cancel command is Ctrl C – hold down the control key and at the same time press the letter C. You will find that AutoCAD releases you and returns you to the **Command:** prompt awaiting the next instruction. You will find that this cancel routine is *built in* to most of the menu commands so that picking a menu item will release you from an existing command – but be careful, this is not

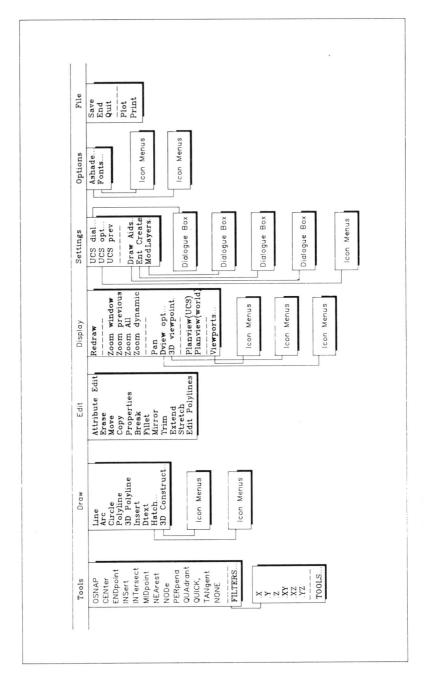

Figure 2.6 Menu bar and pull down menus

so in every case and you may have to use the manual cancel described above. Commands can also be cancelled by picking the word AutoCAD from the top of the screen menu. It is very helpful if one of the mouse or digitiser buttons is programmed to give this CANCEL command. (See Section 15.1.)

2.5 HELP

AutoCAD is a large package with over 120 major commands. These are all described in some detail in the reference manual but this is not always conveniently to hand. There is a very useful help facility built in to the package – just type HELP or pick HELP off one of the menus. If you now enter the name of the command for which help is needed the screen will display some notes that should be useful. If further help is available then the relevant page number of the manual will usually be given.

If you type a return after HELP instead of the name of a command the screen will show a complete list of all the AutoCAD commands in the package. If you are already *within* a command and require help, then type 'HELP. The relevant section of the HELP file will then be displayed. (The apostrophe (') makes the command 'transparent' which allows the command to be used while another command is in operation. See Section 3.4.4)

2.6 Saving and Quitting

There are two methods of leaving a drawing and returning to the main menu – the method you choose will depend on whether you require the drawing to be saved or not. Alternatively, you may save the drawing and remain in the drawing editor.

2.6.1 END

The END command automatically saves the current drawing before returning to the main menu. The file name used will be the current drawing name. If your drawing is a new drawing the current drawing name will be that which you supplied under main menu Task 1 to start the drawing. If the current drawing is not a brand new drawing and was retrieved from disk, then the current drawing name will be the name under which the drawing was filed. You are not allowed to have two drawings on disk with the same name so, in this case, when the drawing is saved again using END, the original version of the drawing will be converted to a backup file (extension .BAK) while the new updated drawing will be saved in a drawing file (extension .DWG) with the original filename (Figure 2.7).

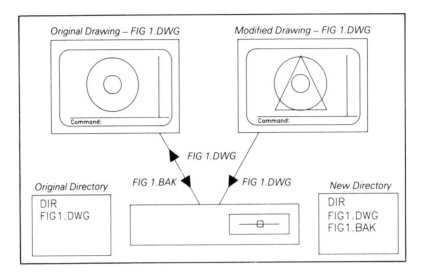

Figure 2.7 Saving an updated drawing

Command: END

2.6.2 QUIT

The QUIT command returns the user to the main menu without saving the current drawing. If an old drawing has been recalled for editing and it is decided that the changes made should not be saved, then QUIT will keep the original drawing file intact and discard any alterations. When using QUIT, AutoCAD will respond with the question **Really want to discard all changes to drawing?** This is a safety feature and if the answer is yes then the user must respond by typing Y from the keyboard.

Command: QUIT
Really want to discard all changes to drawing?: Y

2.6.3 SAVE

It is normal to save a drawing periodically to disk without leaving the drawing editor. This protects the work from accidental loss during its construction but avoids the bother of having to return to the main menu and then re-load the drawing.

Command: SAVE **File name** ‹current file name›:

The current drawing name comes up as the default but, in contrast to the END command, you now have the opportunity to ignore it and substitute a new name. This is very useful if you wish to retain an old drawing intact and save modified versions of it with new titles.

2.7 File Handling and File Types

There are two ways in which AutoCAD allows the user to manipulate files; one leaves the operator in the drawing editor while the other is a task on the AutoCAD main menu – Task 6. Both methods take the user to the file utility menu.

2.7.1 File Handling from the Main Menu

To access the file utilities from the main menu select **6. File utilities**. The file utility menu will appear. Files can be listed, deleted, renamed or copied.

2.7.2 File Handling from within the Drawing Editor

While remaining in the drawing editor the command FILES can be used. Once the FILES command has been invoked the file utility menu appears.

> **Command:** FILES
>   **File Utility Menu**
>   **0 Exit file utility menu**
>   **1 List drawing files**
>   **2 List user specified files**
>   **3 Delete files**
>   **4 Rename files**
>   **5 Copy files**

For all options other than Task 1 the full file name and extension must be given.

1. **List drawing files.** If the user requires to see the drawing files then selection 1 will give a list of all the files with the extension .DWG. AutoCAD needs to know which disk drive and directory to search and will therefore respond:
   Enter drive or directory:
   (press Return for the default directory.)

2. **List user specified files.** This option allows the user to specify an exact file or group of files, AutoCAD will then search the specified drive for files which

match the input criteria. The user can again specify the path to a sub-directory on a given drive. Wild cards such as ? and * can be used as with standard DOS commands.

There are various file types associated with AutoCAD; each has its own special extension which is automatically added by the AutoCAD package:

.bak	Drawing file back-up
.dwg	Drawing file
.dxb	Binary drawing interchange file
.dxf	Drawing interchange file
.dxx	Attribute extract file (dxf format)
.igs	IGES interchange file
.lin	Linetype library file
.lsp	AutoLISP program library file
.lst	Printer plot output file
.mnu	Menu source file
.mnx	Compiled menu file
.old	Original version of converted drawing file
.pat	Hatch pattern library file
.plt	Plot output file
.scr	Command script file
.shp	Shape/font definition source file
.shx	Shape/font definition compiled file
.sld	Slide file
.slb	Slide library
.txt	Attribute extract or template file (cdf/sdf format)

3. **Delete files.** Delete files is used primarily if there is lack of space on a drive to save the current drawing. Files such as back-up files can then be deleted to make room. AutoCAD will ask if the file specified should really be deleted from the disk – if you are sure then respond with a Y.

4. **Rename files.** This option allows the changing of an existing file name to a new name specified by the operator. *Remember to include the file extension.*

    Enter current filename: file1.dwg
    Enter new filename: file2.dwg

It also allows files to be transferred between directories, but not between disks.

    Enter current filename: /dir1/file1.dwg
    Enter new filename: /dir2/file2.dwg

5. Copying files. This allows the copying of files from one disk drive to another.

Enter name of source file: A:filename.dwg
Enter name of destination file: C:filename.dwg

3 · Simple two-dimensional construction

As described in the previous chapter, commands can be issued from the keyboard, from the digitiser tablet or from the screen menus. You should practise with each method and find the one which suits you best. For consistency we will assume the use of the pull downs unless otherwise stated.

However, even if you are using the pull down menus you should always keep an eye on the command line at the bottom of the screen where useful prompts and messages are displayed.

You will find that AutoCAD will sometimes respond slightly differently, depending on which method you choose. For example, if you draw a circle using commands from the keyboard, then only one circle will be drawn, but if you use the pull down menu AutoCAD will assume that you wish to go on drawing circles until you tell it to stop (with a Ctrl C command) or until you give another command from a pull down menu. Don't worry – this is simply because the keyboard command is the basic AutoCAD command but the version from the pull down may have been slightly modified by the person who wrote the menu. When you become more skilled with AutoCAD you will be able to write your own menus – or modify other people's (see Chapter 15).

3.1 Basic Entities

3.1.1 LINEs

One of the simplest drawing entities is a line. Select LINE from the **Draw** pull down menu (Figure 3.1).

Command: LINE

The command line will prompt for a starting point with

From point:

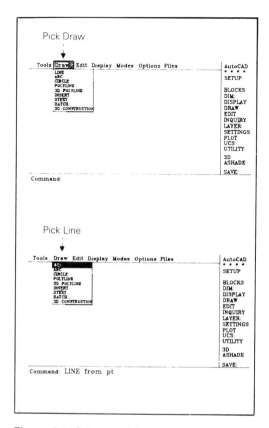

Figure 3.1 Selecting LINE from the Draw menu

To indicate the starting point you may move the cross wires to the required position with the digitiser/mouse and press the Pick button. You will then see that the start point has been fixed and an elastic band cursor joins this point to the current position of the cross wires. The command line prompts for the next point with the words

To point:

The process can be continued indefinitely. When the last point has been specified the command can be terminated by pressing either the Return key or the space bar, after which the elastic band cursor disappears.

> *Note:* If you called the LINE command from the pull down menu then the command will be repeated indefinitely until terminated by CTRL C or by picking another command from a pull down.

An alternative to 'pointing' with the digitiser/mouse is to specify the *absolute coordinates* of the various points from the keyboard.

EXAMPLE

> **Command:** LINE   **From point**   100,120
> **To point:**   50,20

The values of the *XY* coordinates of each point on the line are specified individually.

Alternatively, you may use *relative co-ordinates*, which means that you specify the *X*- and *Y*-distances from the last point on the line to the next point.

EXAMPLE

> **To point:** @200,30

This will result in the next point on the line being located 200 drawing units horizontally and 30 drawing units vertically beyond the previous point. The @ symbol indicates that you are using relative coordinates.

Finally, you may use *relative polar co-ordinates*. These specify the length and the angle of the new line segment relative to the last point on the line (Figure 3.2).

EXAMPLE

> **To point:** @50<45

---

results in a new line segment of length 50 drawing units drawn at an angle of 45 degrees to the horizontal. Remember AutoCAD normally measures angles in degrees, taking positive angles to be measured anticlockwise.

If you make a mistake and wish to remove the last segment of a line it is possible to do this without exiting the LINE command. If you respond to the **To point:** prompt with U (for UNDO):

> **To point:** U

this erases the last segment. Multiple Us backtrack through the line segments, erasing the most recent one each time.

If the last segment of your line is intended to *close* the figure, i.e. to return to the starting point, this can be done automatically by responding with C (Figure 3.3):

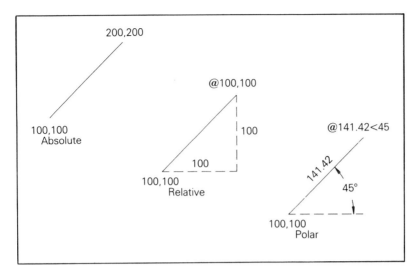

Figure 3.2 Coordinate types

To point: C

If in response to the **From point:** prompt you answer with a return this will take the initial point of the new line to be the final point of the line or arc drawn previously. This is called *continuation mode.*

The start and end coordinates of a line may also be specified in three dimensions by including a *Z* coordinate. See Section 12.3.1.

3.1.2 CIRCLEs

Call up CIRCLE from the pull down menu.

Command: CIRCLE

A screen menu will now appear asking you to choose a method for specifying the circle. This is echoed on the command line

3P/2P/TTR/‹Center point›:Diameter/‹Radius›:

This response is rather confusing. AutoCAD is offering alternative ways of drawing circles. Thus 2P will draw a circle through two specified points on a

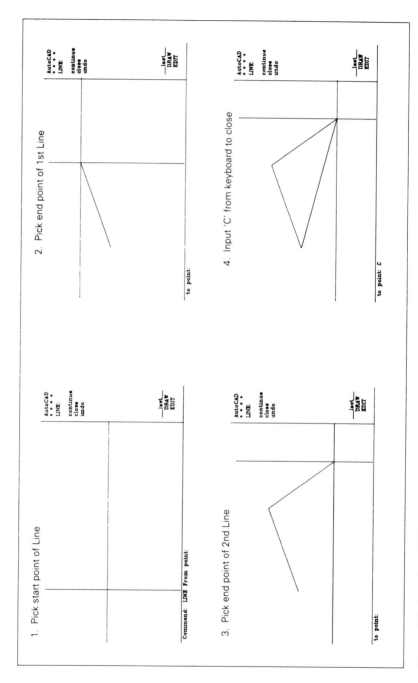

Figure 3.3 Drawing LINEs

diameter, 3P will draw the unique circle passing through any three specified points, and TTR will draw a circle of specified radius which is tangential to two other objects.

However, you will probably not use these more complicated circle routines very often and the remaining methods, Center,Rad and Center,Dia are the simplest.

To draw a circle using Center,Rad simply select a centre point with the mouse/digitiser. The command line will now prompt for a radius. An elastic band cursor will indicate the appearance of circles with this centre and with a radius as specified by the cross wires. When you are satisfied with the size of the circle, press the pick button and the circle will be drawn in.

Alternatively, the centre point and/or the radius may be specified numerically from the keyboard.

Use of Center,Dia is similar except that, after setting the centre point, the cross wires are used to indicate the diameter rather than the radius (Figure 3.4).

3.1.3 ARCs

Arcs are called up by the ARC command and the drawing technique is similar to that for circles. However, AutoCAD allows the arc to be specified in 8 different ways and this again can lead to confusion. The simplest technique is to use the three-point method. (If you are giving commands from the keyboard this is the

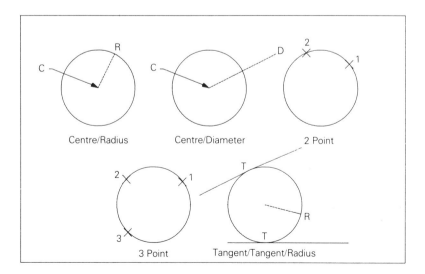

Figure 3.4 CIRCLE definition options

default route as indicated by the angle brackets ‹›). This defines the unique arc which passes through three specified points.

> **Command:** ARC **Center/‹Start point›:**   (Supply start point)
> **Centre/End/‹Second point›:**   (Supply second point.)
> **End point:**   (Supply end point.)

The other routes for specifying an arc are shown in Figure 3.5. The default routes are shown as dotted paths at each decision point. Some duplication occurs in the process – for example there are three possible routes for drawing an arc with specified centre, second point and end point – but other routes are unique and offer useful alternatives for arc specification.

Arcs may also be called up from the screen menu but here the different routes are identified by initials. Thus SCE refers to definition by start point, centre and end point; CSA by centre, start point and the included angle, etc.

The final route is called *Continuation mode*. This may be picked up from the last item on the screen menu or by responding with a return at the first ARC prompt from the keyboard. The effect is to make the end point of the previously drawn line or arc be the start point of the new arc. Since this also specifies the initial direction it is only necessary to supply the End point for the arc to be drawn.

Remember – AutoCAD draws circles and arcs anticlockwise by default. Therefore if the arc you specify goes the wrong way then reverse your start and end points.

A common use of arcs is shown in Figure 3.6, where a triangle may be constructed from a knowledge of the lengths of each of the sides.

3.1.4 ELLIPSEs

The ELLIPSE command can specify an ellipse in a number of ways, as shown in Figure 3.7. The default route is to specify one axis of the ellipse by defining its two end points, P1 and P2. The second axis is then defined as a distance from the centre point of this axis to P3. Alternatively, the first axis may be defined from a centre point and P2.

> **Command:** ELLIPSE
> **‹Axis endpoint 1›/Center:**
> **Axis endpoint 2:**
> **‹Other axis distance›/Rotation:**

Instead of specifying the point P3, the 'roundness' of the ellipse may be set by an angle of Rotation. If this route is taken, the points P1 and P2 are considered as

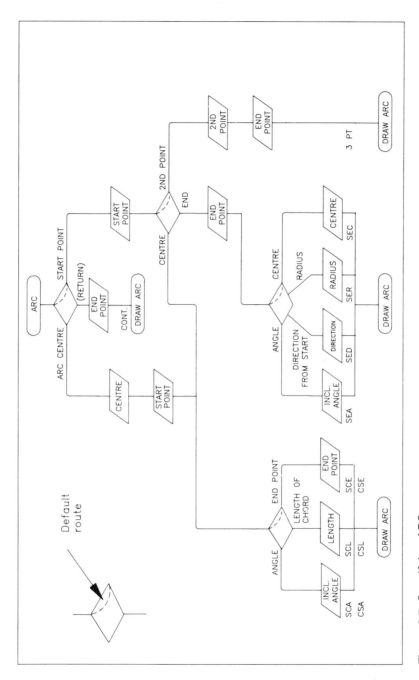

Figure 3.5 Specifying ARCs

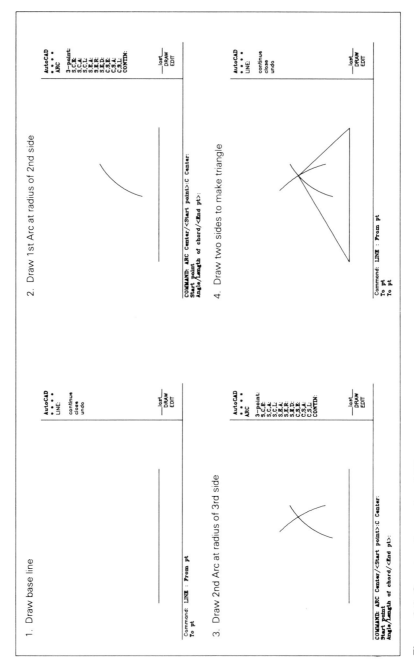

Figure 3.6 Construction using ARCs

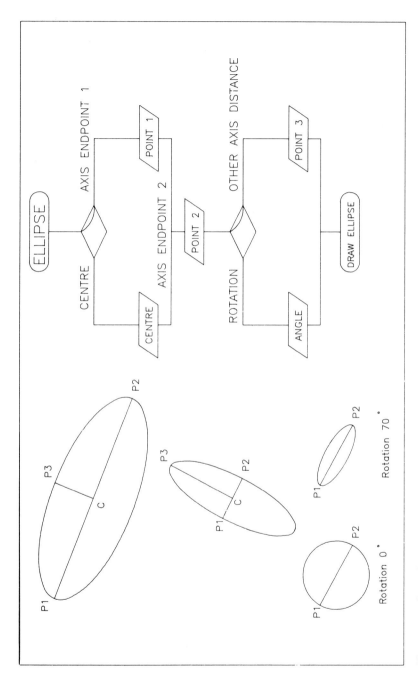

Figure 3.7 Specifying ELLIPSEs

points on the diameter of a circle. If the angle of rotation is set at 0° then the ellipse is drawn circular, i.e. as a circle viewed from above. As the rotation angle increases towards 90° the circle is assumed to be rotated, presenting an increasingly elliptical view and tending to a straight line at an angle of 90°. (The package will accept angles only up to 89.4°.)

3.1.5 POLYGONs

This is a useful command for drawing regular shapes with between 3 and 1024 sides.

> **Command**: POLYGON
> **Number of sides**: 5
> **Edge/‹Center of polygon›**:   (Supply a centre point.)
> **Inscribed in circle/Circumscribed about a circle (I/C):**

If you reply with I you will be prompted for the radius of the circle within which the polygon will just fit. If you reply with a C you will be prompted for the radius of the circle which the polygon will just fit around (Figure 3.8).

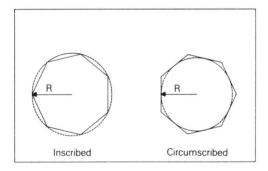

Figure 3.8 POLYGON definition

If you reply with E at the earlier prompt:

Edge/‹Center of polygon›: E

you can specify the size and position of the polygon by giving the two end points of one of the sides or edges.

Although it may seem complicated at first sight, POLYGON is a really useful command – try using it for drawing squares or triangles for instance.

3.1.6 DOUGHNUTs or DONUTs

This command will draw filled circles or rings.

>**Command:** DOUGHNUT   (or DONUT)
>**Inside diameter:** 25
>**Outside diameter:** 80
>**Center of doughnut:**   (Supply centre point.)

Even when DOUGHNUT is called up from the keyboard, this last prompt is repeated indefinitely (until terminated with a return) allowing the figure to be replicated at will.

    If a solid doughnut (without the hole in the middle) is required the internal diameter may be set to zero.

    The doughnut is normally drawn as a 'solid' figure i.e. FILLed in. This can be changed to an unfilled figure if the FILL command is used to switch the fill function off (Figure 3.9):

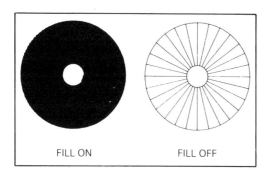

        FILL ON   FILL OFF

Figure 3.9 DOUGHNUT – FILL On/Off

>**Command:** FILL **ON/OFF**‹default›

3.1.7 POINTs

The POINT command allows the positioning of a point on the drawing.

>**Command:** POINT **point:**

The POINT can be positioned using a mouse, a digitiser or by entering the *XY* coordinates.

    Two system variables control POINT mode: PDMODE controls the style of the point (see Section 6.1.14) whilst PDSIZE controls its size. PDSIZE can be set both positive and negative; a positive value causes all points to be an absolute size, a negative value gives the point a relative size so that it always appears the same size on the screen (after a regeneration).

> *Note:* When changing PDMODE it is possible to have a number of different POINT styles on the screen at one time. This is an illusion – after regeneration *all* the points will assume the current PDMODE style.

3.2 Aids to Construction

The drawing modes **Snap, Grid, Ortho, Axis, Blip** etc are provided as drawing aids to make life easier. Correct and frequent use of these aids is one of the secrets of getting the most out of AutoCAD. These modes can be toggled ON/OFF as many times as you like during the drawing but this does *not* affect the default setting. If you wish to change the defaults then use the SETVAR command.

3.2.1 SNAP

The Snap mode causes an imaginary rectangular grid to be set up; all input coordinates are then locked onto the intersections of the grid. When Snap is in operation you will see that the cross wires 'snap' from one intersection point to the next – it is impossible to force them to take up an intermediate position.

Snap allows the input of accurately placed points and the perfect alignment of lines, circle centres and other entities. The size of the imaginary grid (grid spacing) is referred to as the Snap resolution and can be altered at any time. (To make this grid visible, see the GRID command.)

The Snap mode may be invoked by typing SNAP

Command: SNAP
Snap spacing or ON/OFF/Aspect/Rotate/Style‹10›

The Snap options are:

> **On**   The ON option invokes the previous Snap grid resolution.
>
> **Off**   The OFF option deactivates Snap but remembers the settings so that they can be reactivated.
>
> **S**pacing   If you respond to the Snap option prompt with a numeric input, Snap will be activated using the input as the Snap resolution, e.g. if the value is 10 then the Snap grid will be set up with a resolution of 10 drawing units.

Aspect   The spacings along the *x*- and *y*-axes are normally equal but they can be independently set using this option. If the aspect option is not invoked the *x*- and *y*-spacings will default to the same value.

Rotate   The Snap grid can be rotated about a designated point between −90 and 90 degrees. A positive angle rotates the grid counterclockwise whereas a negative angle rotates the grid clockwise.

Style   There are two *Styles* available: Standard and Isometric. Standard refers to the standard rectangular grid. Isometric refers to a grid designed for isometric drawing with grid points aligned at 30, 90, 150, 210 and 330 degrees (Chapter 11).

It is not necessary to use the SNAP command simply to switch Snap on and off – this can be done at any time, even from within another command, by pressing either Ctrl B or function key F9. Repeated use of these keys has the effect of toggling Snap on and off. You can easily keep track of this because, when Snap is On, the word Snap is displayed in the top left-hand corner of the drawing.

3.2.2 ORTHO

Ortho mode is used primarily with the LINE command. It ensures that all lines are drawn orthogonal with respect to the current Snap grid. Assuming that the snap style is standard i.e. the grid has not been rotated, then all lines or traces will be either vertical or horizontal (Figure 3.10). If the Snap grid has been rotated then the ortho rotates accordingly; the same applies to the isometric Snap style mentioned above.

Command: ORTHO **ON/OFF**:

Alternatively, Ortho can be toggled using either Ctrl O or function key F8. Like Snap, the current state of Ortho is displayed in the top left-hand corner of the drawing.

Ortho is certainly a useful aid but the beginner may well find the behaviour of the elastic band cursor very confusing when Ortho is operative. It is not recommended that Ortho be switched on all the time.

3.2.3 GRID

The GRID command displays a reference grid of dots with any desired spacing and is displayed over the area specified by the limits. It is usually set up so that the grid dots occur at the Snap intersection points, thus making them visible. The

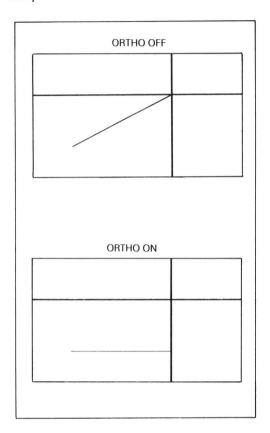

ORTHO OFF

ORTHO ON

Figure 3.10 ORTHO

grid is not part of the drawing and will not be reproduced when the drawing is plotted out. It is used purely as a drawing aid to give a 'feel' for the size of drawing entities.

Command: GRID
Grid spacing(X) or ON/OFF/Snap/Aspect‹20›

The main options **Spacing, ON, OFF** and **Aspect** have the same function as the Snap options of the same name.

> **Snap** The Snap option provides a method of locking the grid to the set Snap resolution. If the value of the Snap resolution is altered the grid is automatically changed to the new Snap value. A numerical spacing of 0.000 has the same effect.

3.2.4 AXIS

The AXIS command can be used to place graduation marks on the drawing axes which, like grid, are helpful in maintaining a feeling for the scale of a drawing. However, again like grid, they are *not* part of the drawing and will not be reproduced on a plot.

Command: AXIS
Tick spacing (X) or ON/OFF/Snap/Aspect‹0.0000›

3.2.5 BLIPMODE

The Blip mode provides a temporary mark, +, on the screen whenever you pick an object or place a point within the drawing. For example, when drawing a circle, the first requirement is to position the centre point. A blip mark will be placed at this point. It is only temporary and will be erased on REDRAW, REGEN, ZOOM and PAN. Blips are used primarily as construction marks. If you wish you can disable the blips:

Command: BLIPMODE **ON/OFF**‹current›:

3.2.6 Setting the Mode from the Pull Down Menu – Dialogue boxes

The pull down dialogue boxes give an 'at a glance' display of some of the current drawing parameters and provide a very convenient means of changing them within the drawing. There are four dialogue boxes which may be accessed from the pull down menu, (under **Settings**) or from the keyboard.

Menu Item	Keyboard Command	Options
Drawing Aids (Figure 3.11)	DDRMODES	Grid Snap Ortho Axis Blip
Entity Create (Figure 3.12)	DDEMODES	Colour Linetype Layer name Elevation Thickness
Modify Layer (Figure 3.13)	DDLMODES	On/Off Freeze/Thaw New Set Colour Linetype
UCS Dialogue (Figure 3.14)	DDUCS	User coordinate system data

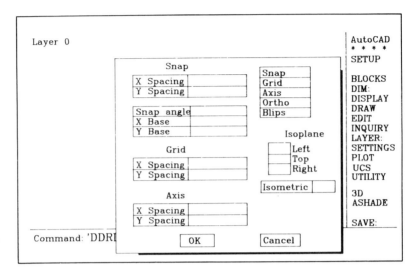

Figure 3.11 Drawing Aids dialogue box

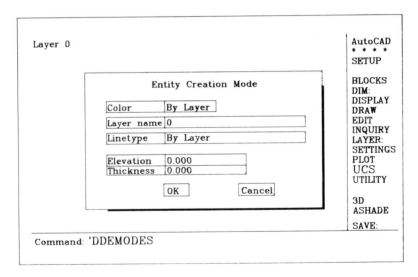

Figure 3.12 Entity Creation dialogue box

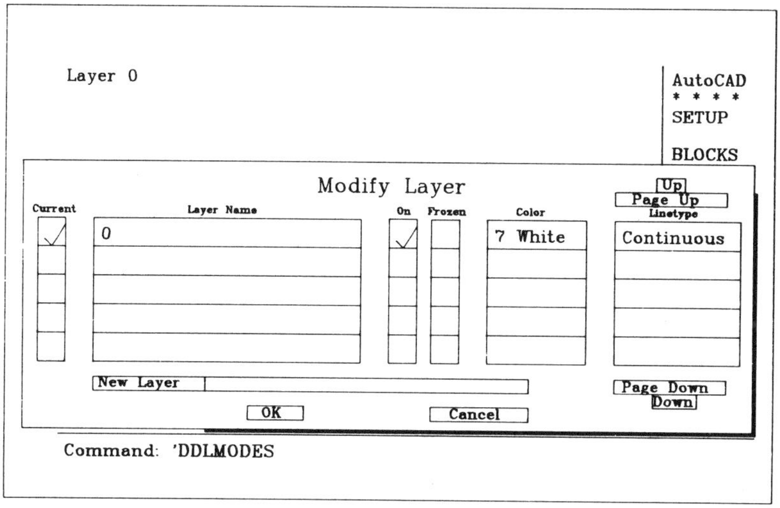

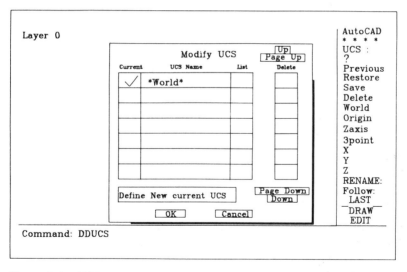

Figure 3.13 Layer dialogue box

Figure 3.14 UCS dialogue box

The drawing aids dialogue box gives immediate access to the Snap, Grid, Ortho, Axis and Blip modes and is probably the most convenient way to set their values. If you wish to toggle one of the mode settings, move the screen arrow to the relevant section of the dialogue box and press the pick button to set the tick symbol. When you are satisfied with all the mode settings you must tick the OK box to return to the drawing.

The dialogue boxes may also be called up via the keyboard with the commands:

DDRMODES   to access the drawing aids dialogue box.
DDEMODES   to access the entity creation dialogue box.
DDLMODES   to access the layer control dialogue box.
DDUCS   to access the UCS dialogue box.

3.2.7 Setting and Saving a Mode using SETVAR

If you wish to make a more permanent change to Snap, Grid, Ortho, Axis and Blip then SETVAR should be used together with the corresponding system variables SNAPMODE, GRIDMODE, ORTHOMODE, AXISMODE and BLIPMODE. These changes will then be saved with the drawing, whereas changes made via the commands SNAP, GRID, ORTHO etc or via a dialogue box are only temporary.

3.3 Editing

3.3.1 Selecting Objects

When editing a drawing it is necessary first to select the objects which are to be edited. AutoCAD has a number of different selection modes including:

• pointing to a specific object
• using one of the window commands (window or crossing; Figure 3.15)
• selecting the last object drawn
• selecting a set of previously selected objects.

When any of the editing commands is invoked AutoCAD automatically drops into its SELECT routine to allow you to build up a *selection set*. The cross wires are temporarily replaced by a small square called the pickbox. The size of this box may be adjusted by using the SETVAR command to alter the value of the system variable PICKBOX.

The command line gives the prompt:

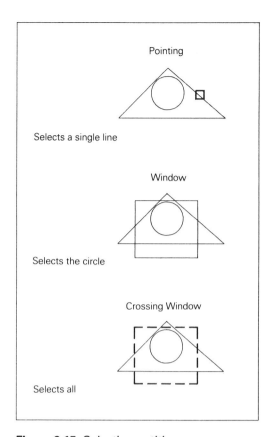

Figure 3.15 Selecting entities

Select objects:

Point   Whenever the select objects routine is invoked a small square box
appears instead of the cross wires; this can be moved around the screen
with the mouse, 'picking' the objects to be selected. As always, keep an
eye on the command line – this will tell you when an object has been
selected, when it is a duplicate selection and so on. The select routine
will allow you to continue indefinitely until you turn it off with a
Return. This signifies that the selection set is complete.

Remove   An R at the **Select objects:** prompt changes the prompt to
Remove objects: and allows you to remove subsequently selected
objects from the selection set. This is useful if you have included some
objects by mistake.

Add   After removing objects from a selection set you can return to the
default **Select objects:** prompt, Addition mode, by entering an A.

Undo If an object(s) is selected by mistake its selection can be cancelled by using Undo. This may be applied repeatedly to step back and undo previous selections.

Window Inputting a W at the **Select objects**: prompt allows the user to use the mouse to specify two opposite corners of a window. Any objects *totally* enclosed by this window will be selected. After this you will be returned to point selection mode and selection can continue.

Crossing Inputting a C at the **Select objects**: prompt again allows the user to specify two corners of a window. Any objects enclosed *or touched* by the crossing window will be selected, after which you will be returned to point mode. The crossing window is displayed as a dashed box to differentiate it from the standard window.

Last Inputting an L at the **Select objects**: prompt selects the last object drawn.

Previous Inputting a P at the **Select objects**: prompt selects the previously selected objects set.

BOX Inputting BOX at the **Select objects**: prompt lets the user specify two corners of a window (as for Window and Crossing). If the second point is to the right of the first then a standard window is invoked, if it is to the left then a crossing window is invoked.

AUto Inputting AU at the **Select objects**: prompt puts the select mode into automatic selection mode. A point is first requested for a single object selection. If no object is found when the pick button is pressed then the point selected will become the first corner of the BOX sub-command (Figure 3.16)

Note: If the select routine is invoked within a command called from a pull down menu you may find that a full selection set is not built up before the main command is executed. Selection and execution are repeated as often as required. As explained earlier, this is because the command from the menu is operated as a mini program and uses more than the 'raw' AutoCAD commands.

3.3.2 ERASE

The ERASE command allows specific entities to be removed from the drawing.

Command: ERASE
Select objects: (Assemble the desired selection set.)

Erase is a clear example of a command which behaves differently when invoked from a pull down compared with simply typing the command from the command line. When called from the pull down, each selected sub-set is erased as soon as it

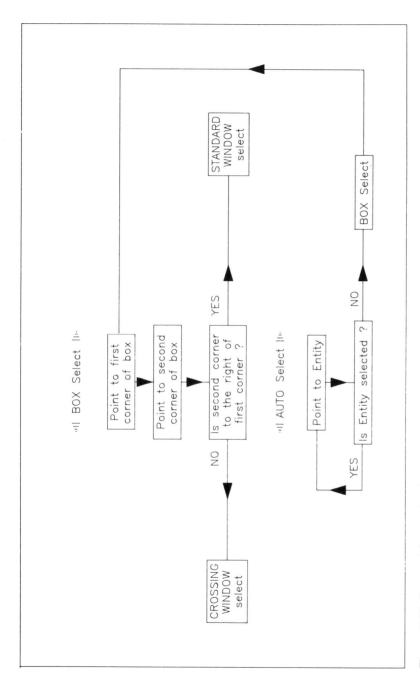

Figure 3.16 Box and Auto selection

is chosen (by pointing or windowing etc.) and then the **Select objects**: prompt returns to allow further selection. Auto mode is the normal mode in this case. Last can be used to erase the last entity to be drawn; if it is repeated then you can step back through the drawing, erasing entities in the reverse order to that in which they were drawn.

3.3.3 OOPS

The OOPS command restores entities which have been inadvertently erased. OOPS will only be effective if invoked *immediately* after an ERASE command.

3.3.4 U and UNDO

The simplest way to undo an error is to use the command U. This simply undoes the previously executed command.

> **Command:** U

> AutoCAD responds with the name of the previously executed command.
> The UNDO command is more comprehensive than the U command and in
some ways is over complicated.

> **Command:** UNDO
> **Auto/Back/Control/End/Group/Mark/‹Number›:**

If you wish to step backwards through the drawing undoing one command at a time then it is sufficient to respond repeatedly with Returns (this is the same as repeated use of the U command).

Alternatively, you may undo a specified number of previous commands at a single stroke by responding to the above prompt with the required number.

All previous commands may be undone in a single operation by responding with Back. This in effect completely erases any new drawing produced under Task 1 of the main menu or any new modifications to an existing drawing introduced under Task 2. This is an extremely powerful aspect of the UNDO command and should be used with care. If you wish to limit the scope of the Back option then you may insert a Mark at any point during the construction of a drawing and this will act as a stop beyond which UNDO Back is inoperative.

Control may be used to limit the scope of the UNDO command so that it may either be totally disabled or limited to a single operation. End and Group are little used except in customised menu writing.

3.3.5 REDO

REDO is only active after an UNDO or U has been performed. It may be used to recover those commands which were removed by the *single preceding* UNDO or U command.

3.3.6 MOVE

The MOVE command allows the movement of entities from one position on the drawing to another. Once the objects to be moved have been selected AutoCAD will ask for two points of displacement, these are the 'Base point' (move from) and the 'Second point' (move to).

> **Command:** MOVE
> **Select objects:** (Assemble the desired selection set.)
> **Base point or displacement:**
> **Second point of displacement:**

If you respond to **Base point** with DRAG this allows you to drag the selected objects around the drawing to the correct position if the DRAGMODE system variable is set to ON. If the DRAGMODE system variable is set to AUTO, drag will be invoked automatically. See Section 3.3.10.

3.3.7 COPY

The COPY command is similar to the MOVE command but instead of moving the selected objects around the drawing it places copies of the selected object(s) at the specified point(s), leaving the original(s) intact.

> **Command:** COPY
> **Select objects:** (Assemble the desired selection set.)
> **‹Base point or displacement›/Multiple:**
> **Second point of displacement:**

Each copy is totally independent of the original and can be edited etc. as if drawn as a separate entity (Figure 3.17).

Multiple copies of the selected objects can be made by answering Multiple after the objects have been chosen. Repeated copies of the selected items can then be positioned throughut the drawing.

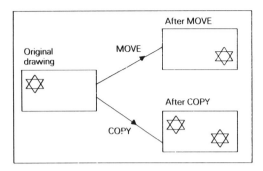

Figure 3.17 COPY and MOVE commands

3.3.8 ROTATE

Entities can be rotated about a specified point by a specified number of degrees.

Command: ROTATE
Select objects: (Assemble the desired selection set.)
Base point: (This is the point about which rotation will occur.)
‹Rotation angle›/Reference:

A positive angle will rotate the selected objects anticlockwise. Responding with an R invokes reference mode which allows the specification of a reference or base angle. The new value of this angle is then supplied and AutoCAD calculates the degree of rotation necessary to achieve this.

3.3.9 MIRROR

The MIRROR command allows mirror images of selected objects to be made, while allowing the original objects to remain or be erased as required.

Command: MIRROR
Select objects: (Assemble the desired selection set.)
First point of mirror line:
Second point:
Delete old objects?‹N›

The mirror line represents the axis about which the objects are mirrored and can be at any orientation. The selected object(s) may be deleted or left in its original position as required.

If an object and its connected text are mirrored then the text will also be a mirror image of the original and so will not be much use. To mirror objects and their connected text but keeping the text readable, use the MIRRTEXT system variable. Set MIRRTEXT to 0 (default value = 1) using the SETVAR command (Figure 3.18).

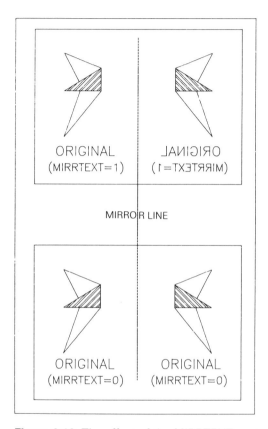

Figure 3.18 The effect of the MIRRTEXT system variable

3.3.10 DRAGMODE

DRAG is used in conjunction with editing commands such as COPY, MOVE, SCALE, ROTATE etc., and also some of the drawing commands e.g. for circles arcs and polylines. It allows dynamic dragging of the chosen object about the drawing area to the required position.

DRAG is accessed using the DRAGMODE command:

Command: DRAGMODE
ON/OFF/AUTO‹current›:

If DRAGMODE is set to AUTO it will automatically be invoked when a command is used which supports drag. In some instances, depending on the speed of your computer, the process of dragging can be time consuming. Under these circumstances DRAGMODE can be set to ON – it will only then be activated if the subcommand DRAG is executed with a command which supports it.

The initial setting of the DRAGMODE system variable is governed by the default value which is set by the prototype drawing.

3.4 Display Controls

As their name implies, the display controls allow you to alter the way a drawing is displayed on the screen. They *do not* alter the drawing itself – in particular, the size of the drawing in terms of drawing units will be unchanged.

3.4.1 REDRAW

This causes the redrawing of the current screen display, deleting any blips present and redrawing objects which have been partially erased from the screen (but not from the drawing) due to editing of other objects.

3.4.2 REGEN

This completely regenerates the entire drawing by recalculating the positions of all the component entities and adjusts the resolution to suit the current screen 'magnification'. Regeneration will in some cases be performed automatically as a consequence of using other display commands such as ZOOM. (This feature may be disabled by use of the REGENAUTO command)

3.4.3 ZOOM

The ZOOM command allows areas of the current drawing to be either increased or decreased in size on the screen while keeping the actual size of the areas constant. By increasing the apparent size of an object you view a smaller area of the drawing; decreasing the apparent size allows you to view a larger area of the drawing.

Zoom may be called up from the keyboard by typing ZOOM

Command: ZOOM All/Center/Dynamic/Extents/Left/Previous/
Window/‹Scale(X)›:

Alternatively, Zoom may be called from the screen or pull down menus, in which case the options offered will be slightly different but the basic Zoom functions will be the same.

The various ZOOM options are:

All   Changes the display so that the complete drawing is shown on the screen.

Center   Allows the entry of the centre point of the region to be displayed. The height of the new display can be entered which in effect magnifies the display (Figure 3.19)

> **Command:** ZOOM
> **All/Center/Dynamic/Extents/Left/Previous/Window/**
> **‹Scale(X)›:C**
> **Center point:**
> **Magnification or Height ‹5›:**

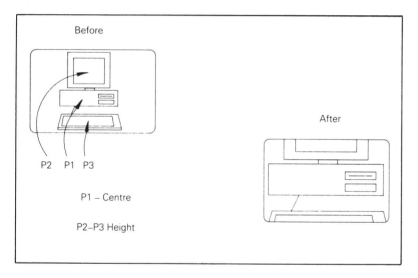

Figure 3.19 ZOOM Centre

Dynamic   When zoom dynamic is used various boxes are drawn on the screen. The original drawing extents will be surrounded by a box made up of a continuous line, whereas the generated area (area which may be viewed at high speed) is surrounded by four corners. The view box can be positioned anywhere on the drawing and also expanded or reduced to the desired size. If a zoom of the original drawing was previously in operation then a box made up of dotted lines will also appear on the

screen indicating the area previously zoomed. If not, then the four
corners will be joined by dotted lines showing that the generated area
was the previous view (Figure 3.20).

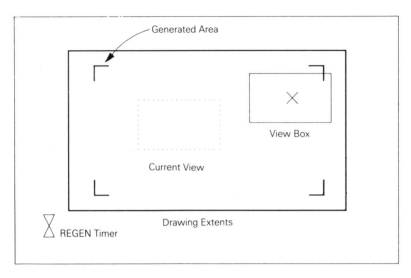

Figure 3.20 ZOOM Dynamic

A view box (containing a cross) the same size as the current
screen will initially be displayed, and can be moved to any part of the
drawing. To adjust the size of the view box press the pick button on the
mouse and an arrow will appear against the right-hand side of the box.
Moving the mouse now sets the size of this box; pressing the pick
button a second time fixes the size and allows the movement of the view
box to the part of the drawing to be zoomed. To zoom to the chosen
area, press the Return key on the keyboard. If the viewbox is
positioned outside the generated area then an hourglass symbol will
appear in the bottom left-hand corner indicating that a regeneration of
the display will occur.

Extent   The zoom extents mode zooms the current drawing to the largest
possible size to fill the screen.

Left   Zoom left is the same as zoom center but instead of specifying the
centre point of the zoomed window the lower left-hand corner is
specified (Figure 3.21).

Previous   Zoom previous is useful as it allows the operator to return to
previous views of the drawing. Zoom previous can be used sequentially
to return through all the previously executed zoom commands.

Window   The window command is probably the most frequently used of
all the zoom commands. It prompts for input of two corners of the

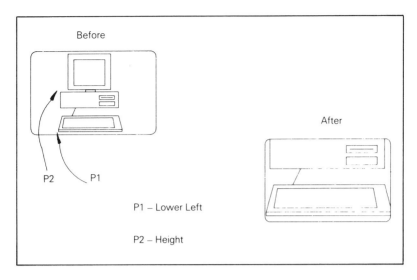

Figure 3.21 ZOOM Left

zoom window, either by coordinates or, more usually, from tne mouse. The window can be any size and in any position on the drawing.

Command: ZOOM
All/Center/Dynamic/Extents/Left/Previous/Window/
‹Scale(X)›:W
First corner:
Other corner:

Scale   The scale subcommand allows the input of a single value which is the magnification factor relative to the complete drawing, i.e. if a factor of 1 is used then the complete drawing will be displayed on the screen, a factor of two will double the size of the drawing whereas a factor of 0.5 will halve the size of the drawing.

If the magnification value is followed by an X the scaling will be computed for the current view on screen and not the complete drawing.

When the Scale option is chosen AutoCAD will display the zoomed drawing relative to the centre point of the drawing and therefore objects at the edge of the drawing could well be forced out of view, off the edge of the screen.

3.4.4 Transparent ZOOM

A transparent command is one which can be used while another command is in operation. For instance, transparent ZOOM could be used within the LINE command to enable the second point of a line to be positioned with greater accuracy. This is *very* useful.

Command: LINE
From point: (Point to start position.)
To point: 'ZOOM (The apostrophe denotes transparent mode.)
«Center/Dynamic/Left/Previous/Window»:W (Select zoom window.)
To point: (Point to next line point.)

Most of the ZOOM commands offered by the pull down menu are transparent, as can be seen from the preceding apostrophe on the menu.

Transparent commands cannot always be used. If the command requires a regeneration of the drawing then the transparent command will be ignored.

3.4.5 PAN

The PAN command allows you to move about a drawing without changing the magnification i.e. objects that are not visible (off the screen) can be panned into view. The direction and distance which the drawing moves is called the displacement and is entered, either as a relative displacement by typing in the corresponding X and Y displacement values followed by a Return, or as two separate coordinate points which pans the drawing from the first point to the second (Figure 3.22).

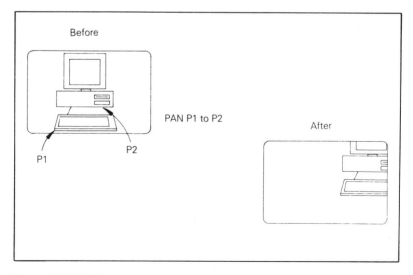

Figure 3.22 PAN

Command: PAN **Displacement:** ‹coordinates›
Second point: (Return.) (Indicates relative displacement.)

or

Command: PAN **Displacement:** ‹1st coordinates›
Second point: ‹2nd coordinates›

Input of the coordinates can be made through the keyboard or via the mouse. Pan can be made transparent by using an apostrophe prefix, i.e. 'PAN.

3.4.6 VIEW

When a large drawing is being undertaken it is often very useful to be able to call up specific views of the drawing. VIEW nominates a specified area of the drawing on the screen which can then be recalled at any time.

Command: VIEW **?/Delete/Restore/Save/Window:**
View name:

? Lists the names of all the saved views relating to the current drawing.
Delete Deletes a currently saved view.
Restore Changes the current display for the view requested, assuming that the view requested has previously been saved.
Save The area of the drawing which you require to save has first to be displayed on the screen as it is the screen display which will be saved for later retrieval. If the name you give to this view already exists then the new view replaces it. Once saved the view can be called at any time – it is saved with the drawing file.
Window Window allows a specified area of the screen display to be saved without the need to invoke a ZOOM command.

Like ZOOM and PAN, VIEW can also be used transparently.

3.4.7 ViewPORTS

The VPORTS command allows you to split the viewing screen into a number of separate areas, each of which can contain a different view of the current drawing. The maximum number of viewing areas is four. When the VPORTS command is invoked one of the viewports created will be the 'active' viewport, identified by the presence of the cross wires. Moving the cursor into one of the other viewports produces the arrow symbol instead of the cross wires.

It is possible to modify any view of the current drawing in any of the defined viewports by taking the cursor into the required viewport and pressing the pick button – the cross wires appear in this viewport indicating that it is now active. A major feature of viewports is that any modifications made to the drawing is automatically reflected in all viewports. In addition it is possible to work in more than one viewport, e.g. a line may be started in one viewport and terminated in another.

There are three different ways of accessing the VPORTS command – from the command line, the screen menu or from the pull down icon (Figure 3.23) on the **Display** pull down. From the command line:

Command: VPORTS
Save/Restore/Delete/Join/SIngle/?/2/‹3›/4:

Save   Save the current viewport configuration under a user-defined name.
Restore   Restores a previously saved viewport configuration.
Delete   Deletes a previously saved viewport configuration.
Join   Converts two adjacent viewports into a single larger viewport. The
         drawing resident in the dominant viewport will be drawn in the single
         viewport. AutoCAD prompts:

   Select dominant viewport ‹current›:
   Select viewport to join:

SIngle   Returns to the standard single viewport mode.
?   Returns a list of the current and saved viewports. This list is made up of
     the name of the saved viewports together with the special coordinates
     used to define each individual viewport. These special coordinates use
     the convention 0,0 for the bottom left-hand corner of the screen and 1,1
     for top right corner. Thus 0,0 0.5,1 and 0.5,0 1,1 describes the two
     viewports obtained by equally dividing the screen vertically
     (Figure 3.24).
2   Splits the active viewport into equal halves – either vertically or
     horizontally.
3   Divides the active viewport into three areas. AutoCAD prompts:

   Horizontal/Vertical/Above/Below/Left/‹Right›:

   Horizontal and Vertical divide the area into three equal viewports.
   Above and Below divide the area horizontally into three – one large
   and two small. Left and Right divide the area vertically into
   three – again one large and two small.
4   Divides the screen into four equal viewports.

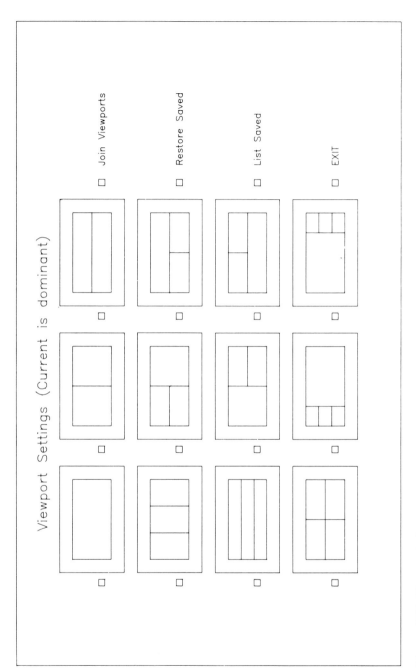

Figure 3.23 Viewports icon

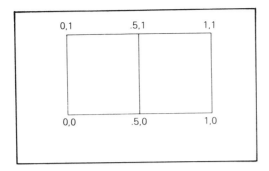

Figure 3.24 Viewports coordinate notation (two vertical ports)

When using the pull down Viewports icon you are limited to a choice of twelve predefined viewport configurations.

> *Note:* If your current drawing is relatively complicated and you choose one of the unequal 4-viewport configurations then you may find that it takes a considerable time before the final chosen configuration is achieved.

3.4.8 REDRAWALL and REGENALL

The normal REDRAW and REGEN commands will only work on the active viewport. If you require all the current viewports to be redrawn then use the REDRAWALL command. Similarly to regenerate all the current viewports use REGENALL.

3.5 SKETCH Mode

Most people who are unfamiliar with the way a CAD system operates assume that drawings are produced by using the mouse or digitiser as a sort of magic pen to draw directly on to the screen. In fact, as we have seen already, this is not how drawings are usually constructed. However, there are occasions when it is useful to be able to sketch irregular shapes. Sketch mode allows you to do this. A simple example is shown in Figure 3.25.

Although it is possible to use a mouse in sketch mode, in practice you will obtain better results when using a digitiser. This is because the digitiser puck/pen is designed to allow you to follow outlines accurately using its cross wires or pen-like tip. The mouse has no such corresponding feature.

When in sketch mode it is almost as if you have temporarily left AutoCAD and entered a separate, simple package which has only *seven* commands.

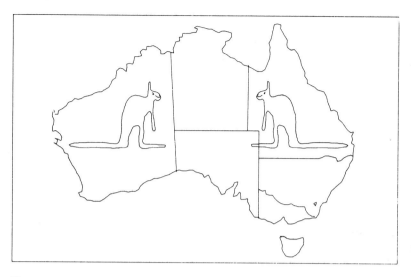

Figure 3.25 Use of SKETCH

Sketch mode is initiated by the SKETCH command:

Command: SKETCH
Record increment:

The prompt here is for a distance which will set the coarseness of the sketch. The sketch is divided up into sequential elements and the length of each element is equal to the record increment. Clearly, you will obtain much smoother sketches if the increment is small, but remember that a large sketch will contain an enormous number of elements which will take up a significant amount of computer storage space.

Sketch. Pen eXit Quit Record Erase Connect .

P Raise/lower 'pen'
X, space, Return Record lines and exit to AutoCAD
Q, Ctrl C Discard lines and exit to AutoCAD
R Record lines
E Erase
C Connect
. Line to point

P The puck is considered to be a pen in sketch mode. A P command from the keyboard (or pressing the pick button on the puck) acts as a toggle and controls whether this 'pen' is down – and hence makes a line – or up, when no line is made. The pen up/down mode has no *physical* significance.

R This Records the sketch, i.e. any sketched lines drawn to date are imported into the AutoCAD drawing. After this they are outside the control of the Sketch commands but they can, of course, be manipulated by the normal AutoCAD commands and are treated as a series of separate elements. Whether these elements are treated by AutoCAD as lines or polylines depends on the value of the system variable SKPOLY (0=line , 1=polyline). Use of the R command leaves you still in Sketch mode.

X, space, Return These commands all have the effect of recording the sketch but they also return you from Sketch mode to normal AutoCAD mode.

Q, Ctrl C These commands discard all sketch lines not previously recorded and return you to AutoCAD.

E The Erase sub-command produces the prompt

Erase:Select end of delete

Point to that element of the sketch preceding the error(s) to be erased. The sketch will then be blanked out on the screen *from this element to the last-drawn element of the sketch*. (Depending on your computer and the complexity of the sketch, the speed with which this occurs may range from instantaneous to very slow.) Pressing P or the 'pick' button then permanently erases the blanked-out section and returns you to the SKETCH menu.

Elements of a sketch which have previously been recorded cannot be erased by this method. Pressing E a second time will abort the erase.

C The Connect command allows you to continue with a sketch from the previous end point. Assuming that the 'pen' is up, approach the end point, and when you are *within one elemental length* the 'pen' is automatically lowered and sketching continues. Again, this will work only for elements of a sketch which have not yet been recorded. If your record length is very small you will find it difficult to make this connection.

. (period) This will draw a straight line from the end of the previously drawn sketch line to the current position of the 'pen', which must initially be up.

Snap and Ortho settings will still apply in sketch mode. Ortho is very limiting when sketching and should not normally be used. The Snap setting will dominate the record increment so that the 'coarseness' of the sketch will be controlled by the Snap setting. There is thus no point in setting the record increment on the sketch to be smaller than the Snap interval if Snap is on.

3.5.1 Calibrating the Digitiser

When using a digitiser in Sketch mode the length of line (in drawing units) on the screen is proportional to the distance travelled by the puck on the tablet but this will NOT be an exact 1:1 relationship. It will depend primarily on the size of the screen pointing area as defined on the tablet (see Section 15.5). Thus, if you wish to use the puck to trace the outline of an object placed on the tablet, the shape will be transferred into your drawing but the size and position on the screen will be arbitrary.

Calibration of the tablet allows you to map the tablet area onto the screen at any suitable scale and position.

Suppose that you have an accurate outline of an irregular object and you wish to transfer this *to a particular position and scale* in an existing drawing.

First, attach the outline to the digitiser tablet, then use the CALibrate option of the TABLET command:

Command: TABLET
ON/OFF/CAL/CFG: CAL

You are then prompted to digitise one point on the outline and type in the known coordinates of this point. This is repeated for a second point. The tablet is then calibrated. You may notice, depending on the scales involved, that the movement of the cross-wires on the screen is now much reduced – even for full movement of the puck across the tablet surface.

EXAMPLE

For example, if one point of the outline is to be positioned at point 100,150 in the drawing and a second point at 300,350, then:

Command: TABLET
ON/OFF/CAL/CFG: CAL
Calibrate tablet for use. . .
Digitize first known point:
Enter coordinates for first point: 100,150
Digitize second known point:
Enter coordinates for second point: 300,350

You can now use the SKETCH command in the normal way and the outline will be introduced into the drawing at the correct scale and position. Even if the outline has been attached to the tablet 'on the skew' AutoCAD will compensate for this and reproduce the shape squarely into the drawing.

If you wish to return the digitiser to its normal uncalibrated mode you simply have to switch it OFF with the TABLET command. Alternatively, the tablet may be toggled on and off at any time using the F10 key.

> *Note:* If the digitiser has been configured to allow the use of template menus (see Section 15.5), only the designated screen pointing area on the digitiser may be used for sketching whether or not you are in calibrated mode. You may digitise points outside this area when setting up the calibration but you will not be able to access them for sketching – they remain reserved for issuing commands from the template menus irrespective of whether TABLET is in the ON or the OFF state.

4 · Two-dimensional polylines

Polylines incorporate the properties of both lines and arcs. They also have a number of additional properties which include variable line width (parallel or tapered), curve fitting and the construction of complex *single entities* composed of both lines and arcs (Figure 4.1).

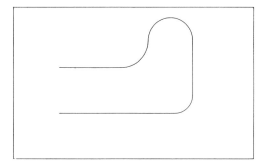

Figure 4.1 Single polyline made up of arcs and lines

A major feature is that an existing polyline may be extensively modified by comprehensive special editing facilities (see section 4.3).

Command: PLINE
From point:

When the starting point of the polyline is given the currently set line width will be displayed. This can be changed at any time during the use of PLINE.

4.1 Straight lines

Initially PLINE will assume that a straight line is to be drawn.
The following prompt will be displayed:

Arc/Close/Halfwidth/Length/Undo/Width/‹Endpoint›:

Arc Switches to arc mode (new prompt)

Close Allows the closing of a group of lines/arcs, with a line or arc connecting the last point to the original starting point.

Length Produces a line connected to the last segment (at the same angle as that segment), of the length specified.

Undo Removes the last segment drawn, whether it was a line or an arc.

Width Allows the setting of the line width; this can be set to produce a parallel or tapered line/arc (Figure 4.2).

Halfwidth Same as width but half the total width is specified.

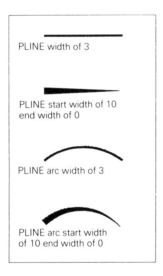

PLINE width of 3

PLINE start width of 10 end width of 0

PLINE arc width of 3

PLINE arc start width of 10 end width of 0

Figure 4.2 Variation of width

4.2 Arcs

Arcs are drawn by convention in the *anticlockwise* direction. If Arc is selected from the above prompt then a new prompt will be displayed:

Angle/CEntre/CLose/Direction/Halfwidth/Line/Radius/Second pt/ Undo/Width/‹Endpoint of arc›:

Angle Allows the setting of the included angle – the angle the arc will span (Figure 4.3). For an arc to be drawn clockwise input a negative angle.

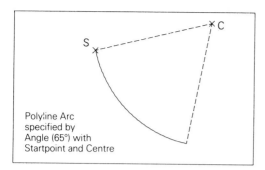

Figure 4.3 Polyline arc: angle specification

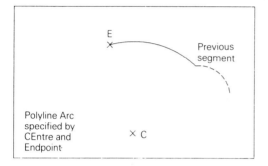

Figure 4.4 Polyline arc: centre, endpoint specification

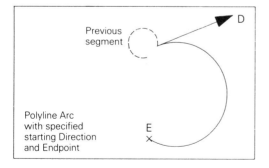

Figure 4.5 Polyline arc: direction specification

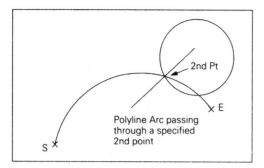

Figure 4.6 Polyline arc: second point specification

CEntre   Normally an arc will be drawn at a tangent to the previous
   segment: Centre allows a specific centre point to be set (Figure 4.4).
CLose   Same as Close for the line option but closes with an arc.
Direction   Allows the setting of an explicit starting direction (Figure 4.5).
Line   Switches back to line mode.
Radius   Allows the setting of a specific radius.
Second pt   Allows the input of a second point through which the arc must
   pass (Figure 4.6).

4.3 PEDIT – The special Polyline Edit Command

The special command PEDIT is used to edit polylines in the following way:

1. Change the width of the entire polyline.
2. Change the width or taper of individual segments of a polyline.
3. Open a closed polyline, or close an open polyline.
4. Straighten lines and arcs between two specified points.
5. Break the polyline into two or more segments.
6. Join individual polylines to make one single polyline.
7. Move a selected vertex or add a new one.
8. Curve fit.
9. Convert a non-polyline into a polyline.

Polyline editing is accessed by the PEDIT command:

   Command: PEDIT
   Select Polyline:

The chosen line will be checked to see whether it is a polyline; if it is not you
will be asked if you wish to change it into a polyline. Once a polyline has been
selected the following prompt will be displayed:

Close/Join/Width/Edit vertex/Fit curve/Spline curve/Decurve/Undo/ eXit ‹X›

Close: If the chosen polyline is 'open' then the Close command effects the true closing of the polyline. Even a polyline which has been drawn to start and finish at the same point is considered 'open'. In this case applying Close will have no visible effect but the polyline will now be treated as a closed figure. When a polyline is closed the Open command will be displayed at the prompt in place of Close (Figure 4.7).

Join: Allows the joining of arcs, lines and other polylines to the selected polyline (Figure 4.8). The selected objects to be joined must be positioned *exactly* at one end point of the polyline. Lines meeting a polyline to form a T will not be joined. Join will not work with closed polylines.

Width: Allows the polyline to be given a new uniform width (Figure 4.9).

Fit curve: A smooth curve is fitted to the polyline vertices (Figure 4.10). This can be edited using the Edit vertex command.

Spline curve   There are two spline curve options available – quadratic and cubic – controlled by the system variable SPLINETYPE (5 = quadratic and 6 = cubic). Each produces a far more accurate curve than the one produced by the Fit curve command (Figure 4.11). The vertices are used as control points, the curve passing through the first and last points. It is pulled towards the other points but not necessarily through them. The more points the more accurate the curve. Setting the system variable SPLFRAME to 1 allows the original polyline to be displayed in addition to the spline curve. The system variable SPLINESEGS controls the number of line segments generated to produce the curve (default = 8). The above system variables may be accessed from an icon menu by picking Polyvars from the PEDIT screen menu (see Section 12.5.5).

Decurve: Reverses the fit curve command.

Undo: Undoes the last PEDIT sub-command. By repeating this command you are allowed to step back through the PEDIT sub-commands.

eXit: Exit from the PEDIT command.

Edit vertex: When using this option a cross will be drawn on the first vertex of the selected polyline (Figure 4.12) and the following prompt will be displayed:

Next/Previous/Break/Insert/Move/Regen/Straighten/Tangent/ Width/eXit ‹N›:

Next/**P**revious: Moves the cross to the next/previous vertex.

Break: Splits the polyline into two at the position of the cross. If two

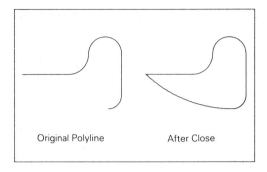

Figure 4.7 Closing a polyline

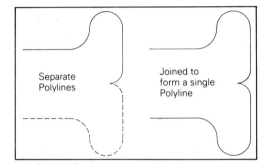

Figure 4.8 Joining polylines

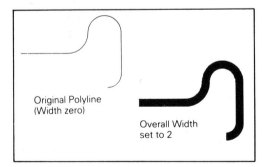

Figure 4.9 Width adjustment

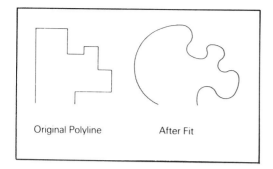

Figure 4.10 Smoothing

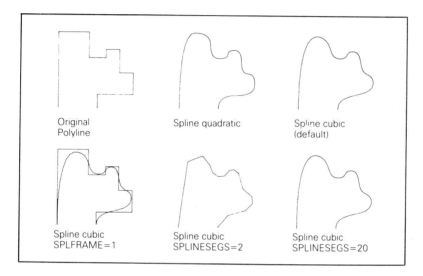

Figure 4.11 Spline curve options

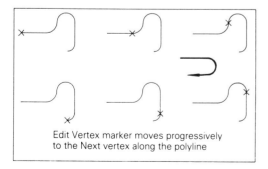

Figure 4.12 Edit vertex marker

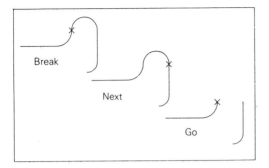

Figure 4.13 Stages in breaking a polyline

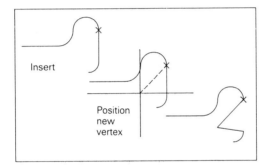

Figure 4.14 Inserting an extra vertex

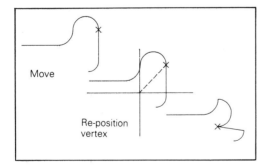

Figure 4.15 Moving an existing vertex

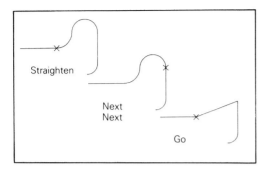

Figure 4.16 Stages in straightening a polyline

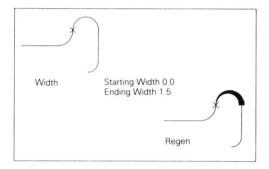

Figure 4.17 Altering the width of a segment

vertices are selected the section of the polyline between them will be deleted (Figure 4.13).

Insert: Allows the insertion of a new vertex into the selected polyline (Figure 4.14).

Move: Allows the movement of the currently selected vertex to a new position (Figure 4.15).

Regen: Regenerates the polyline, removing construction lines etc.

Straighten: Allows the straightening of the section of a polyline between selected vertices (Figure 4.16).

Tangent: Allows the input of a tangent direction to use with the curve fitting option.

Width: Allows the changing of width for the segment *following* the marked vertex. To see the result of this command the Regen command must be given (Figure 4.17).

4.4 Exploding a Polyline

EXPLODE is a special command used with blocks, dimensions and meshes as well as with polylines. After EXPLODE has been executed the segments of a polyline will no longer be a single entity but will now be treated as individual line and arc entities. All information about the original polyline, such as its width, will be discarded – the resulting lines and arcs will follow the old centre line.

Command: EXPLODE
Select block reference, polyline, dimension or mesh

5 · Layers, colours and blocks

5.1 LAYERS and COLOURS

An AutoCAD drawing is usually made up from a number of 'layers'. The layers themselves are invisible and it is probably helpful to think of them as a group of transparent sheets of film on which the different parts of the drawing are placed. By looking down through the sheets a complete picture is obtained (Figure 5.1). By removing or colouring certain sheets, selected parts of the picture can be hidden or emphasized.

The AutoCAD LAYER command is very powerful, and correct handling of layers is essential in order to make the best use of the package.

Layers are most easily demonstrated when using a colour monitor but their use is by no means limited to a colour installation. There is no limit to the number of layers you may have in a drawing, nor to the number of entities that can be held on a single layer.

A typical use of a layer would be to group together related objects such as electric wiring, pipework etc. Similarly text and dimensions may be more easily handled if grouped together onto their own layers.

When starting a new drawing you will only have one layer – Layer 0. This layer cannot be deleted or re-named and has special properties relating to blocks. Extra layers can be created at any time. One of the layers of a drawing may be nominated as the *current layer* – any new entity drawn will be placed on this layer by default. The current layer name is displayed in the top left-hand corner of the screen.

5.1.1 Properties of Layers

- Name. A layer must be given a unique name to distinguish it from all other layers. The 'name' may simply be a number: 1, 5, 65, . . . , or it may be a word (up to 31 characters long) which is in some way descriptive of the contents of the layer, e.g. ELECTRICWIRING or SECOND_FLOOR. The

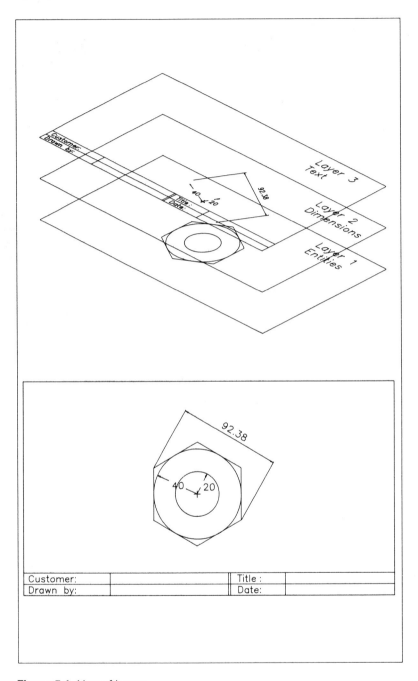

Figure 5.1 Use of layers

first 8 characters of the name of the current layer are always displayed in the top left-hand corner of the drawing.

> *Note:* Spaces in names are not allowed – a hyphen or an underscore may be used instead.

- On/Off. A layer, together with all its contents, can be switched on or off at any time. When Off the contents of the layer become invisible although they are still handled by the package for certain functions such as ZOOM, PAN and REGENeration. Layers that are Off are not plotted but they are still included in a drawing when it is saved.
- Colour. A layer normally has a colour assigned to it so that all entities drawn on the layer will automatically take the same colour. This is a default situation which can be over-ridden when required so that individual entities on the layer can be forced to take any desired colour (see the COLOR command).

   The colours are referred to by number from 1 to 255. Unfortunately, there is little standardization between different hardware systems as to the interpretation of colours by number. However, the first 7 numbers can be considered to be standard:

   1. Red
   2. Yellow
   3. Green
   4. Cyan
   5. Blue
   6. Magenta
   7. White   (default).

   Any new layer and any layer which does not have a specified colour will default to colour 7 (white). Nearly all colour systems (colour board and VDU) will support these seven colours but beyond colour 7 different systems vary tremendously. You certainly can *not* assume that all 255 colours will be represented. Try running one of the AutoCAD-supplied colour drawings such as CHROMA or 256COLOR to see how your system performs. You may get a shock.

   If you are using a monochrome system the colours will all be represented identically on screen. The colours are still useful because each colour can be assigned to a different pen on a pen plotter.
- Linetype. The treatment of linetypes within a layer closely follows that of the treatment of colours. All lines within a layer normally take up the linetype previously assigned to that layer, e.g. dashed or dotted. Individual entities can be forced to take up a linetype which is different from that of the layer. The default linetype for new layers is CONTINUOUS.

● Freeze/Thaw. The Freeze/Thaw state of a layer is superficially similar to On/Off. A frozen layer is invisible both on screen and on the plotter. The main difference is that a frozen layer is completely ignored by the package for virtually all commands other than Save. This means that a complicated frozen layer will not slow down the ZOOM, PAN and REGENeration processes – so it is good practice to freeze any layers that are not currently being used. They can easily be thawed out later.

5.1.2 Changing and creating layers

By far the easiest way to control layers is through the layers dialogue box. This may be accessed by selecting Modify Layer from the **Settings** pull down or alternatively by typing DDLMODES as previously described.

The dialogue box clearly shows the layers which have already been created for use with the current drawing (Figure 5.2). It also shows for each layer its name, On/Off state, Freeze/Thaw state, Colour and Linetype. A tick in the Current box shows which layer is current, i.e. the layer on to which any new entities will be drawn. There is also a box for creating new layers to be added to the set.

It is very easy to change any of these settings – simply use the mouse to move the arrow to the relevant box and press the pick button. In the case of colours (Figure 5.3) and linetypes (Figure 5.4), a subsidiary dialogue box will appear. When you have made your selection, pick the OK box and you will be returned to the main dialogue box. When you have finished making all the

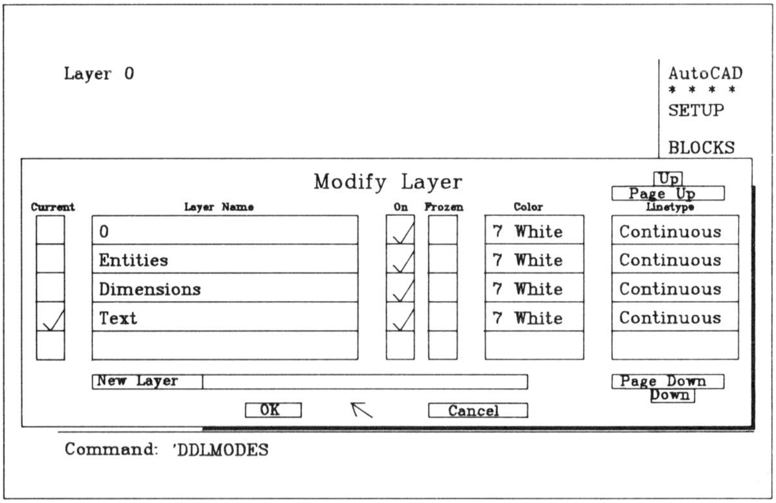

Figure 5.2 Layer editing

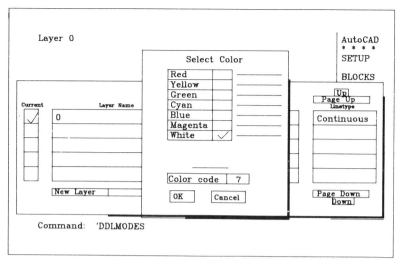

Figure 5.3 Layer colour editing

required changes, again tick the OK box and you will be returned to the drawing.

If you do not have access to the dialogue boxes you must use the LAYER command. This gives access to all the properties in the dialogue box but it is rather more cumbersome to use.

Command: LAYER
?/Make/Set/New/ON/OFF/Color/Ltype/Freeze/Thaw

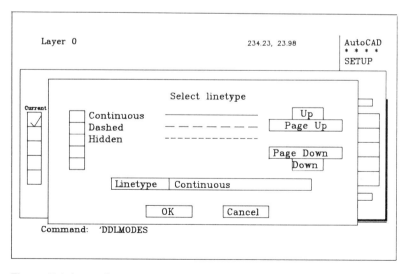

Figure 5.4 Layer linetype editing

Because you will often need to specify more than one property of a layer at a time, the AutoCAD response to a request for, say, a change in layer colour is not immediate but instead you are returned to the above menu. This can be confusing because the requested change will not have occurred. The rule is that, after you have made all the required changes to the layer and you have been returned to the layer menu yet again – give a final Return. This 'fixes' all your requests which will at last be obeyed and the **Command:** prompt will reappear.

Some of the items on the layer menu are obvious, some less so.

? The question mark response gives a display of the names of all the layers incorporated in your drawing, together with their on/off state, colour and linetype. To return to the drawing simply press the F1 function key.

Make When you start a new drawing only one layer exists. This is always called layer 0, it always has a default colour of white and a continuous linetype (which cannot be changed). Make allows you to define a new layer and in addition *sets that layer to be the current layer*. Other features of the new layer such as colour, linetype etc. can be set before exiting the layer menu with a Return.

Set This sets the new current layer but the layer must already be in existence.

New This creates a new layer but it does not set it to be the current layer.

ON/OFF Controls the visibility of a layer or layers. Several layers can be specified by a single On or Off statement provided that the layer names are separated by commas. All layers may be switched On or Off by using the * wild card.

Color The colour of specified layers can be set by responding with a valid colour number between 1 and 255 or by the name of one of the seven standard colours, e.g. Red. When prompted for the layer name to which the new colour applies you can again reply with multiple layer names. A null response will be taken to indicate the current layer only.

Ltype The response to this request is:

Linetype (or ?) ‹CONTINUOUS›

The **?** will result in a list of linetypes *in current use in the drawing*. Other linetypes are available but they must be loaded from the file ACAD.LIN. Don't worry – this is done automatically for you when you request the new linetype.

Freeze Freezes a given layer or layers.
Thaw Thaws a given layer or layers.

5.2 The COLOR or COLOUR Command

There is a separate COLOR command which allows you to force the colour of an individual entity, no matter what colour is set for the layer on which it is drawn.

Command: COLOR
New entity color: RED

This sequence will over-ride the layer colour for all subsequently drawn entities. To return to the colouring-by-layer system the COLOR command is repeated but the response is BYLAYER.

The entity colour can also be set by entering the Entity Creation dialogue box (DDEMODES), picking Color and entering a subsidiary dialogue box (Figure 5.5).

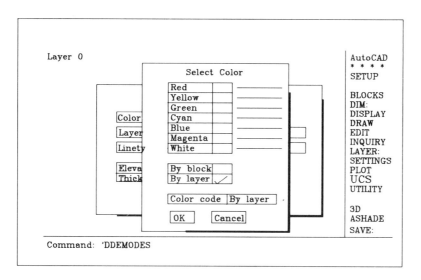

Figure 5.5 Setting entity colours

5.3 BLOCKs and Associated Commands

A block is a series of objects grouped together to form a single entity. Once the objects have been chosen they are given a block name (specified by the user), saved under that name and can then be recalled at any time and inserted in the drawing at any point and at any scale and orientation (Figure 5.6).

After insertion blocks are treated as single entities and as such can be selected for scaling, rotating, moving, erasing etc. by simply pointing to any part of that block.

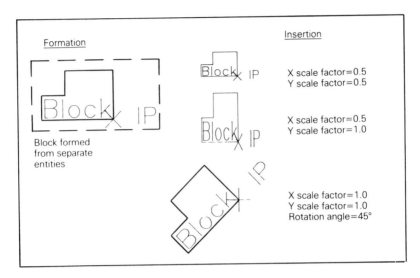

Figure 5.6 Use of blocks

Blocks normally reside within the original drawing but they can also be saved separately on to disk to be available for use in other drawings. This makes it possible to build up libraries of commonly used parts/objects which can be inserted as needed, thus simplifying the drawing procedure.

It is possible for blocks to be made up of entities taken from any number of layers, and of any number of colours and linetypes. When the block is inserted into a drawing these layers, colours and linetypes will be recreated.

There are a few exceptions to this:

1. Any block made from objects drawn on layer 0 will be inserted into the current drawing layer and not onto layer 0.
2. Objects drawn with the colour BYBLOCK or BYLAYER will take the current entity or layer colour when inserted.
3. Objects drawn with the linetype BYBLOCK or BYLAYER will take the current entity or layer linetype when inserted.

It is easy to produce nested blocks i.e. blocks within blocks, but the rules regarding colour, linetype etc. become more complicated.

5.3.1 BLOCK

The BLOCK command is used to define the block – to name it, choose an appropriate insertion point and select the objects which will become part of the final block.

Command: BLOCK **Block name (or ?):**

Enter the block name, or the **?** to see a list of the block names already in use in the current drawing.

Insertion base point:

This prompt is requesting a reference point to assign to the block. When the block is recalled it will be positioned with respect to this reference point.

Select objects:

Use the standard **Select objects** methods to choose the objects/entities which are to become part of the block; these can also include other blocks. After all the objects have been chosen press Return to create the block.

When the block has been created the objects chosen will always be erased from the drawing. If you wish to retrieve then *immediately* use the OOPS command.

Blocks can also include text information as *attributes*. This is covered in detail in Section 5.4.

5.3.2 INSERT

The command INSERT is used to retrieve a previously saved block and add it to the current drawing. The inserted block can be scaled in the X-, Y- and Z-directions and rotated about the reference (insertion) point. This can be achieved before (see Preset insertion) or after the block has been dragged to its final position.

Command: INSERT **Block name (or ?):**
Insertion point:
X scale factor‹1›/Corner/XYZ:
Y scale factor (default=X):
Rotation angle:

Some of these prompts need a bit of explanation:

1. **Insertion point.** The position within the drawing where the block is to be placed. When the block was originally saved an insertion base point was specified; this will be located at the insertion point.

2. **X scale factor‹1›/Corner/XYZ.** The **X scale factor** can be set to whatever value is required. If the Return key is the response to this prompt the block

will be inserted with its original scale. A negative scale factor can also be used – this has the effect of 'mirroring' the block. **Corner** is used to specify both the *X*- and *Y*-scales at the same time, using the insertion point and another user-specified point as the corners of a box. **XYZ** relates to 3D visualisation.

3. **Y scale factor (default=X).** The **Y scale factor** will default to the *X*-axis scale if the return key is the response, otherwise a separate *Y*-scale can be entered.

4. **Rotation angle.** The angle by which the block is rotated about its insertion point can be specified here.

See Figure 5.6.

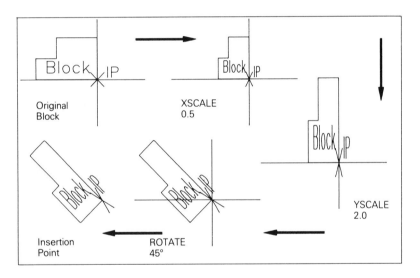

Figure 5.7 Scale and rotate before insertion

5.3.3 Preset Insertion

As described above, when the **Insertion point** prompt is displayed the block is normally dragged to the required position in the drawing and then scaled and rotated. However, there are a number of very useful alternative inputs which can be used at the **Insertion point** prompt *before* positioning the block (Figure 5.7):

Scale   Allows the overall scale to be preset.
Xscale   Presets the *X*-scale factor.
Yscale   Presets the *Y*-scale factor.
Zscale   Presets the *Z*-scale factor.

Rotate Presets the rotation angle.
PScale Same as **Scale** but after the object has been positioned a scale
    factor is requested again.
PXscale Same as **PScale** but only affects the X-scale.
PYscale Same as **PScale** but only affects the Y-scale.
PZscale Same as **PScale** but only affects the Z-scale.
PRotate Same as **Rotate**, but after the block is in its final position the
    rotation angle is requested again.

See Figure 5.8.

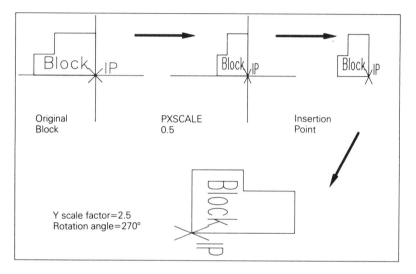

Figure 5.8 Preset insertion using PXscale

5.3.4 EXPLODE

EXPLODE is a special command used with blocks, polylines, dimensions and
three-dimensional polygon meshes. When a block has been inserted it is treated
as a single entity and can therefore be erased, moved, copied etc. by selecting a
single point of that block. EXPLODE is used to change the block from its single
entity form to its component parts. This makes it is possible to edit individual
parts of the block.

Command: EXPLODE
Select block reference, polyline, dimension or mesh

5.3.5 INSERT*

The special command INSERT* is used to insert the block while keeping the individual entities within that block separate, i.e. as if EXPLODEd.

> **Command: INSERT Block name (or ?):** *‹Block name›
> **Insertion point:**
> **Scale factor ‹1›:**
> **Rotation angle ‹0›:**

Only one scale factor is requested and this is then applied to both X- and Y-scales; negative scale factors cannot be used.

5.3.6 MINSERT

The MINSERT command allows a rectangular array of the chosen block to be inserted into the drawing. When MINSERT is called up the standard Insert prompts appear followed by the Array prompts.

> **Command: MINSERT**
> **Insertion point:**
> **X scale factor ‹1›/corner/XYZ:**
> **Y scale factor (default=X):**
> **Rotation angle:**
> **Number of rows(---)‹1›:**
> **Number of columns (||||)‹1›:**
> **Unit cell or distance between cells (---):**
> **Distance between columns:**

After the standard INSERT prompts AutoCAD will ask for the number of rows and columns, followed by a request for the distances between them (Figure 5.9). See Section 6.1.1 for a fuller treatment of arrays.

5.3.7 WBLOCK

Ordinary blocks may only be used within the drawing in which they were created.

WBLOCK, which stands for Write Block, is used to write a block out to disk so that it can be inserted into other drawings. A block saved to disk by WBLOCK carries a .DWG extension and is therefore indistinguishable from an ordinary drawing file. Conversely, a previously saved drawing may be treated as a block and inserted into the current drawing (Figure 5.10).

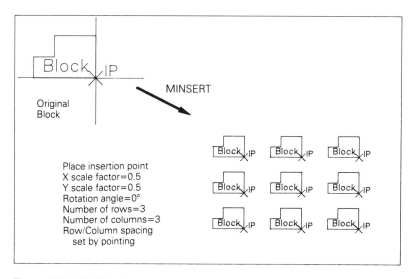

Figure 5.9 Multiple inserts

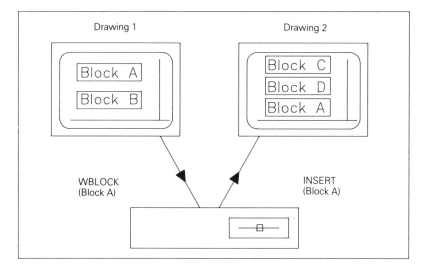

Figure 5.10 Block transfer between drawings

Command: WBLOCK **File name:**
(this is the name under which the block will be filed on the disk – it is your choice)

Block name:

There are four allowed responses to **Block name**. This can be rather confusing. If the entities which are to comprise the Wblock have already been defined in an ordinary block, then it would be a waste of time to re-define them. The first two of the following responses are alternative ways of referencing this block.

name   This names the ordinary block whose entities will be used in the Wblock.

=   This is used when you have arranged that the Wblock file name is the same as that of an existing block.

*   The entire drawing is made the Wblock – this has the same effect as the SAVE command.

(blank)   AutoCAD will ask for the user to select objects and an insertion point as with the ordinary BLOCK command.

5.4 Block Attributes

It is possible to include in a block information other than just the geometric shapes which make up its visible structure. Such data are called *attributes*. An attribute is treated as text and may consist of letters, numbers or symbols. When a block is defined, any attribute text strings are included in the block definition. Subsequent insertions of the block will include the attribute data.

The simplest attribute is a *constant*. A constant attribute has the same value for every occurrence of the block and it cannot easily be changed. A typical example would be a part code number associated with a component in an engineering drawing. Every insertion of that particular component would thus carry the identifying code.

Conversely, the attribute may be made *variable* so that the text may be changed at every insertion. In this case a prompt for the text is given as part of the block insertion sequence. The wording of the prompt is your choice and is saved with the block. Variable attributes are invaluable for grouping otherwise identical blocks under suitable headings, for example Room Number, Owner or Process Type.

Finally, there are the *preset* attributes. These are attributes which are variable but normally take up their default value on insertion – i.e. there is normally no prompt. In this respect they behave as constant attributes. Where preset attributes differ from both constant and variable attributes is in the method of insertion of the block. If the block is inserted via keyboard or menu commands then the preset attribute is automatically set to its default value. If however the block is inserted using the dialogue box (accessed via the INSERT command if the ATTDIA system variable is set to 1) then the preset attribute is treated as a variable and a prompt is issued on insertion.

Attributes, either constant, variable or preset, are stored in the block definition together with an identifying text label called an *attribute tag*. The tag has a similar function to a field name in a database and allows you to access the

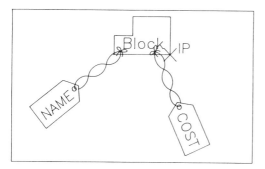

Figure 5.11 Attribute tags

attributes separately. Multiple attribute tags may be appended to a single block provided that tag names are not duplicated (Figure 5.11).

After a block has been inserted into a drawing the associated attribute values are added (Figure 5.12) and may be made *visible* or *invisible* as required. Any change made to the overall visibility will force a regeneration of the drawing. If all the attributes are visible the process of regeneration can be slowed down significantly while the attribute data are printed on the screen.

5.4.1 Defining Block Attributes

Attributes must be defined before the block definition process.

Command: ATTDEF
Attribute modes – Invisible:N   Constant:N   Verify:N   Preset:N

This prompt allows you to set three features of the attribute:

1. The visibility of the attribute (although this can be overridden after insertion using the ATTDISP command).
2. Whether the attribute is to be treated as a constant, a variable or a preset.

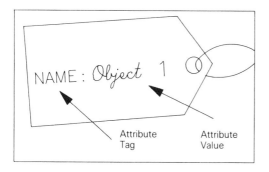

Figure 5.12 Adding attribute values

3. Whether you wish to have a chance during the insertion process to verify that its value is correct.

The initial response to all four alternatives is No, as shown. To alter any response to Yes you must return an I, C, V or P as required. The prompt will then reappear with the relevant N changed to a Y. When all four responses are satisfactory press Return to accept. AutoCAD then prompts:

Attribute tag
Define the attribute tag using any characters except blanks.

Attribute prompt
Enter text to be used to prompt for the attribute value on insertion of the block. *This is not applicable if the attribute is to be a constant; in this case the prompt is omitted.*

Attribute value
If the attribute is to be a constant this prompts for the constant value. If the attribute is to be a variable or preset this prompt is used to offer a default value on insertion of the block. This may be a null if desired.

AutoCAD now proceeds to prompt for the positioning of the text of the attribute, exactly as for a TEXT command, i.e. centred, right-justified, aligned, etc. The attribute tags will then be displayed on the drawing as specified. You can automatically align a series of attributes as with a series of text strings – simply enter a space or Return when prompted for the text starting point – AutoCAD will align each new attribute tag below the previous one.

EXAMPLE

For example, to define a variable attribute with a tag NAME and a default value of OBJECT 1:

> **Command:** ATTDEF
> **Attribute modes – Invisible:N   Constant:N   Verify:N   Preset:N**
> **Attribute tag:**   NAME
> **Attribute prompt:**   (Please name this item.)
> **Default attribute value:** OBJECT 1
> **Start point or Align/Center/Fit/Middle/Right/Style:**
> **Height:**
> **Rotation angle:**

When all the required attribute definitions have been entered the block can be defined. Proceed as normal with the block definition. When prompted to select the objects of the block simply include the attribute tags as displayed – using a window to include all the tags is probably the easiest method. When selection is complete the block will be defined and, as usual, will disappear from the screen. The attribute tags will also disappear and will not normally be seen again.

5.4.2 Inserting a Block with Attributes

It is important when inserting a block with preset attributes into a drawing to remember the following points:

1. If the preset attributes are to be considered constant, then the commands can be entered from the keyboard or from any of the screen, pull down or tablet menus.
2. If the preset attributes are to be treated as variable then the pop up dialogue box *must* be used.

When the block is to be inserted into a drawing the usual prompts about position, scale, and orientation are given. If the attributes of the block are all constants then block insertion occurs immediately. If the attributes are set to 'visible' then the *attribute values* (not the *attribute tags*) are displayed with the same text style, position and justification etc as was specified for the tags at the definition stage.

If any of the attributes are variable attributes then the prompt for their value is issued together with the specified default. This is repeated for all the variable attributes, after which the block is inserted as before.

5.4.3 Insertion using the Dialogue Box

To insert a block with attributes using the pop up dialogue box the system variable ATTDIA must be set to 1 (default zero). The dialogue box displays all the variable and preset attribute names along with their default values. The desired values can then be modified and once all are correctly set the block is inserted by picking the 'OK' square in the dialogue box (Figure 5.13).

> *Note:* If you call INSERT from the draw pull down menu then ATTDIA is automatically set to 1 and you will therefore not need to invoke the SETVAR command.

5.4.4 Suppression of Attribute Request

The system variable ATTREQ controls the suppression of the attribute request prompts. The default setting for this variable is 1 and therefore normal attribute

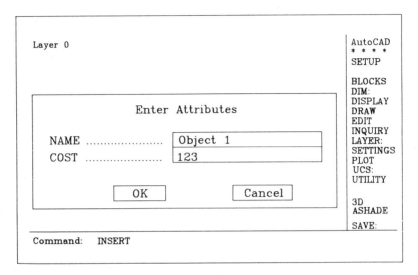

Figure 5.13 Insertion using dialogue box

request prompts appear. If ATTREQ is set to zero then, on block insertion, no attributes prompts appear, and all attributes take up their default values.

5.4.5 Visibility

The visibility of the attribute values after block insertion may be controlled by the ATTDISP command.

Command: ATTDISP
Normal/On/Off:

The Normal mode allows the visibility of each attribute to be as specified during the ATTDEF process. The On mode overrides this and makes all attributes visible. Similarly, the Off mode makes all attributes invisible.

5.4.6 Editing Attribute Tags

If you wish to add, remove or modify the attribute tags of a block there is no alternative – *the block must be redefined.*

Insert the block into the drawing at some convenient place and execute the EXPLODE command. The block will reappear apparently unchanged but you will notice that the *attribute values* have been replaced by the *attribute tags*. An unwanted attribute can now be removed by ERASE. New attributes can be specified by ATTDEF. Attributes to be modified should be erased and then respecified. When all is correct the block may be redefined with its original name, wiping out the original specification.

> *Note:* The drawing will then be regenerated using the new block definition so that any previously inserted blocks with that name will be changed.

5.4.7 Editing Attribute Values

If the *value* of an attribute is to be changed then the DDATTE or the ATTEDIT commands can be used.

> *Note:* The editing functions cannot be applied to constant attributes.

The DDATTE command is dialogue box orientated and is very similar in operation to the insert dialogue box. When DDATTE is invoked you will be prompted to select the block to be edited. Once chosen a dialogue box will appear with the chosen block preset and/or variable attribute names and existing values. These values can then be modified as required (Figure 5.14).

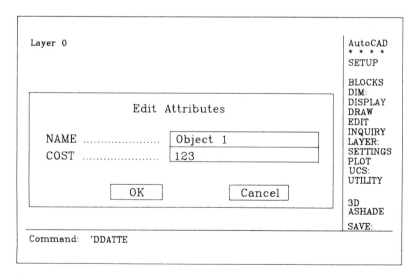

Figure 5.14 Edit Attribute dialogue box

The ATTEDIT command gives wide scope in the editing of attribute values. Thus, it allows you to edit all or selected attributes of all or selected blocks. The scope of the command is first set by specifying which attributes or groups of attributes are to be edited and which blocks are to be considered. AutoCAD then searches the drawing for all attributes which match this pattern and presents them for modification.

The ATTEDIT command can be applied either to individual attributes or globally to all the attributes in the drawing. The command is very powerful and requires some practice to use effectively.

5.4.8 Individual Attribute Property Editing

If the individual attribute editing route is chosen, then in addition to changing the attribute value it is also possible to change other properties such as colour, layer, position etc.

Command: ATTEDIT
Edit Attributes one at a time ?‹Y›:   Y

Block name specification ‹*›:
Attribute tag specification ‹*›:
Attribute value specification ‹*›:

These three questions allow you to specify the scope of the command. By using the wild card symbol * you can apply the ATTEDIT command to every attribute within the drawing.

Select attributes:

Point to individual blocks or use a window to select a number of blocks – those which satisfy the scope criteria may then be edited. The first attribute to be edited is marked with a cross 'X'.

Value/Position/Height/Angle/Style/Layer/Color/Next‹N›:   V

These property options are largely self explanatory, but in the case of Value a subsidiary question is asked.

Change or Replace ?‹R›:

If you select Replace then you are allowed to change the complete attribute entry, whereas if you select Change then AutoCAD prompts

String to change:
New string:

which allows you to change part of the attribute string.

EXAMPLE

For example: if the old attribute value represents a serial part number LS127649/341/000 then by selecting Change:

String to change: 341
New string: 678

a new attribute value of LS127649/678/000 is attained.

Other properties of the same attribute can be modified until the Next option is selected. The marker cross 'X' then moves on to the next attribute to be edited.

> *Note:* Unlike the PEDIT Edit vertex option, it is not possible to return to an attribute once the Next option has been selected i.e. there is no Previous option.

5.4.9 Global Attribute Editing

If the individual attribute editing route is not chosen, then the global option is invoked. This allows the multiple editing of all the selected blocks in one operation. However, the only editing allowed is the changing of all or part of the attribute value string (as described above – Change option).

Command: ATTEDIT
Edit Attributes one at a time ?‹Y›:   N

Global edit of attribute values.
Edit only attributes visible on screen? ‹Y›:
Y   (Only attributes selected from the screen will be edited.)
N   (Every attribute within the drawing which fits the scope will be edited.)

Block name specification ‹*›:
Attribute tag specification ‹*›:
Attribute value specification ‹*›:
Select attributes:
(This prompt is displayed only when editing attributes visible on screen – Use a suitable window.)

nnn **attributes selected.**
String to change:
New string:

6·Additional editing and inquiry commands

6.1 ADVANCED EDITING

6.1.1 ARRAY

The ARRAY command allows the user to take a single drawn entity or block and replicate it to form either a rectangular or a polar array.

The array element must be on the screen before ARRAY is called up. This is true even if the element is a named block.

Command: ARRAY
Select objects: (Assemble the desired selection set.)
Rectangular/Polar array (R/P): R
Number of rows (---)‹1›:
Number of columns (||||)‹1›
Unit cell or distance between rows (---):
Distance between columns (||||):

Instead of supplying the distances between rows and columns from the keyboard you can respond to the **. . . distance between rows . . .** prompt by picking a point with the mouse. You will be then be prompted for the **Second point** of a window which defines both the row and column separation of the array. The rectangular array is now drawn (Figure 6.1).

A polar array is produced in a similar manner:

Command: ARRAY
Select objects: (Assemble the desired selection set.)
Rectangular/Polar array (R/P): P
Center point of array: (Point to centre or give coordinates.)
Number of items: 7 (say)
Angle to fill (+=CCW,-=CW)‹360›:

This is requesting the angular rotation, clockwise or counterclockwise, through

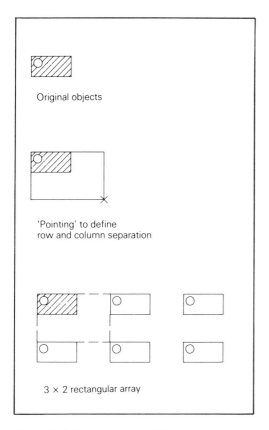

Original objects

'Pointing' to define
row and column separation

3 × 2 rectangular array

Figure 6.1 A rectangular ARRAY

which the whole array is to be rotated. A return selects the default value of 360°.

Rotate objects as they are copied?:   Y

The whole circular array is now drawn (Figure 6.2).

Note: If you are not using AutoCAD Release 10 be careful when you request
the objects not to be rotated. On earlier versions, if the selection set is
composed of a number of separate entities rather than a single entity or a
block, then you will find that the objects seem to 'explode' as they are arrayed.
This is because, without rotation, the distance from each entity in the set to the
centre of the array is variable and, while this looks all right in the original
position, it will cause the elements apparently to fly apart as they are arrayed.
The best way round this problem is to make the offending elements into a
block.

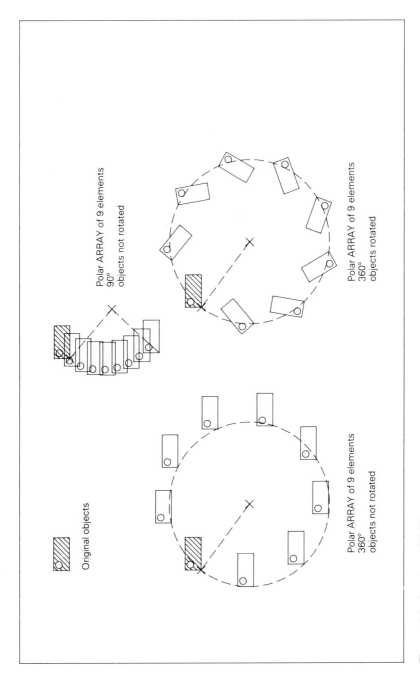

Figure 6.2 A polar ARRAY

6.1.2 CHANGE

CHANGE is a very powerful editing command in that it can be used to alter both the size and position of an entity and also other entity properties such as layer, colour etc.

> **Command:** CHANGE
> **Select objects:**   (Select entity(s).)
> **Properties/‹Change point›:**

The default response requests a Change Point (CP). This may be supplied from either the mouse or the keyboard. Depending on the entity selected, the CHANGE command will modify the entity relative to the CP. Thus if a line is selected then the end point closest to the CP will be moved to the CP. In the case of a circle the radius will be adjusted so that the circle passes through the CP while the centre point remains fixed. If a block is selected then the CP becomes the new insertion point and you will be prompted for a new rotation angle. Text may be moved to the specified CP and in addition the height, rotation angle, style and content may be altered. If multiple lines are selected they will *all* be modified to meet at the CP. When a number of different entities are selected the lines will all be treated as above but circles will trigger a prompt for a new radius and blocks a prompt for a new insertion point. See Figure 6.3.

If you require to change a property of the selected entity(s) then respond with a P at the **Properties/‹Change point›** prompt.

> **Properties/‹Change point›:**   P
> **Change what property(Color/Elev/LAyer/LType/Thickness)?**

Each time you select a change in a property you will be returned to the above menu allowing further changes to be made. Only when you respond with a Return at the above prompt will the changes be executed.

6.1.3 CHPROP

If you wish only to change the properties of an entity then the CHPROP command may be used.

> **Command:** CHPROP
> **Select objects:**
> **Change what property(Color/LAyer/LType/Thickness)?**

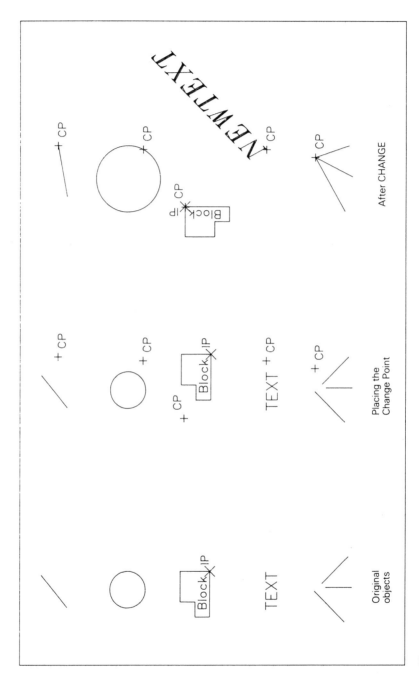

Figure 6.3 The versatile CHANGE command

6.1.4 RENAME

Several AutoCAD features require a user-defined name, e.g. blocks, views, text styles etc. RENAME allows these names to be changed at any time.

> **Command:** RENAME
> **Block/LAyer/LType/Style/Ucs/VIew/Vport:**
> **Old (object) name:**
> **New (object) name:**

6.1.5 PURGE

This is the only command which allows existing user-defined features to be deleted from a drawing. In practice PURGE may *only* be used *immediately* after loading a previously saved drawing and before any new entities have been added or any existing entities have been modified.

> **Command:** PURGE
> **Purge unused Blocks/LAyers/LTypes/SHapes/STyles/All:**

AutoCAD responds by offering the selected items one at a time for deletion.

6.1.6 SCALE

This command enables you to change the size of existing entities.

> **Command:** SCALE
> **Select objects:**   (Assemble the desired selection set.)
> **Base point:**   (Give base point.)
> **‹Scale factor›/Reference:**

The default response must be a numerical scale factor. To reduce the object in size the scale factor must lie between 0 and 1; to enlarge it the scale factor must be greater than 1 (Figure 6.4).

The same result may be achieved with less accuracy by dragging using the mouse, when the result can be assessed visually to give the desired effect. The base point may be anywhere in the drawing – if part of the object lies on the base point it will remain stationary as the rest of the object is scaled.

Remember that scaling is applied equally in the *X*- and the *Y*-directions, so it is not possible to change an object's shape – such as changing an ellipse into a circle – using SCALE.

The alternative response to **Scale factor** is **Reference**. This simply performs

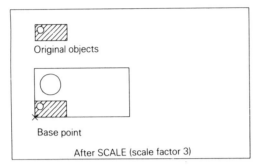

Figure 6.4 Scaling

the scale factor calculation for you. If you enter an existing length (either numerically or by pointing) followed by the desired new length (again you may point or drag if you prefer) then the correct scaling is performed automatically (Figure 6.5). This is very useful for scaling an entire drawing to a desired final size.

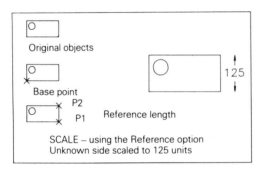

Figure 6.5 SCALE: reference option

EXAMPLE

‹**Scale factor›/Reference:**   R
Reference length: 525
New length: 125

This will apply the correct reduction factor of 0.2381, to the selected objects.

6.1.7 BREAK

The BREAK command can be used to erase parts of entities such as lines, circles, arcs or polylines.

> **Command:** BREAK
> **Select object:** (Use last, window, pointing etc.)
> **Enter first point:** (Point to one end of deletion.)
> **Enter second point:** (Point to other end of deletion.)

The selected section will then be removed.

If you use pointing to select the object then the **Enter first point:** prompt is omitted and the second prompt is modified to:

Enter second point (or F for first point):

This is because AutoCAD assumes that the point used to select the entity is actually the point specifying one end of the deletion. If this is not the case then typing F invokes a prompt for the first point.

The second point need not actually lie on the entity to be erased – AutoCAD will find the nearest point on the entity. If the second point lies within the entity then the region between the points will be removed. If it lies beyond the end of an open entity such as a line or an arc then the region between the first point and the end will be erased. This is useful because it avoids the danger of leaving a minute piece of the entity behind when you erase.

If you wish simply to break the entity into two without erasing an appreciable part of it then you should enter the same point at both the first and second prompts. This can be done by entering an @ symbol at the second prompt – this will be interpreted as 'repeat of last coordinate'. See Figure 6.6.

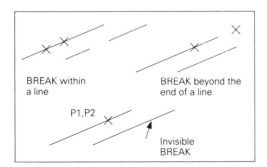

Figure 6.6 BREAKing lines

When breaking a circle, care must be taken when choosing the first and second break points. Remember that AutoCAD always works counterclockwise

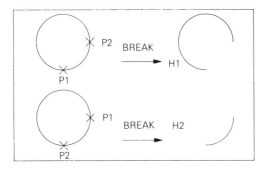

Figure 6.7 BREAKing a circle

and so the relative position of the two break points will affect which section of the circle is removed (Figure 6.7).

6.1.8 TRIM

It is often difficult to ensure that two objects meet each other exactly without any overshoot. With TRIM this is made easy. One of the objects must be considered as a cutting edge acting on the other.

> **Command:** TRIM
> **Select cutting edge(s). . .**   (Point to the cutting object.)
> **Select objects:**
> (Be careful. This is *still* asking you to select cutting edges: you may select lines, arcs, circles or polylines)
> **Select objects to trim:**
> (Select object(s) by pointing, not by windowing. Make sure you *point to the part of the object to be deleted* or you may delete the wrong bit.)

An example of the use of TRIM is shown in Figure 6.8.

The following error messages are sometimes encountered:

No edges selected:
(None of the selected cutting edges is suitable.)

Entity does not intersect an edge:
(No cutting possible.)

Cannot TRIM this entity:
(Invalid entity for trimming, e.g. a trace or text.)

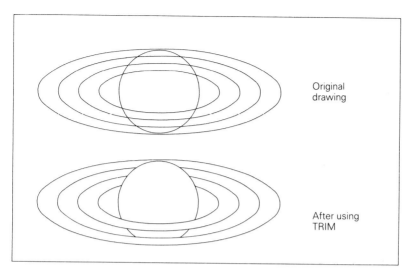

Original
drawing

After using
TRIM

Figure 6.8 Use of TRIM

Circle must intersect twice:
(You can only trim a chord off a circle if it intersects the cutting edge twice – obvious when you think about it.)

6.1.9 EXTEND

EXTEND can be thought of as the reverse of TRIM. A selected object will be extended until it meets a specified boundary such as a second object. Thus lines will be extended indefinitely in their original direction (Figure 6.9) and arcs will be extended with their original radius of curvature (Figure 6.10). If the extensions cannot reach the required boundary the command is aborted.

Command: EXTEND
Select boundary edge(s)   (Point to final boundary of extended line.)
Select object:
(This enables other boundaries to be specified: you may select lines, arcs, circles or polylines.)

Select object to extend:
(Point to (do not window) the object to be extended.)

Objects are extended from the end closest to the point by which the object was selected. If multiple boundary edges are specified the selected object will be extended to the nearest edge. The object may be extended to successive edges by

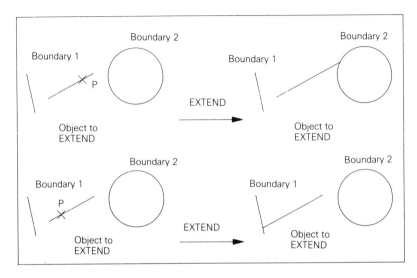

Figure 6.9 EXTENDing lines

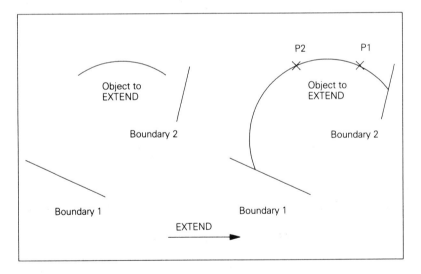

Figure 6.10 EXTENDing arcs

picking it repeatedly. Remember that arcs will be extended in their positive direction, i.e. counterclockwise.

6.1.10 STRETCH

This very useful command allows you to move a group of objects around within a drawing while at the same time stretching or compressing any lines, arcs, traces, solids or polylines which connect the group to the rest of the drawing. Such connecting lines behave as if they were elastic bands while the objects of the group remain unaltered (Figure 6.11).

The command is simple in operation but the syntax used is confusing.

Command: STRETCH
Select objects to stretch by window: C

This is the confusing bit. The selected objects form the group to be *moved* – these objects are not in fact 'stretched'. Also, you *must* use a window to select the group but it is best not to respond with the standard W for Window. This would not select the entities joining the group to the rest of the drawing and STRETCH would not work. Instead you should always type C for Crossing window.

Select object:

This is the standard object selection prompt. It is not normally needed unless you have used a Window selection in which case you must now point to every line crossing the Window boundary.

Base point:

Select a convenient base point relevant to the group to be moved.

New point:

Specify final position of the group. You may use 'drag' to observe the effect.

Entities other than lines, arcs, traces, solids or polylines are not affected by STRETCH – they are either moved, if their definition point lies within the specified window, or they are left alone. (The definition point is the centre of a circle, the location point of a point, the insertion point of a block or shape and the left-hand end of the base line of any text or attribute definition.)

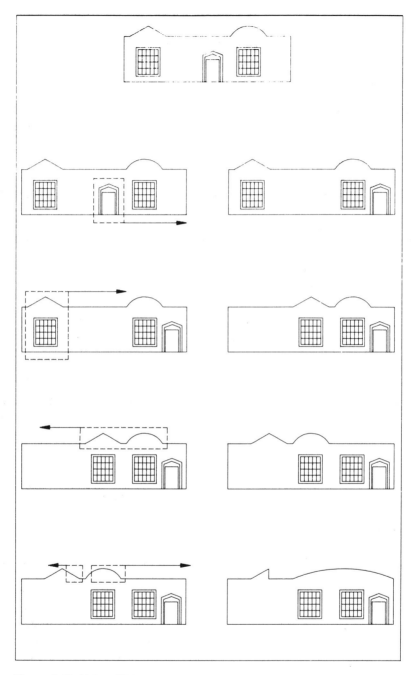

Figure 6.11 Using STRETCH to transform a drawing

6.1.11 FILLET

Adjacent lines which may or may not be touching can be filleted to a desired radius using the FILLET command.

Command: FILLET
Polyline/Radius/‹Select two lines›:

It is first necessary to specify the desired radius by responding with an R

Enter fillet radius ‹0.000›:

Then re-invoke FILLET and select two lines.
   If you respond with a P you may select a polyline instead of two separate lines.

Select polyline:

See Figure 6.12.

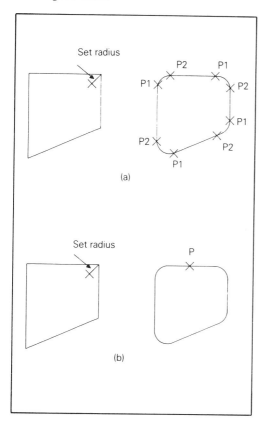

(a)

(b)

Figure 6.12(a) FILLETing a set of lines
Figure 6.12(b) FILLETing a polyline

6.1.12 CHAMFER

CHAMFER follows the same rules as FILLET but instead of supplying a radius AutoCAD will ask for two distances. These represent the distance along each line to which the chamfer will be taken (Figure 6.13).

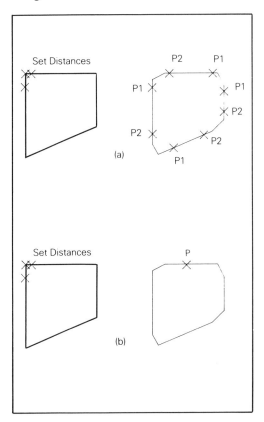

Figure 6.13(a) CHAMFERing a set of lines
Figure 6.13(b) CHAMFERing a polyline

Command: CHAMFER
Polyline/Distance/‹Select first line›:   D
Enter first chamfer distance ‹0.000›:
Enter second chamfer distance ‹0.000›:

6.1.13 OFFSET

The OFFSET command can be used with all the standard AutoCAD entities, i.e lines, circles, arcs. etc and produces a parallel entity separated from the original by a *constant* distance. In the simplest case the offset of a straight line will be an identical line parallel to the first. However, in most other cases the offset entity will differ in length and shape from the original as shown in Figure 6.14.

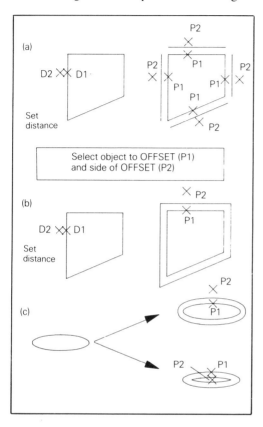

Figure 6.14(a) OFFSETing a set of lines
Figure 6.14(b) OFFSETing a polyline
Figure 6.14(c) OFFSET distortion

Command: OFFSET
Offset distance or Through ‹Through›: T
Select object to offset:
Throughpoint:

If you take the default (Through) option you will be prompted for the position of a point Through which the offset will pass.

Alternatively, if you input an *Offset distance* instead of the default a further prompt will ask which side of the original object the offset should be drawn.

Select object to offset:
Side to offset

6.1.14 DIVIDE and MEASURE

DIVIDE allows you to divide up an entity such as a line or an arc into a specified number of parts (Figure 6.15). The entity is not broken, the division is achieved by placing point entities as markers along its length.

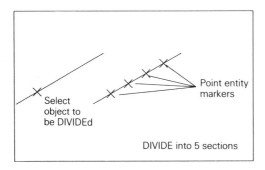

Figure 6.15 Dividing a line

MEASURE operates in a very similar manner but in this case the spacing between the markers, rather than their number, is specified (Figure 6.16).

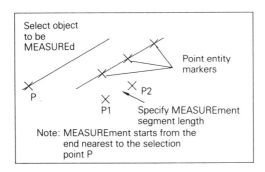

Figure 6.16 Measuring a line

Command: DIVIDE
Select object to divide: (Point to object.)
‹Number of segments›/Block: (Enter a number between 2 and 32767!)

Command: MEASURE
Select object to measure: (Point to object.)
‹Segment length›/Block:

(Reply with a numerical distance or use the mouse to indicate the segment length)

The object will then be divided as requested with point entity markers inserted at each division. *These may well be invisible*. A point entity may only be seen when it is separate from any other object. However, the invisible points can still be used, for instance with 'Node' Object Snap to attach new entities at each division. See Chapter 7.

The marker points are automatically added to the 'last selection' set. This means that they may be referred to as a group the next time a **Select objects:** prompt is encountered. Thus, all the points may be removed, after you have used them, by a single command:

Command: ERASE
Select objects: P(revious)

Alternatively, you may wish to make the points visible. The representation of a point entity can be varied according to the setting of the system variables PDMODE and PDSIZE. The first variable, PDMODE, represents point entities as follows:

PDMODE	Point representation
0	A dot (default value)
1	Invisible
2	A cross (like a + sign)
3	A cross (like an X)
4	A short vertical line extending upwards

These choices may be further extended by plotting any of the above inside a circle (add 32 to the above numbers, e.g. 32, 33, 34 etc.), a square (add 64), or both (add 96). See Figure 6.17.

PDSIZE controls the point size for all settings of PDMODE except 0 or 1. If positive PDSIZE specifies the absolute point size: if negative it is interpreted as a percentage of the screen size causing points to remain the same size irrespective of the amount of zoom, in or out.

Both PDMODE and PDSIZE are set via the SETVAR command. Old points will remain unchanged until the next REGENeration.

Returning to DIVIDE and MEASURE, in either case you can replace the point entity division markers with a previously defined block. If you respond to

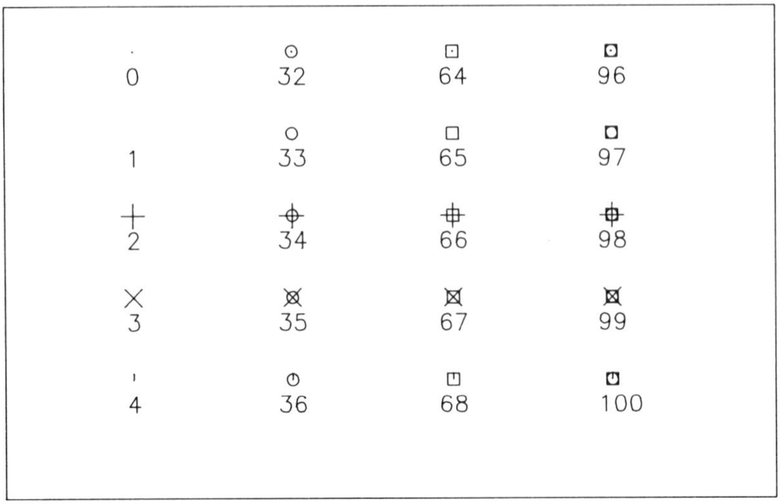

Figure 6.17 POINT modes set with the system variable PDMODE

the second prompt with BLOCK or just B then AutoCAD will prompt for the name of a block. This must be a block *currently defined within the drawing*. A block stored on disk using WBLOCK *cannot* be used here.

AutoCAD will then ask if the block is to be aligned with the object and after this the division or measurement will be performed and the marker blocks inserted in place of point entities. This can be very useful – for instance if you wished to insert a block representing an electrical outlet at regular intervals along a wall in a room plan drawing then DIVIDE could handle this in one operation (Figure 6.18).

6.2 Inquiry Commands

6.2.1 LIST

LIST is a generally useful command which gives full details of any entity specified and is particularly useful when editing.

Command: LIST
Select objects:

AutoCAD responds with a list of the coordinates and tangent direction of selected lines, the centre and radius of circles and arcs, together with information about layer, colour, linetype etc. The area and perimeter of a closed polyline, circle, polygon and ellipse is also given.

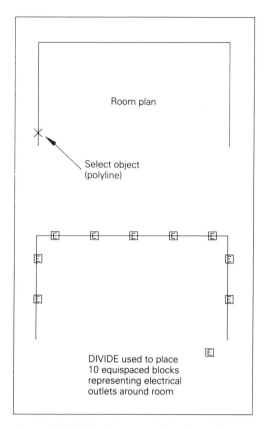

Figure 6.18 Dividing using block markers

6.2.2 DBLIST

This is the same as List, but the data for the *complete* drawing is displayed. DBLIST can take a very long time if the drawing is large.

6.2.3 ID

The ID command displays the coordinates of a chosen point in the drawing.

Command: ID
Point:

This can be very useful when positioning an entity at an exact distance from an unknown point in a drawing.

EXAMPLE

For example, if a line is to be drawn 50 units away from an unknown point in the 0° direction, first use the ID command to select and identify the point, then enter the line command. At the prompt **From point:** enter the relative coordinate @50‹0. AutoCAD uses the ID point as a point to which the relative coordinate is referenced.

6.2.4 DISTANCE

The DISTANCE command responds with the distance and angle between any two specified points whether two- or three-dimensional.

    Command: DIST First point: Second point:

6.2.5 AREA

The AREA command allows the specification of an entity or any number of points enclosing a space, the last point specified is assumed to be connected to the first point specified. The area command calculates both the area and the perimeter of the specified region.

    Command: AREA
    ‹First point›/Entity/Add/Subtract:
    Next point:
    .
    .
    .
    Next point: Return
    Area=‹calculated area›, **Perimeter**=‹calculated perimeter›

6.2.6 STATUS

The STATUS command lists the following drawing parameters:

0 Entities in Drawing 1				
Limits are	*X*:	0.00	420.00	(off) (world)
	Y:	0.00	297.00	
Drawing uses	*X*:	0.00	420.00	
	Y:	0.00	297.00	

Display shows	*X*:	0.00	420.00			
	Y:	0.00	297.00			
Insertion base is	*X*:	0.00	*Y*:	0.00	*Z*:	0.00
Snap resolution is	*X*:	10.00	*Y*:	10.00		
Grid spacing is	*X*:	0.0000	*Y*:	0.0000		

Current layer: 0
Current colour: BYLAYER – – 0   (White)
Current linetype: BYLAYER – – CONTINUOUS
Current elevation: 0.0000   thickness: 0.0000
Axis off   Fill on   Grid off   Ortho off Qtext off Snap on   Tablet off
Object snap modes: None
Free RAM: 14 452 bytes   Free disk: 1 249 280 bytes
I/O page space: 93k bytes   Extended I/O page space: 19k bytes

7 · Object Snap

Object Snap allows you to snap the cross wires of the cursor on to a variety of key points related to existing objects in the drawing. This complements the basic snap facility which locks on to the coordinate system. This greatly enhances the accuracy with which drawings may be constructed.

For instance, it can be very difficult to draw a line to meet the centre point of an existing circle if the centre point is not marked and the circle was not drawn with basic Snap in operation. Object Snap allows this hidden point to be accessed immediately.

Object Snap may be operated either continuously by default (background mode) or it may be called up for a *single* drawing operation (override mode) – such as drawing a single line originating from the exact midpoint of another.

The precise feature of an object onto which the cursor snaps is determined by the *Object Snap mode(s)* which are currently invoked. There are several of these modes to choose from and it is possible to use a combination of several modes at one time. They are listed either on the **Tools** pull down menu or on the corresponding screen menu (which is called up by picking the **** symbol near the top of the screen menu under the word AutoCAD).

When Object Snap is operating there is no visible effect until AutoCAD requests a point e.g. the **From point:** prompt encountered within the LINE command. The normal cross wires of the cursor are then supplemented with a square target box at their intersection (Figure 7.1). The size of the target box may be adjusted through the APERTURE command.

Command: APERTURE
Object snap target height (1–50 pixels)‹10›:

This indicates the search area within which AutoCAD will look for entities which are able to satisfy the current Object Snap mode.

For example, if within the LINE command the Object Snap mode is set to look for the centres of circles (CENter mode), then if the target box overlaps part

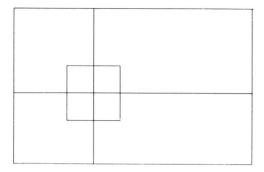

Figure 7.1 The Object snap target box

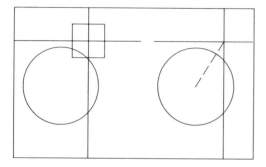

Figure 7.2 Drawing a line from an unknown centre point

of a circle and the 'pick' button is pressed, AutoCAD will place the start point of the line at the centre of the circle (Figure 7.2).

7.1 Object Snap Modes

The following available Object Snap modes are illustrated in Figures 7.3 and 7.4.

NEArest*. Snaps to the *nearest position* on any line, circle or arc
ENDpoint. Snaps to the nearest *endpoint* of a line or arc
MIDpoint. Snaps to the *midpoint* of a line or arc
CENter. Snaps to the *centre* of an arc or circle
NODe. Snaps to a *point* entity
QUAdrant. Snaps to nearest *quadrant* point of an arc or circle, i.e.
    12 o'clock, 3 o'clock, 6 o'clock or 9 o'clock.

> *Note:* If the circle or arc has been rotated these quadrant points will be rotated also.

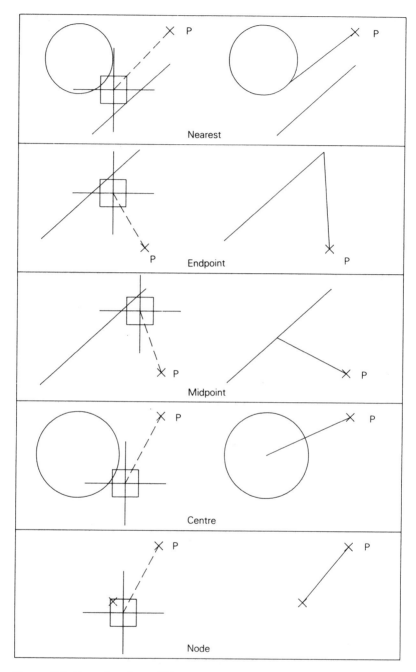

Figure 7.3 Use of various Object snap modes

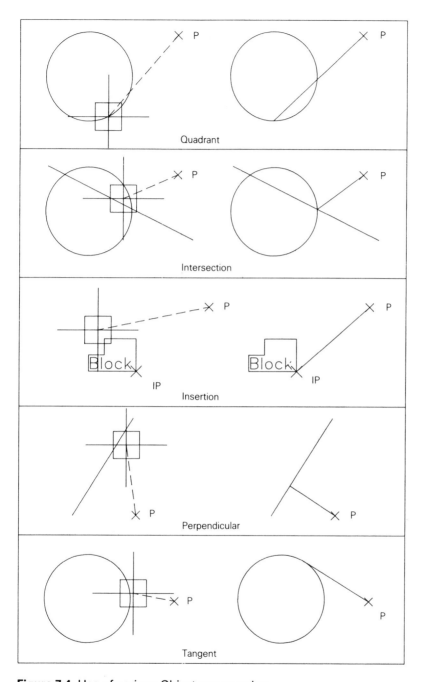

Figure 7.4 Use of various Object snap modes

INTersection*. Snaps to the *intersection* of any lines, circles or arcs which lies nearest to the centre of the target box.

INSert. Snaps to the *insertion point* of a block, shape or text entity.

PERpendicular*. Snaps to that point on a line, circle or arc which, when connected by a straight line to the *last point specified*, forms a *normal* to the line, circle or arc.

TANgent*. Snaps to that point on a circle or arc which, when connected by a straight line to the *last point specified*, forms a *tangent* to the circle or arc.

QUIck. This mode is used *only* in conjunction with other Object Snap modes. It ensures that the point selected is the *first one* which satisfies the mode criteria. Without Quick all possible candidate points are examined to see which is nearest to the centre of the target box.

NONe. *Disables* Object Snap

Notes
(a) Some Object Snap modes will not operate or are restricted when used with objects which are contained in blocks. These modes are indicated with a *.
(b) Each section of a polyline is treated as a separate line or arc entity.
(c) Object Snap considers only the centre line of wide polylines (Figure 7.5).

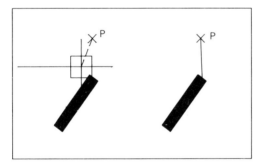

Figure 7.5 Object snap finds the centre of a wide polyline

7.2 Invoking Object Snap

7.2.1 Background or Osnap Mode

Object snap may be set up in its background mode by giving the command OSNAP.

Command: OSNAP
Object snap modes: END,MID,QUA

This has the effect of setting the running Object Snap modes to ENDpoint, MIDpoint and QUAdrant.

> *Note:* Only the first 3 letters of any mode name form a sufficient response.

The snap point chosen will be the one which satisfies at least one of these modes and which is nearest to the centre of the target box. These background modes, unless changed, will remain in operation throughout the drawing and will be saved as part of the drawing.

7.2.2 Single Point Override Mode

This is often more useful than the background mode. It allows you to select the mode(s) you want but it will only remain in force for just one point selection. As the name implies, it can be used to override the background mode for the current point, after which the background mode will take over again. Single point override can be used even when there is no background mode set, i.e. it can be used when Object Snap is inoperative.

To invoke this single point Object Snap you can simply respond to any AutoCAD point prompt with the required mode name. This may be picked up from the pull down or screen menus or typed in directly. AutoCAD then responds appropriately, supplying helpful prompt words such as **of** or **to** on the command line.

For example, suppose that your drawing included a circle and an arc and that you wished to construct a line from the centre of the circle to the midpoint of the arc. Using Object Snap the task is very simple:

      Command: LINE
      From point: CEN **of**   (point to the circle)
      To point: MID **of**   (point to the arc)

See Figure 7.6.
If you don't think that was clever, try doing it without Object Snap!

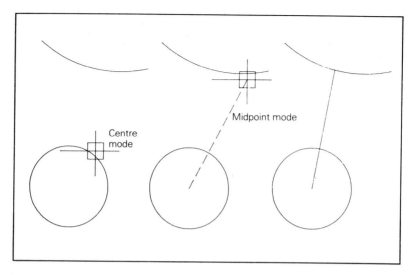

Figure 7.6 Constructing line from centre of circle to mid-point of arc

8 · Text and dimensioning

8.1 TEXT

Text can be incorporated into an AutoCAD drawing using the TEXT or DTEXT commands. The text positioning, justification and height can be altered as required, as can the text style and font.

> **Command:** TEXT
> **Start point or Align/Center/Fit/Middle/Right/Style:**
> **Height:**   (Type in a height or point using the mouse.)
> **Rotation angle:**   (0 for horizontal text.)
> **Text:**

The majority of the options are concerned with the positioning of the subsequent text within the drawing:

> **Start point**   This is the default response. The indicated point sets the left-hand extremity of the base line of the text.
> **Align**   This prompts for two points which set the extremities of the text *base line*. The overall character size and orientation of the text is adjusted to fit these limits. Consequently there will be no prompts for Height or Angle.
> **Center**   This prompts for a point which sets the centre point of the *base line* of the text.
> **Fit**   Similar to Align. The two points requested set the limits of the text but the height is separately specified. The character width is then stretched or compressed to fit.
> **Middle**   Similar to Center. The specified point sets the midpoint of the *body* of the text.
> **Right**   The text base line is right justified from the specified point.

See Figure 8.1.

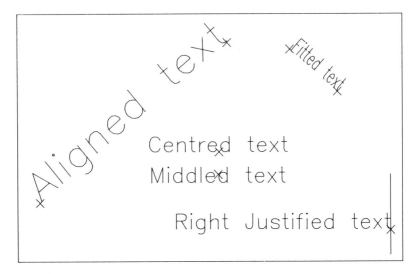

Figure 8.1 Text options

Note: If you have previously used the TEXT command in your drawing then, if you respond to the **Start point** prompt with a Return, the height and the angle of the last text entry will be assumed. In addition, the new text will adopt the previous alignment mode and automatically will be positioned immediately below the previous text.

8.1.1 Text Styles

The remaining option is **Style**. This determines the appearance of the text rather than its position. It selects a text style which has previously been defined using the STYLE command. The default style supplied is called STANDARD and uses a simple text font.

8.1.2 STYLE Command

If you do not wish to use the STANDARD style then you can define your own using the STYLE command.

A user-defined text style determines the text *font* to be used, e.g. Monotext, Roman, Gothic etc. There are over twenty font styles available, ranging from Italic to music symbols – Figure 8.2. If you select the Fonts option of the **Options** pull down menu an icon menu is displayed giving a visual representation of the fonts available.

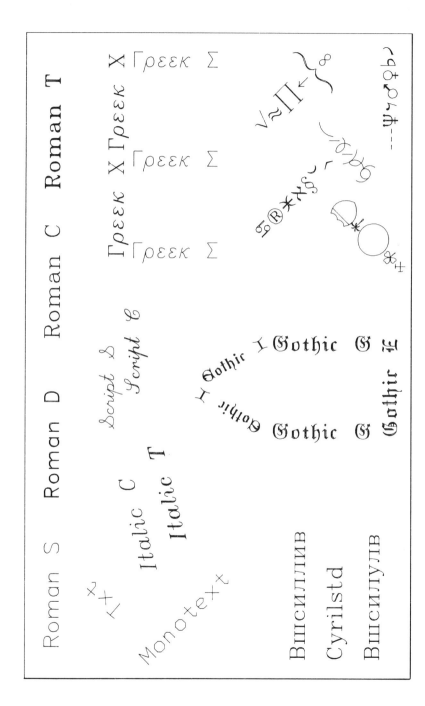

Figure 8.2 Text fonts

The style also determines the height, width factor, and obliquing angle of the text together with options for backwards, upside-down and vertical orientation (Figure 8.3).

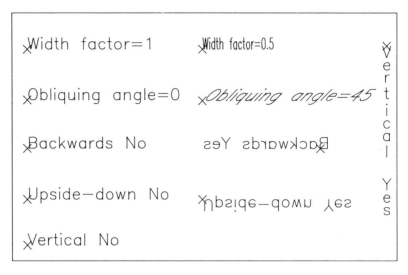

Figure 8.3 Aspects of text style

Command: STYLE
Text style name (or ?) ‹STANDARD›: MYSTYLE
New style.
Font file ‹txt›: GOTHICE
Height ‹0.000›:
Width factor ‹1.00›:
Obliquing angle ‹0.0000›:
Backwards? ‹N›
Upside-down? ‹N›
Vertical? ‹N›
MYSTYLE is now the current style

The default style, STANDARD, has a height of 0 (which allows you to adjust the height each time the style is used), a width factor of 1, an obliquing angle of 0 and it has the backward, upside-down and vertical options all normal.

If you redefine an existing style (using the original style name but changing the font) then any text previously written in this style will be changed to the new font.

A useful quick way to set a new text style is again to use the Fonts icon pull down menu. If you now 'pick' a text font from the icon menu, AutoCAD will proceed to set up a new text style using this font. The only difference from using the STYLE command from the keyboard is that you will not be allowed to give your choice of name to the new style – the style name will default to the name of the font chosen.

8.1.3 Special Characters

AutoCAD supports a limited number of special characters in addition to the standard characters found in the text fonts. These are identified by the %% sign which must be inserted within the text string to warn AutoCAD that a special character is about to be used:

%%u	Toggle underline mode on/off
%%o	Toggle overline mode on/off
%%d	Draw 'degrees' symbol °
%%p	Draw 'plus/minus' symbol ±
%%c	Draw 'circle diameter' symbol ∅

See Figure 8.4.

What you type	What you get
%%uUNDERLINED%%u NORMAL	UNDERLINED NORMAL
%%oOVERLINED%%o NORMAL	OVERLINED NORMAL
25%%dC	25°C
%%p0.1mm	±0.1mm
%%c50mm	∅50mm

Figure 8.4 Special character definitions

In addition to the above, it is possible to specify *any* of the characters in a font file by way of their ASCII code numbers. The ASCII (American Standard Code for Information Interchange) code numbers used in an AutoCAD font range from 1 to 126 (although codes 1–31 are control characters which are not normally used). The remaining characters may be specified using

%%nnn

Where nnn represents the three digits of the ASCII code. This allows you to have access to all the characters of the font *even if they do not appear on your keyboard*.

It is also possible to add non-standard symbols to the character set and assign them code numbers between 130 and 255. In this case the %%nnn method is the *only* way that you will be able to access them. See Section 13.5.7.

8.1.4 Dynamic Text (DTEXT)

DTEXT is an improvement on TEXT in that it allows you to see the text appearing on the screen as you type it on the keyboard. You can also edit each line with the Backspace key and enter multiple lines of text within one command.

The command sequence is initially identical to TEXT.

Command: DTEXT
Start point or Align/Center/Fit/Middle/Right/Style:
Height:
Rotation angle:
Text:

When the **Text:** prompt appears a box is drawn on the screen indicating the position, height and angle of the first character. As the text is entered it is echoed on the screen as well as in the text prompt area. As each line of text is returned the box cursor drops to the position one line below the starting point and the **Text:** prompt is repeated. A final Return terminates DTEXT by re-writing all the text on the screen in its final form, obeying any **Fit**, **Middle** or other justification criteria.

Successive characters or lines of text within the same DTEXT command can be placed at different points on the screen by using the mouse to point to the new start position.

The special %% characters may be used within DTEXT but they will be printed on the screen verbatim, e.g. as %%p, until the DTEXT command is terminated, at which time they will be translated into the relevant special symbol.

8.1.5 Quick Text (QTEXT)

QTEXT acts as a toggle that can be switched On or Off at any time.

Command: QTEXT
ON/OFF: ON

When QTEXT is On, any existing text will be replaced at the next Regeneration by a simple rectangular box outline which approximately covers the position previously occupied by the text (Figure 8.5). This greatly speeds up the regeneration process because the box is much quicker to draw than the text, particularly if a complex text font is employed. At the same time the position of the text is clearly shown to facilitate layout of the drawing.

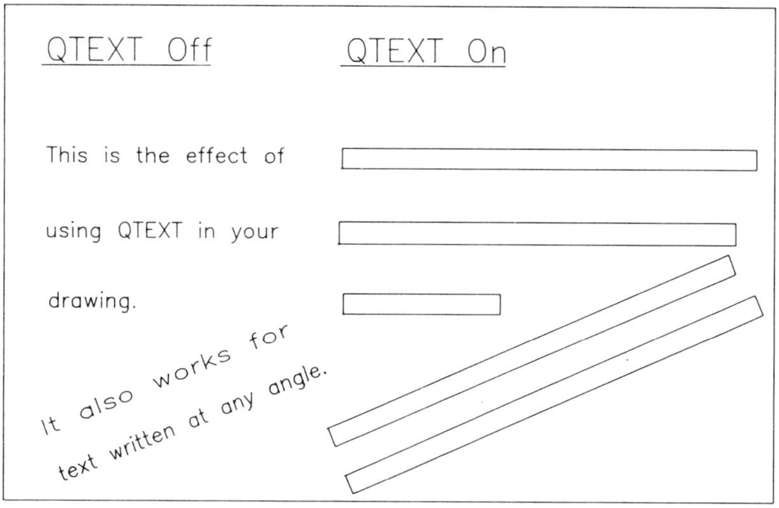

Figure 8.5 Effect of QTEXT

Text entered after Qtext mode has been turned On will initially be displayed normally, but after the next regeneration it also will be displayed in rectangular box form.

The current Qtext mode prevailing when the drawing is saved will be preserved and reinstated when the drawing is retrieved. When you wish to plot the full drawing, enter QTEXT: Off followed by REGEN.

8.2 DIMensioning

Dimensions can be added to a drawing by the rather tedious method of drawing each dimension line and adding the dimension via the TEXT command. A much easier, more efficient way is to use AutoCAD's comprehensive in-built DIM command.

AutoCAD provides four basic types of dimensioning – linear, angular, diameter and radius.

8.2.1 Dimension Terminology

There are various terms which are used to describe the way in which an entity is dimensioned and it is essential to be familiar with these. See Figures 8.6 and 8.7.

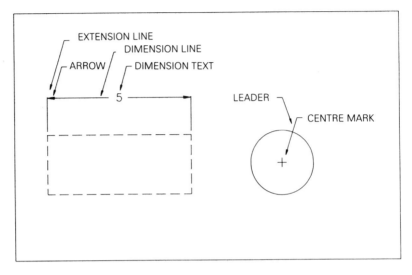

Figure 8.6 Dimension terminology

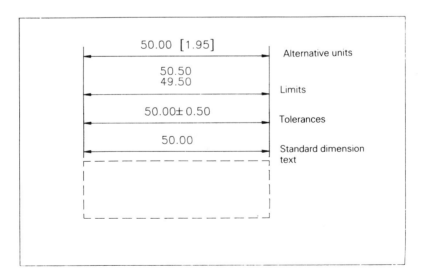

Figure 8.7 Dimension units

- *Dimension line.* A line with 'arrows' which marks out the dimension boundary; the dimension text is either positioned alongside the dimension line or it divides the dimension line in two. If the dimension is too small to take the text then the dimension lines will take the form of two 'arrows' pointing inward to two short lines which mark the positions of the measured object.
- *Arrows.* Different countries and professions have a variety of different drafting standards; for this reason AutoCAD allows the drawing of arrows, tick marks or an arbitrary arrow block (defining a symbol of your choice) at the end of the dimension line.
- *Extension lines.* If the dimension line is drawn outside the limits of the object being measured then extension lines are drawn, perpendicular to the dimension line. They are used only with linear and angular dimensioning.
- *Dimension text.* This is the text string which is used to indicate the measured dimension. AutoCAD will automatically compute the dimension text from the drawing (the default); this can be put directly into the drawing. Alternatively, this response can be overridden and the dimension text can be input from the keyboard. The dimension text will be in the current text style and default units (these can be changed by invoking the UNITS command).
- *Tolerances.* Dimension tolerances can be appended to the dimension text automatically. The plus and minus quantities may be equal or may be different. If they are equal then AutoCAD will use the ± symbol, if they are different then they will be displayed one above the other.
- *Limits.* The tolerance values can be added and subtracted from the dimension value giving the limits for the measured line rather than the nominal value. The upper and lower limits will be displayed one above the other.
- *Alternate units.* Two sets of units can be used simultaneously, e.g. the dimension text can be displayed in both inches and millimetres.
- *Leaders.* A leader is a line drawn from the object being measured to an area of the drawing free to take the dimension text, e.g. if a circle is too small to have the radius drawn within it then a leader would be used to position the dimension text in a free area outside the circle.
- *Centre mark/line.* The centre of a circle or arc can be shown by using either a centre mark (a small cross) or a centre line (broken lines crossing at the centre and intersecting the circumference of the circle or arc).
- *Variables.* The presentation of dimensions in a drawing is controlled by a set of dimension variables, some being simple on/off types while others have numerical values. These can be changed at any time from within the drawing.

8.2.2 DIM and DIM1

The two commands DIM and DIM1 are used to access the dimension function. DIM1 is used for single dimension commands, whereas DIM is used when a number of dimension commands are to executed.

When using DIM the only way to exit the command is by using Ctrl C, or by selecting EXIT from the DIM menu.

The screen menu which appears when either the DIM or DIM1 command is invoked is as follows:

AUTOCAD
* * * *
DIM:
DIM1:

LINEAR
angular
diameter
radius
center
leader
dim vars
redraw
status
undo
style
EXIT
next ----------------› **Hometext**
DRAW   **Update**
EDIT   **Newtext**

8.2.3 Linear Dimensioning

When the linear dimensioning option is chosen from the main dimension menu the following new menu appears:

horiz
vertical
aligned
rotated

baseline
continue

previous
last
--   --
DRAW
EDIT

There are four linear dimensioning options: horizontal, vertical, aligned or rotated (Figure 8.8). The only difference between these four options is the angle at which the dimension line is drawn.

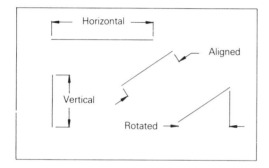

Figure 8.8 Linear dimension types

horiz   Draws the linear dimension line horizontally.
vertical   Draws the linear dimension line vertically.
aligned   Aligns the dimension line to the object being dimensioned.
rotated   Allows the specification of an angle for the dimension line.

The two other commands available in the linear menu are BASELINE and CONTINUE.

baseline   Continues the linear dimension from the first extension line
(baseline) of the previous dimension, i.e. several points along a line can
be dimensioned from the start of the line.
continue   Continues the linear dimension from the last extension line
defined in
the previous dimension, i.e. the distance between points along a line
can be
dimensioned without having to specify the first point each time.

The difference between these two methods is shown in Figure 8.9.

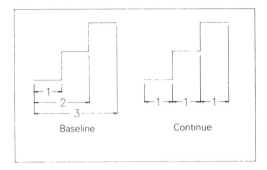

Figure 8.9 Further linear dimension options

The command sequence for linear dimensioning is as follows:

Pick LINEAR from the menu
dim: HORIZ or VERTICAL or ALIGNED or ROTATED

First extension line origin or RETURN to select:

There are two valid responses to the above prompt:

1. Specify a point on the drawing – the first extension line origin
   AutoCAD will then prompt:

   Second extension line origin:

   Specify the position of the start of the second extension line.

2. A Return (or pressing the space bar) allows you to choose a line arc or circle
   for dimensioning.
   AutoCAD will then prompt:

   Select line, arc or circle:

   Specify the line, arc or circle to be dimensioned by pointing or by using a
   window.

Once the extents of the dimension line have been given AutoCAD will ask for the
position of the dimension line, i.e a point through which the dimension line will
pass.

Dimension line location:

It then just remains to input the dimension text:

Dimension text ‹measured length›:

There are two ways of entering the dimension text:

AutoCAD will compute the distance between the two extension lines and give the value in drawing units. This is the default response and so pressing the Return will automatically add this dimension to your drawing. If you wish to add a prefix or suffix to the computed value then this can be achieved by inputting the prefix followed by ‹›, or by inputting ‹› followed by the suffix. The ‹› represents the computed value.

Alternatively, you can input your own value by simply entering it as text at this point.

8.2.4 ANGULAR Dimensioning

The dimension line in this case is an arc spanning the angle between the two extension lines. Normally the angle to be dimensioned will be between two intersecting lines but this does not have to be the case, AutoCAD allows the dimensioning of the angle between two lines which do not touch at all.

dim: ANGULAR
Select first line:
Second line:
Enter the dimension line arc location:
Dimension text ‹measured angle›:
Enter text location:

The prompts above are similar to those used in linear dimensioning apart from the request for text location. A Return at this point will cause AutoCAD to position the text across the dimension line, breaking the line first to allow room for the text. If there is not enough room for the text AutoCAD will ask for a new location. If you specify a location for the text AutoCAD will assume that there is enough room and will not check to see if it is overwriting other work.

8.2.5 DIAMETER Dimensioning

Both circles and arcs can be dimensioned using this command.

dim: DIAMETER
Select arc or circle:

The dimension line will run through the centre of the circle and also the point used to select the circle. It is therefore important to select the point with care to ensure that the dimension line is positioned correctly.

Dimension text ‹measured value›:

If the text will not fit inside the circle then AutoCAD will prompt:

Text does not fit. Enter leader length for text:

Enter the leader line length – this will cause a line to be drawn from the point chosen on the diameter to the text.

8.2.6 RADIUS Dimensioning

The radius command is almost identical to the diameter command – a line is drawn from the centre of the circle to the point used to specify the circle. The text is drawn along the radius line; if the text will not fit then a leader will be drawn – this can be located at either end of the radius line. See Figure 8.10.

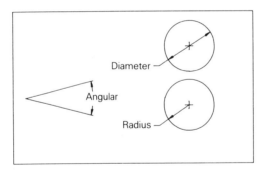

Figure 8.10 Radius and diameter dimensioning

8.2.7 Dimensioning Utilities

- CENTER. Draws a centre mark or lines in a circle or arc, dependent on the setting of the DIMCEN variable.
- LEADER. The main role of leaders, as described earlier, is the positioning of dimension text in a free area of the drawing when the allowable space within the dimension line is insufficient. The command LEADER can be invoked independently of other DIM commands and allows the construction of fairly complex leaders. When invoked you will be prompted for a **Leader**

start followed by any number of **To** points. Any point can be undone by typing a U; a null response allows dimension text to be input.

- REDRAW. This causes the redrawing of the entire drawing, deleting any point entities present.
- STATUS. The STATUS command gives a list of the dimension variables, their associated 'status' and a brief description of each, as in the list of variables below.
- UNDO. This lets you delete the last dimension command; by repeatedly using UNDO you can step back through the dimension commands to the beginning of the sequence.
- STYLE. Allows the changing of the dimension text style (as with the standard text STYLE command)
- EXIT. Allows you to exit from the DIM command mode.
- HOMETEXT. If the dimension text has been positioned away from the dimension line then Hometext causes the repositioning of the dimension text to its 'home' position. For example, if a dimensioned line has been stretched then the dimension text will be 'out of position'. HOMETEXT places the dimension text correctly relative to the stretched line – at its centre point (Figure 8.11).

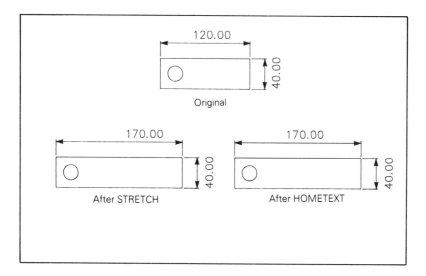

Figure 8.11 HOMETEXT

- UPDATE. If it is decided that dimensions already added to a drawing are not completely correct, e.g. the dimension text size is too small, it is necessary to change the dimension variables. Therefore to update the old dimensions, change the desired dimension variable, invoke the UPDATE command, select the dimensions to be updated and execute with a Return.

● NEWTEXT. Used to respecify the text for a dimension entity without having first to erase the old dimension and then respecify it.

8.2.8 Dim Variables

The appearance of dimensions in a drawing is totally governed by the setting of the dimension variables. Some variables are of the on/off variety while the remainder represent sizes and distances. Normally the dimension variables will be preset by the user in the prototype drawing, but occasionally it will be found necessary to change the odd one. This is achieved by simply selecting Dim Vars from the dimension menu, picking the variable name and making the required change.

This is simple enough. The main problem with the dimension variables is in remembering which is which. A series of diagrams is shown in Figures 8.12 and 8.13 which illustrate the functions of the different variables.

Some alternative versions of the AutoCAD menu supply similar diagrams as icons which also give access to each variable so that its value can be changed. This is the preferred method for editing dimension variables and you should enquire from your AutoCAD dealer whether such alternative menu software is available. In the UK this is supplied as an extra menu file called ACADUK.MNU and the associated slide library ACADUK.SLB. (See Section 15.2 to learn about menu changing.)

The full list of dimension variables is given below together with the normal default settings:

DIMALT	Off	Alternate units selected
DIMALTD	2	Alternate units decimal places
DIMALTF	25.4000	Alternate units scale factor
DIMAPOST		Default suffix for alternate text
DIMASO	On	Create associative dimension
DIMASZ	0.1800	Arrow size
DIMBLK		Arrow block name
DIMBLK1		First arrow block name
DIMBLK2		Second arrow block name
DIMCEN	0.0900	Centre mark size
DIMDLE	0.0000	Dimension line extension
DIMDLI	0.3800	Dimension line increment for continuation
DIMEXE	0.1800	Extension above dimension line
DIMEXO	0.0625	Extension line origin offset
DIMLFAC	1.0000	Linear unit scale factor
DIMLIM	Off	Generate dimension limits
DIMPOST		Default suffix for dimension text
DIMRND	0.0000	Rounding value

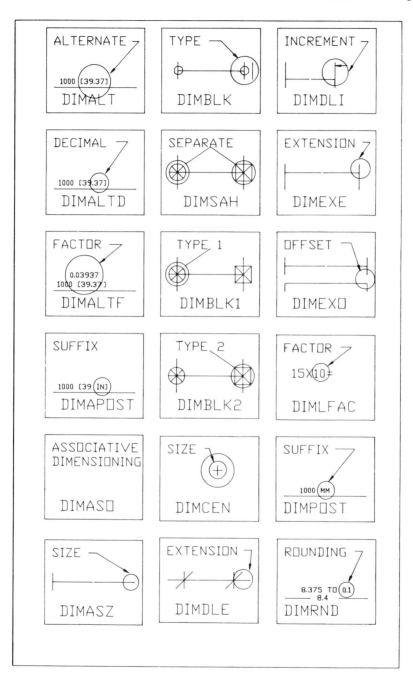

Figure 8.12 Dimension variables

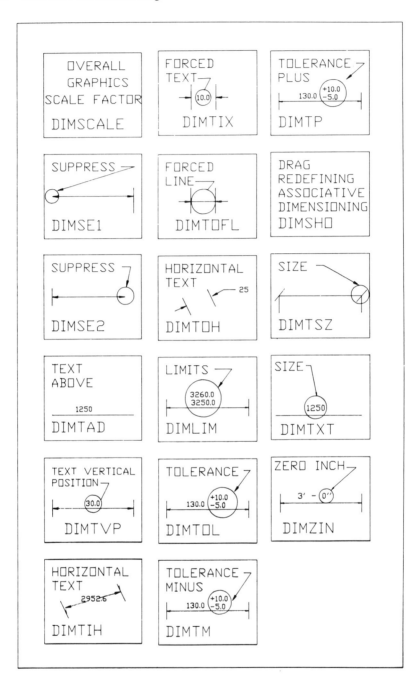

Figure 8.13 Dimension variables

DIMSAH	Off	Separate arrow blocks
DIMSCALE	1.0000	Overall scale factor
DIMSE1	Off	Suppress the first extension line
DIMSE2	Off	Suppress the second extension line
DIMSHO	Off	Update dimensions while dragging
DIMSOXD	Off	Suppress outside extension dimension
DIMTAD	Off	Place text above the extension line
DIMTIH	On	Text inside extensions is horizontal
DIMTIX	Off	Place text inside extensions
DIMTM	0.0000	Minus tolerance
DIMTOFL	Off	Force line inside extension lines
DIMTOH	On	Text outside extensions is horizontal
DIMTOL	Off	Generate dimension tolerances
DIMTP	0.0000	Plus tolerance
DIMTSZ	0.0000	Tick size
DIMTVP	0.0000	Text vertical position
DIMTXT	0.1800	Text height
DIMZIN	0	Zero inches/feet control

8.2.9 Associated Dimension Commands

There are various commands which edit dimension entities automatically when changing a drawing. The dimension entities must be included in the selection set together with the drawn entities which are to be altered or edited.

The commands are:

ARRAY	Polar array only
EXTEND	Linear dimensions only
MIRROR	
ROTATE	
SCALE	
STRETCH	Linear and angular dimensions only
TRIM	Linear dimensions only

The command EXPLODE can be used to split a dimension into its component parts, which can later be edited individually.

9·Linetypes and hatching

9.1 Linetypes

AutoCAD contains a library of various linetypes which can be called at any time during the drawing execution. The standard AutoCAD linetypes are kept in a library file called ACAD.LIN (Figure 9.1). It is possible to create your own linetypes (containing only dots and dashes) and library file. See Section 13.3.

It is possible to change the linetype for entities drawn on a specific layer by using the Ltype subcommand (found when the LAYER command is invoked) as long as the desired linetype has already been loaded into the drawing file. AutoCAD will perform an automatic REGEN using the new linetype definition and therefore all entities previously drawn on that layer will take up the new linetype.

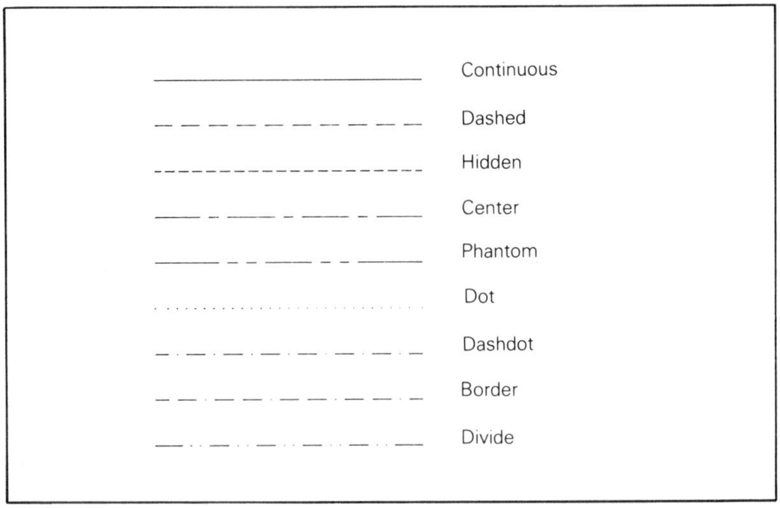

Figure 9.1 Linetypes

> *Note:* There are certain rules which must be observed when using the linetype command:
>
> 1. Only lines, arcs, circles, ellipses, polygons and polylines can have their linetype changed. All other entities are drawn with the 'continuous' linetype.
> 2. A linetype definition must exist in a linetype library before it can be loaded into a drawing or assigned to a layer.
> 3. When the linetype has been loaded into the drawing its definition is read into the drawing file, it is therefore not necessary to reload the linetype from the library file for subsequent use.

All commands associated with LINETYPE can be executed either from the screen menu or directly from the keyboard, but the Entity Creation dialogue box, Figure 9.2, (found under **Settings** pull down menu) can only be used to Set the current linetype.

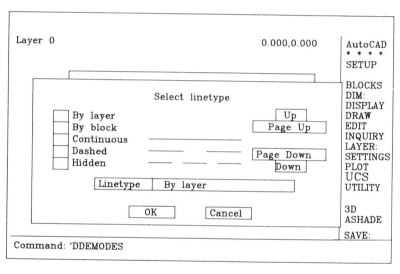

Figure 9.2 Linetype dialogue box

Command: LINETYPE
?/Create/Load/Set:

?   The ? will show the linetypes which are available for loading into your drawing file from the requested library file. If the only library file which exists is the AutoCAD standard linetype library file then this will be the default. If you have created your own library file then this can be called and will then become the default. AutoCAD prompts:

File to list ‹default›:

Load   Before a linetype can be loaded into a drawing file it must exist in a
        library file. When Load is called then the linetype name has to be
        entered followed by the library file name. AutoCAD will search
        this file for the requested linetype.

Name of linetype to load: (* will load all linetypes)
File to search ‹default›:

Note: Linetypes may not be loaded using the dialogue box.

Set   When the linetype has been loaded into the drawing file it can then
       be made the current linetype by using the Set option. All new
       drawing entities will then take the new linetype.

New entity linetype (or ?) ‹current›

        There are also a number of other responses which are allowed at
        this point: If you respond with BYLAYER then the linetype will
        be that which has previously been set for the layer on which the
        entities are being drawn. The special instruction BYBLOCK causes
        all entities to be drawn with a 'continuous' linetype until they are
        grouped together into a block. Whenever the block is inserted it
        will then inherit the current entity-linetype. The final special
        instruction is the ? which lists the currently loaded linetypes.

Create   Allows you to create your own simple linetypes. (section 13.3.1)

The Linetype of an entity may be altered by using the CHANGE or CHPROP
command. If the requested linetype is not resident in the drawing file AutoCAD
will search the standard library file (ACAD.LIN) automatically. If the linetype
cannot be found AutoCAD will then check to see whether it is in another library
file – if so *you* must load the linetype using the LINETYPE command.

9.1.1 LTSCALE

The linetype dash specification is in terms of drawing units. As these can be
thought of as, say, 'inches' or 'kilometres' it is useful to be able to scale the
linetype. LTSCALE allows this.

A linetype scale of 25 drawing units is the usual default value. When the
scale is changed then the drawing is automatically regenerated.

Command: LTSCALE
New scale factor ‹default›:

> *Note:* If LTSCALE is set too large or too small then the effect is to make most linetypes appear to be continuous (Figure 9.3).

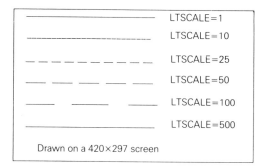

Figure showing:
- LTSCALE=1
- LTSCALE=10
- LTSCALE=25
- LTSCALE=50
- LTSCALE=100
- LTSCALE=500

Drawn on a 420×297 screen

Figure 9.3 The effect of LTSCALE

9.2 HATCHing

As with linetypes AutoCAD has a built-in library of hatch patterns stored in a library file called ACAD.PAT. These are shown in Figures 9.4 and 9.5. It is possible to create your own hatch patterns and store them for future use (see Section 13.4), or create simple patterns for one time use from within the hatch command.

A hatch pattern is made of a number of hatch lines *of the current linetype* which have a particular angle and spacing.

Command: HATCH
Pattern (? or name/U,style) ‹default›:
Scale for pattern ‹1.0000›:
Angle for pattern ‹0.0000›:
Select objects:

> *Note:* The resulting hatched pattern area in all but the most simple cases may differ depending upon the method of selection used, i.e. if a window is used rather than picking individual entities (Figure 9.6).

? Lists the standard hatch patterns stored in the library file ACAD.PAT together with their general use. When the desired pattern has been chosen, input its name to make it the default pattern for all subsequent

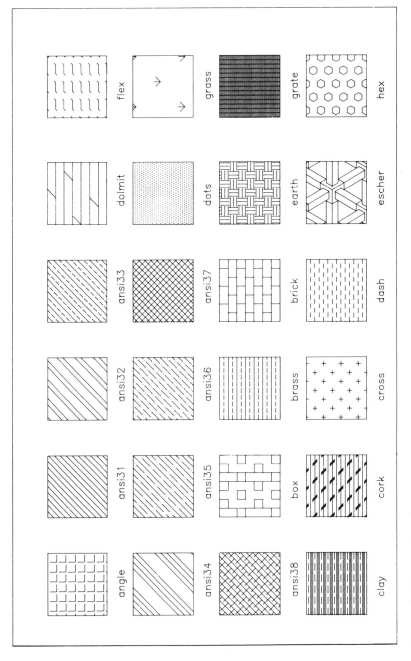

Figure 9.4 Library hatch patterns

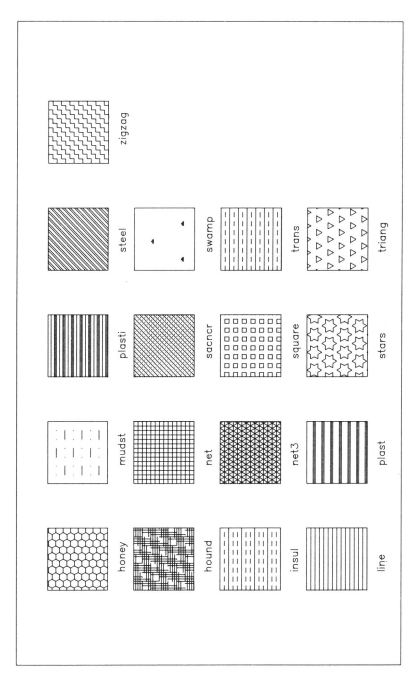

Figure 9.5 Library hatch patterns

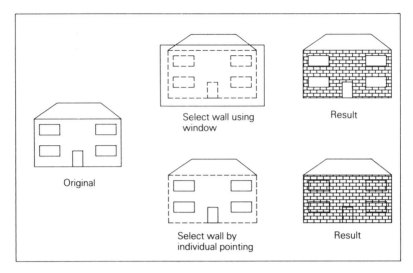

Figure 9.6 The effect of selection methods on the hatched area

hatching. If the name of the hatch pattern is followed by a comma and one of the letters N, O, I, then the hatch style will be changed (see Hatch Styles), e.g.

Pattern (? or name/U,style) ‹default›: escher,o

will change the default to the escher hatch with 'outermost' style.

U   User defined. Simple hatch patterns can be defined for immediate use only. AutoCAD will prompt:

Angle for crosshatch lines ‹default›:
Spacing between lines ‹default›:
Double hatch area? ‹default›:

The double hatch area prompt requires a yes or no input; it refers to whether you require a second set of lines drawn at right angles to the original lines.

Note: If the HATCH command was the last command used and is recalled with a Return then the previously used pattern, scale and angle will be assumed and you will be prompted only to select objects. If you need to respecify any of these parameters then you must give a fresh HATCH command.

9.2.1 Boundary of Hatched Area

The boundary of the area to be hatched has to be specified and it is important that it is made up of single entities which join at their end points. If one of the entities overhangs the hatch area, then the hatch pattern will be generated incorrectly; the overhanging segment must therefore be removed or replaced by two separate entities.

If the areas ABCH and GDEF are to be hatched then the lines AF and BE have to be broken into the separate segments AH, GF, BC and DE using invisible cuts (BREAK command) at points C,D,H and G (Figure 9.7).

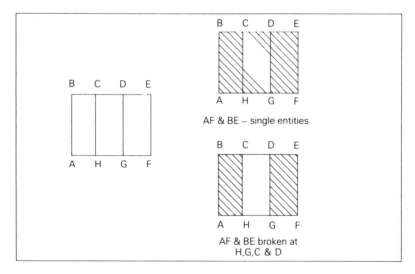

Figure 9.7 Boundary of hatched area

Alternatively, lines BC, CD, DE, AH, HG and GF may be individually drawn.

9.2.2 Hatch Styles

When using HATCH it is important that only the *required* area is cross-hatched. If the space inside the boundary chosen is empty then there are no problems, but if there are separate entities within the boundary then it is necessary to specify which areas are to be hatched. There are various hatch 'styles' which can be invoked to allow specification of the areas to be hatched (Figure 9.8).

Normal: Normal is the default setting. It causes the hatch lines to extend from the outer boundary wall to the next intersecting line; the hatch

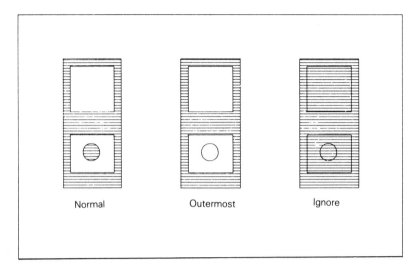

Normal   Outermost   Ignore

Figure 9.8 Hatch styles

line is then turned off until it meets the next intersecting line which reactivates the hatch line etc. If the boundary lines are numbered from the outermost inwards, areas which are surrounded by an odd-numbered line will be hatched whereas areas surrounded by an even-numbered line will not (Figure 9.9).

Outermost: This again hatches inward from the area boundary. If an intersecting line is encountered, then the hatch line is turned off and does not turn back on again as in the Normal case, with the result that only the outermost area is hatched.

Ignore: Any entity within the boundary area is ignored, the hatch lines extending over them to the opposite boundary line.

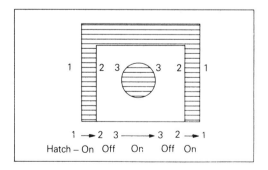

Figure 9.9 Normal hatch style mechanism

When hatch lines encounter attributes, text, shapes, traces or solids then the hatch line is turned off. An invisible box exists around attribute shape or text which, if the objects have been selected using a window, will not be hatched (unless the 'ignore' option has been selected). See Figure 9.10.

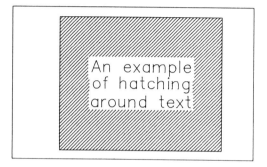

Figure 9.10 Hatching inhibited by text

10 · Plotting

The end product of most drawings will be a 'hard copy' or plot. Plotting may be performed using a plotter or a dot matrix printer. In general, the plotter will give a much more satisfactory result but the printer will probably be cheaper and quicker. Most of the following, with the exception of the section covering pens and colours, will be applicable to both plotting and printer plotting.

Plotting with a plotter is initiated from main menu Task 3 or from the PLOT command. The corresponding printer plot comes from main menu Task 4 or the PRPLOT command.

If you are plotting from the main menu you must specify the drawing title. PLOT and PRPLOT are used with a drawing currently loaded. The advantage of the latter methods is that you have a more visual choice of which sections of the drawing are plotted.

10.1 Choosing What to PLOT

Let us assume that you have developed a drawing and wish to plot it on a plotter. The golden rule is that, before you do anything else, you *must save the drawing*. It is possible for things to go wrong during plotting and you can find yourself in a situation where the machine 'hangs up' and you have to switch off and lose the drawing.

> **Command:** PLOT
> **What to plot -- Display, Extents, Limits, View, or Window ‹D›:**

This first prompt will occur with the drawing still on the screen. It is asking which part of the drawing should be plotted. The most likely response is the default response – Display – which simply means the drawing as presently displayed on the screen. This need not necessarily be the complete drawing, it could be a small view produced by ZOOM. The alternatives are reasonably self-explanatory:

Extents   Plots the whole drawing rather as ZOOM Extents fills the screen with the drawing contents, leaving no surrounding space.

Limits   Plots the entire drawing area as defined by the drawing limits. This may differ from the area actually in use.

View   Plots a predefined and named view of the drawing.

Window   Allows you to window a small section of the displayed drawing and plot only that area.

As soon as you have chosen one of these alternatives the drawing will vanish from the screen.

10.2 The Plotter Menu

A new and fierce-looking menu will now appear, looking typically like the following:

Plot will NOT be written to a selected file
Sizes are in millimetres
Plot origin is at (0.00,0.00)
Plotting area is 359.92 wide by 269.98 high (MAX size)
Plot is NOT rotated 90 degrees
Pen width is 0.25
Area fill will be adjusted for pen width
Hidden lines will NOT be removed
Plot will be scaled to fit available area

Do you want to change anything? ‹N›

Taking these one by one:

1. **Plot will NOT be written to a selected file**
   This writes your plot to a file for subsequent use. It needs special software not supplied with AutoCAD for it to be of any use. Its most likely application is with desk top publishing where the plot file can be used to introduce the drawing into a mixed text/graphics format.

2. **Sizes are in millimetres**
   The lengths of the lines plotted by the plotter are directly related to the drawing units at the top of the drawing. These units can be considered to be either inches or millimetres.

3. **Plot origin is at (0.00,0.00)**

   The plot origin is normally at 0,0 but it can be shifted by changing these coordinates.

4. **Plotting area is 359.92 wide by 269.98 high (MAX size)**

   This is the plotting area – in millimetres in this case because of entry (2) – which can be handled by your plotter and will vary depending upon which plotter was specified at configuration.

5. **Plot is NOT rotated 90 degrees**

   The plotted drawing can be as it appeared on the screen (landscape format), or rotated clockwise through 90° (portrait format).

6. **Pen width is 0.25**

   This is only important when the plotter is filling in solid areas such as a doughnut. The finer the pen tip the more fill-in strokes will be needed to fill the area.

7. **Area fill will be adjusted for pen width**

   See above.

8. **Hidden lines will NOT be removed**

   This applies only to three-dimensional drawings and is used for changing a wire-frame model into one with a solid appearance.

9. **Plot will be scaled to fit available area**

   If the dimensions of the final plotted drawing are not critical it is usually best to scale the drawing so that it fits the paper. The drawing units will not be faithfully reproduced as either inches or millimetres in this case, although relative sizes will of course be maintained.

   There is a fair chance that you will not wish to change anything from this menu, in which case return the No default. The package will now give you a chance to set up the plotter. If all is ready, give another Return. Depending on the complexity of the drawing the plotter will start immediately or there may first be a delay while the coordinates of the drawing are calculated. After the plot has been completed a further Return will put the drawing back on screen.

   A plot can be terminated at any time by a Ctrl C but the response may not be immediate because the plotter can store blocks of coordinates in its buffer and will insist on working through them before stopping. *Do not switch off the plotter while it is plotting* – you may hang up the computer and may lose your drawing if not previously saved.

10.3 Changing the Plotter Menu

If you do wish to change any of the plotter menu items, then return Y at the **Do**

you wish to change anything? prompt. You will first of all be shown a pen/colour menu. Ignore this using the No default (see below). You will then be prompted with each of the menu items (1)–(9) above. Change the ones which you want to change and Return the others. The prompts are quite helpful.

In the case of the last item

Plot will be scaled to fit available area

if you want to scale the drawing to fit the paper the response is

F

As AutoCAD expects all drawings to be constructed full size it is at this point that the required scale should be specified. When the drawing was originally constructed a drawing unit was considered as, say, 1 millimetre. This can now be related to a real plotted length.

Thus, to specify a true scale of drawing units to real millimetres or inches on the paper the response could be:

1=2

which means that 1 plotted millimetre (or inch if I is specified at item 2) is equal to 2 drawing units. Alternatively,

100=1

would give a scale of 100 plotted millimetres (or inches) = 1 drawing unit.

You should always look carefully at the plotter menu. You will find that *AutoCAD remembers the last menu* and will produce the modified menu rather than the original the next time PLOT is entered.

10.4 Plotting in Different Colours

Most plotters, as distinct from printers, have the ability to change pens and plot in multi-colours. Thus, even if you have a monochrome display, it is possible to produce multi-coloured drawings if the colour options have been correctly invoked in the drawing.

Each colour with a colour number less than 16 can be separately assigned to a numbered pen in a multi-pen plotter. It is up to you to match the actual colours of the pens to the colours of the drawing in an acceptable way. Colours with numbers from 16–255 are automatically assigned to pen number 1.

To check on the current pen/colour configuration, request a plot and choose the required area of the drawing. AutoCAD will respond with the plotter menu described above. Respond with a Y at the end of the menu:

Do you want to change anything? ‹N› Y

You will then be shown the pen/colour menu:

Entity Color	Pen No.	Line Type	Pen Speed
1(red)	1	0	10
2(yellow)	2	0	10
3(green)	3	0	10
4(cyan)	4	0	10
5(blue)	5	0	10
6(magenta)	6	0	10
7(white)	7	0	10
8	8	0	10
:	:	:	:
:	:	:	:
15	1	0	10

Line types	
0 =	continuous line
1 =	....
2 =	....
3 =	---------------------
4 =	————————

Do you want to change any of these parameters? ‹N›

You will almost certainly need to change something so respond with a Y. You will then be presented with each line of the menu separately and will be able to match each colour with a pen number. If you have only a few pens you will have to assign the same pen to a number of different colours. When you have made all the adjustments that you need you can exit to the main plotter menu with an X.

It is advised that you ignore the linetype and pen speed options and leave them at their default values. This is particularly important if you have already introduced different linetypes into your drawing. The AutoCAD manual warns against mixing such software-defined linetypes with hardware-defined linetypes as found in this menu.

If your plotter supports only one pen AutoCAD will recognise this and pause during plotting to allow you to change pens.

11 · Isometric drawing

11.1 Isometric Axes

The isometric features of AutoCAD are provided simply as an aid to producing drawings with an isometric projection and should not be confused with the extensive three-dimensional facilities of the package. The features are closely linked with the SNAP command.

To commence a drawing in isometric projection, SNAP should be invoked and the Style option chosen.

Command: SNAP
Snap spacing or ON/OFF/Aspect/Rotate/Style: S
Standard/Isometric: I
Vertical spacing: 10

You will now see that the cross wires on the screen are no longer at right angle but are set at 60° to each other. When making isometric drawings, surfaces may be represented on one of three planes – Left, Top and Right. Lines defining these surfaces will normally be drawn at 30°, 90° or 150° to the horizontal. The cross wires in the isometric snap style act as an aid in the construction of these lines. Cross wire pairs may be inclined at 90° and 150° (Left-hand plane), 150° and 30° (Top plane) and 90° and 30° (Right-hand plane). These combinations and their associated planes are shown in Figure 11.1.

To switch from one pair of cross wires to another you may use the ISOPLANE command.

Command: ISOPLANE
Left/Top/Right/(Toggle):

Left plane, Top plane or Right plane cross wires may be specified by responding with L, T or R. Alternatively, the plane may be toggled from L to T to R to L etc by repeatedly pressing Return.

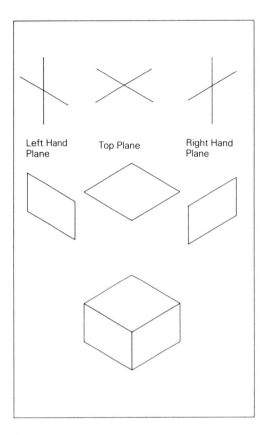

Figure 11.1 Isometric planes

However, you do not need to use ISOPLANE at all. AutoCAD allows you to toggle between each isometric plane by using Ctrl E. This has the advantage of being transparent and so can be used within a drawing command.

ORTHO, GRID and SNAP commands, when used with isometric style, respond exactly in keeping with their normal functions but always with reference to the isometric planes rather than the normal orthogonal planes.

11.2 Isocircles

Most of the drawing commands such as CIRCLE, POLYGON etc. do not take account of the isometric style but there is one drawing facility which is specially aimed at isometric style. This is the ISOCIRCLE section of the ELLIPSE command which is offered *only* when in isometric mode. A circular shape drawn on an isometric projection will, of course, be drawn as an ellipse. If it is assumed that the current drawing is in isometric style, then, to represent a circle :

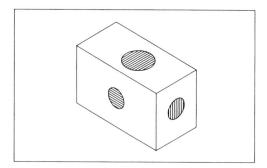

Figure 11.2 The illusion of circles

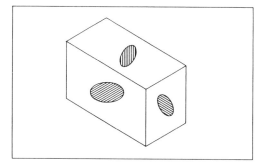

Figure 11.3 The illusion of circles destroyed

Command: ELLIPSE
‹Axis endpoint 1›/Center/Isocircle: |
Center of Circle:
‹Circle radius›/Diameter:

You can then specify the position and size of the 'circle' and the corresponding
ellipse will be drawn with reference to the current isometric plane. Figure 11.2
displays a box drawn with the help of the isometric facilities of AutoCAD and
shows isocircles inserted correctly into three of the plane surfaces. The angle of
the cross hatching has been adjusted to match the isoplanes to enhance the effect.

Be careful not to insert the circle on some plane other than the current
isoplane because the result will look 'wrong'. Figure 11.3 shows exactly the same
isocircles as the previous figure, but inserted on the wrong faces. The illusion that
they are circles has been totally lost.

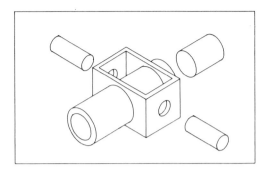

Figure 11.4 An example of an isometric drawing

Note: It is possible to produce very convincing three-dimensional representations using isometric drawing (Figure 11.4) but these are not recognised as three-dimensional drawings by AutoCAD. Any attempt to use the specialised three-dimensional commands such as VPOINT or HIDE on such a drawing will be unsuccessful and confusing.

12 · Three-dimensional drawing with AutoCAD

12.1 Three-dimensional drawing before Release 10

AutoCAD's original three-dimensional (3D) drawing facility could more accurately be referred to as 2.5-dimensional drawing. Simple entities such as lines, circles or arcs could be 'extruded' only in the Z-direction (i.e. perpendicular to the X–Y plane). These parallel-sided 3D entities were of only limited use – they could be rotated *only* about the Z-axis and *only* lines parallel to the Z-axis could be drawn. To overcome this second limitation AutoCAD Release 2.6 introduced two additional commands – 3DLINE and 3DFACE – allowing non-parallel-sided structures to be represented.

The original AutoCAD 3D drawing facility relied upon the specification of both elevation and thickness. Although this original 3D facility was very limited it has provided the basis upon which Release 10's extensive 3D features have been built.

12.1.1 Elevation and Thickness

The original method of 3D realisation was to construct the drawing as a 2D plan view of the object. If the plan is imagined to be drawn on a piece of paper, then the third dimension, the extrusion thickness, will extend either out of (above) or into (below) the paper's surface i.e. in the positive or negative Z-direction. Other items may be added to the plan view which are at another height or ELEVation above or below the paper, although always parallel to it (Figure 12.1). Thus, before any 3D object is drawn, its elevation and thickness must have been specified using the ELEV command or by selecting Entity Creation under the **Settings** pull down menu (DDEMODES). See Figure 12.2.

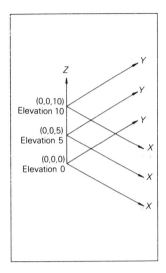

Figure 12.1 Different elevations

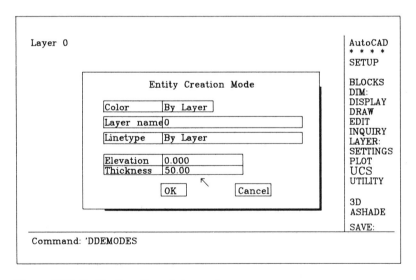

Figure 12.2 Entity Creation dialogue box

EXAMPLE

To draw a cylinder at elevation 0 and height 50 units:

> **Command:** ELEV
> **New current elevation** ‹0.0000›: 0
> **New current thickness:** ‹0.000›: 50

This sets the elevation and extrusion thickness of all subsequently drawn objects until these settings are respecified.

Remember that you are looking at the cylinder in plan view so that it will appear as a simple circle. To view the cylinder from a point other than directly above (Figure 12.3) use the VPOINT command. See Section 12.1.4.

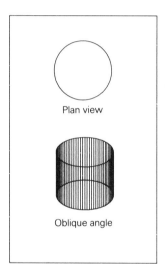

Figure 12.3 Changing the viewpoint

12.1.2 Varying the ELEVation and Thickness

The single cylinder example, when viewed from some oblique angle, clearly demonstrates the effect of setting the extrusion thickness. The thickness determines the height of the object, in the above example this is 50 units. The effect of the ELEVation term will become clearer when extra objects are added to the drawing at various elevations.

> *Note:* Although it is possible to modify and extend drawings from other viewpoints it is always safest to return to the plan view before any changes are made.

The cylinder is based at elevation 0 and has a height of 50. To place another cylinder on top of the first the elevation must be changed before the second cylinder is drawn (Figure 12.4).

Command: ELEV
New current elevation ‹0.0000›: 50
New current thickness: ‹50.00›: 75

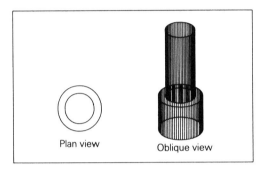

Plan view · Oblique view

Figure 12.4 Placing objects at different heights

12.1.3 Changing the Elevation and Thickness of Existing Entities

The elevation or thickness of any existing entity in a drawing may be altered by use of the CHANGE command. The entities are first selected in the normal manner and then P is returned to show that you wish to change one of the properties, followed by E or T for elevation or thickness.

12.1.4 VPOINT

To obtain the 3D effect we need to change the viewpoint – there are various ways of achieving this although the recently introduced icon method is the most convenient.

The viewpoint may be specified as a set of *XYZ* coordinates relative to the drawing which is assumed to be at the origin. Remember that if perspective views are not generated then these coordinates specify only a direction of view, not a viewing distance. Thus the viewpoint 0,−1,0 will be interpreted as a view from the centre ($X=0$), front ($Y=-1$) and ground level ($Z=0$) but will give just the same view on screen as the more distant viewpoint $0,-10,0$. A view from the left would be given by $-1,0,0$: from the right by $1,0,0$ from the rear by $0,1,0$ and from the top by $0,0,1$ (Figure 12.5).

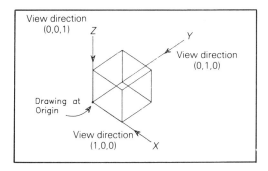

Figure 12.5 Specifying viewpoints

An isometric view from the right, front, top position would be obtained from viewpoint $1,-1,1$:

Command: VPOINT
Enter viewpoint ‹ X,Y,Z ›: $1,-1,1$

A 'wire frame' model of the drawing is now displayed (Figure 12.6). VPOINT may adjust the size of the display on screen, but the real dimensions and position of the object are not lost. To view the object from a different angle, repeat the VPOINT command and change the viewpoint coordinates.

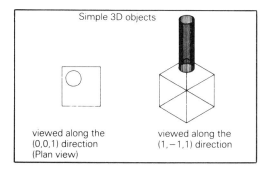

Figure 12.6 Wire frame representation

An alternative means of setting the viewpoint is provided which is more convenient, although less precise, than specifying the coordinates. If a null response (Return) is supplied at the VPOINT prompt the screen will clear and an axes tripod and a compass are displayed (Figure 12.7). Either representation may be used to specify the viewpoint but the compass is probably easier to understand.

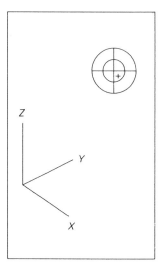

Figure 12.7 Compass method of specifying viewpoint

The compass is a two-dimensional representation of a globe as seen from above. Thus the centre point represents the north pole and if this position is picked with the pointing device the resulting display of the drawing will be a plan view (corresponding to coordinates 0,0,1).

The inner circle of the compass represents the equator and will always give a ground level (Z=0) view. '12 o'clock' on this circle represents a rear elevation (0,1,0), '3 o'clock' and '9 o'clock' represent side elevations (−1,0,0 and 1,0,0) and '6 o'clock' the front elevation (0,−1,0).

All points between the two compass circles represent points in the southern hemisphere and any corresponding viewpoint is from below the model (Z negative). The entire outer circle represents the south pole and gives a view from directly below the model (0,0,−1).

A third method of specifying the viewpoint is by defining the viewpoint angle.

Command: VPOINT
Rotate/‹View point›:   R
Enter angle in X-Y plane from X axis   45
Enter angle from X-Y plane   45

If you imagine the object being drawn in the X–Y plane and extruded in the

Z-plane it would appear as in Figure 12.8. The viewpoint P is defined by setting the two angles shown.

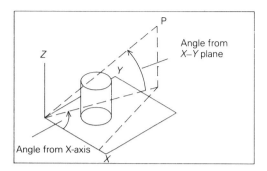

Figure 12.8 Viewpoint defined by angles

12.1.5 Viewpoint Selection by Icon Menu

The most convenient method of viewpoint selection is provided by picking 3D Viewpoint from the **Display** pull down menu. The required direction of view may be chosen from the displayed icons (Figure 12.9) and the viewpoint angle is selected from the corresponding screen menu.

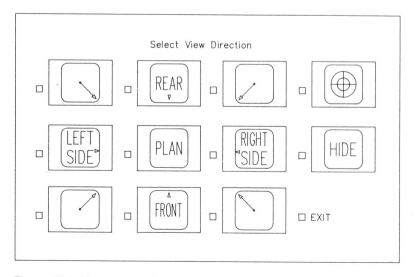

Figure 12.9 Viewpoint selection by icon menu

12.1.6 HIDE

Drawings are normally displayed as wire-frame models. This is acceptable for simple drawings but, as the complexity increases, the number of lines tends to obscure important features. The HIDE command takes a wire-frame model as viewed on the screen and removes those lines which would be hidden from view in a solid object viewed from that angle. The process is slow because each segment of each line must be treated separately. In a very complex drawing the time elapsed may extend to hours. Once the process is completed, the drawing is displayed on screen with hidden lines removed (Figure 12.10).

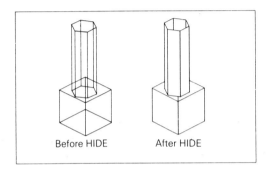

Before HIDE   After HIDE

Figure 12.10 The effect of HIDE

However, if you subsequently change the viewpoint *the drawing will revert to wire frame* because the HIDE operation was only relevant to the view current at the time HIDE was invoked.

The same is true for plotting. It is pointless going through the HIDE routine on screen if you wish only to plot the hidden lines version. Normal plotting will usually result in a wire-frame drawing. A plot with hidden lines removed *must be specified in the plotting menu* and the HIDE process will then be repeated, whether or not the display on screen has been processed by HIDE.

12.1.7 Solid and Hollow Entities

Following HIDE, wire-frame cylinders are represented as cylindrical solids. In many cases this is desirable but it is possible that you may wish to represent a hollow cylinder and yet still use the hidden lines facility. The AutoCAD software has built in to it some (rather arbitrary) decisions of how a particular shape should be considered. It all depends on the original 2D shape that was used in the plan view. Thus a circle, when extruded into a cylinder, is always considered to be a solid, i.e. it has a top and a bottom. If a hollow cylinder is required it must be derived from two arcs (Figure 12.11).

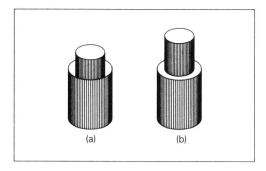

Figure 12.11(a) Hollow cylinder
Figure 12.11(b) Solid cylinder

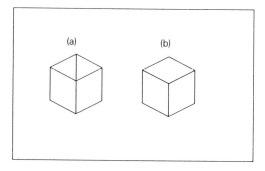

Figure 12.12(a) Open box
Figure 12.12(b) Solid box

Similarly, a box derived from lines will be thought of as having no top or bottom. To avoid this the original rectangle in the plan view may be drawn using a 3D Face, placed on top of the box to act as a lid (Figure 12.12). Circles, solids and wide polylines are all treated, when extruded, as solids by HIDE. Any non-closed entity in the 2D plan view will result in an open 3D structure (Figure 12.13).

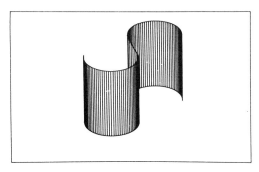

Figure 12.13 Open hidden entity

If SOLID is used as the basis of rectilinear structures it will be treated on screen as a filled area on the plan view but not in any other projection. If this is inconvenient the FILL facility can be turned off.

One of the problems with HIDE is that you cannot save a drawing in hidden form. This is not important for simple drawings but if the drawing is very large the time for a HIDE can be considerable and this must be endured each time a hidden version of the drawing is required.

One solution is to form a SLIDE of the drawing. See Chapter 14.

12.1.8 Hiding Objects that Touch

The decisions taken by the HIDE routine on whether any given object is hidden by another are a matter of accurate calculation of the coordinates. When two objects are drawn to be exactly touching each other the decision becomes almost arbitrary. Minute rounding errors in the calculation can have a disproportionate effect. Thus, in a drawing of a house, the line of an interior wall which touches an exterior wall may sometimes 'appear' on the outside view. This is usually caused when, in the plan view, the two walls are 'snapped' to the same position. In the case of point contacts this is rarely important but, with lines and surfaces in contact, care is required to achieve the desired result.

12.1.9 Displaying the Hidden Lines

It is sometimes useful if the hidden lines, instead of being completely suppressed, can be displayed on a separate layer and in a different colour. To achieve this it is necessary to create an additional special layer for each layer in the original drawing. The special layers must carry the same names as the original layers but prefixed with the word HIDDEN. Thus if the original drawing was on layers called PLANE1 and PLANE2 the new layers *must* be called HIDDENPLANE1 and HIDDENPLANE2. By setting new colours for these special layers the hidden lines are clearly displayed after a HIDE operation.

12.1.10 Turned Off and Frozen Layers

If an object is drawn on a layer that is turned off it is invisible on the screen but it can still be considered by the HIDE command and can thus obscure an object that would otherwise have been visible. If the unwanted layer is frozen instead of turned off this problem will not arise.

12.2 Three-dimensional drawing with Release 10

All the above commands and techniques are still available and relevant to 3D construction in Release 10. The standard 2D drawing commands are now used to create complex 3D constructions by manipulation of the coordinate system.

12.2.1 The User Coordinate System (UCS)

The User Coordinate System (UCS) is fundamental to the treatment of 3D constructions in Release 10.

Originally, AutoCAD made use of the static coordinate system – the coordinate point $X=0$, $Y=0$, $Z=0$ being fixed. All inputs were then made relative to this fixed origin and were therefore unique. This system is now known as the World Coordinate System (WCS). See Figure 12.14.

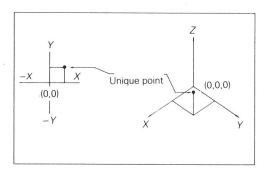

Figure 12.14 World Coordinate System

The user coordinate system allows the 0,0,0 point to be repositioned anywhere with respect to the previously defined origin. Any number of user coordinate systems, together with their user-defined 0,0,0 coordinate points, can now be defined within a drawing (Figure 12.15).

A UCS can be defined at any position and at any angle in space. This immensely simplifies the construction of 3D drawings, allowing 3D objects to be constructed using standard 2D techniques. Thus all the standard 2D entities such as circles, arcs, polygons etc. can be drawn on the current UCS X–Y plane. This is the *only* technique by which these 2D entities can be positioned anywhere in space. The exception to this rule is the LINE entity which has now been given full 3D properties, i.e. X-, Y- and Z-co-ordinates of the start and end points can now be specified to define uniquely its position in space. See Section 12.3.1.

All the original (pre-Release 10) 3D techniques, such as setting the extrusion thickness, can be applied to entities drawn on any defined UCS. For example, it is now possible to construct cylinders at any orientation in space (Figure 12.16).

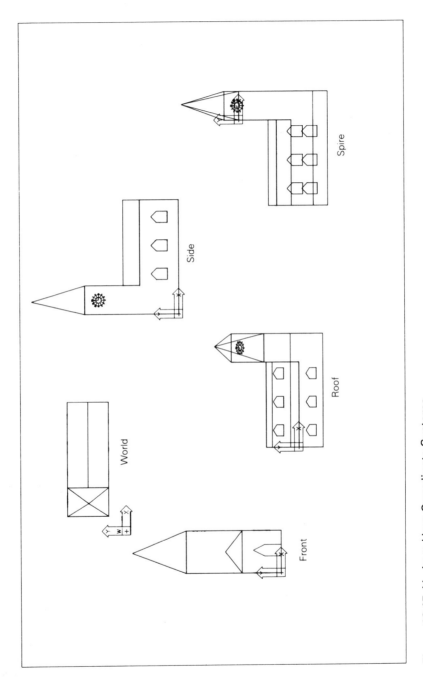

Figure 12.15 Various User Coordinate Systems

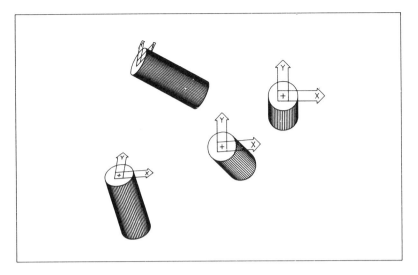

Figure 12.16 Cylinders at various orientations

Once a UCS has been defined it can be recalled at any time and made the current UCS, all inputs will then be relative to the 0,0,0 defined by this current UCS.

> *Note:* Learning to create and manipulate user coordinate systems is fundamental to 3D drawing. You should persevere – it will be worth it eventually.
> The examples given in Appendix 6 have been structured to introduce you to the concept of the UCS and other advanced 3D techniques.

12.2.2 The UCS Icon

The UCS icon is an aid to visualising the position and angle of the current UCS with respect to the previous UCS. The icon consists of two orthogonal arrows pointing in the positive *X*- and *Y*-directions.

If you are presently using the WCS then a W will appear within the *Y*-arrow.

If the UCS icon is positioned at the origin of the current UCS, then a + symbol will appear at the intersection of the arrows.

If you are viewing the drawing from any position above the current UCS (i.e. positive *Z*), then a square box will also appear at this intersection.

If you are viewing the drawing exactly edge on (± 1°) to the current UCS, then the UCS icon will be replaced by a broken pencil symbol – positioning a coordinate point may now be impossible.

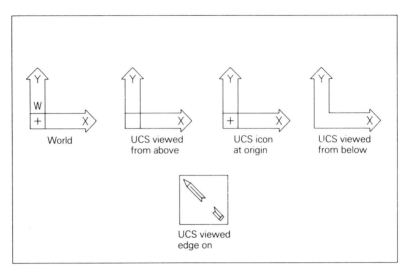

World   UCS viewed from above   UCS icon at origin   UCS viewed from below

UCS viewed edge on

Figure 12.17 UCS icons

The various UCS icons are shown in Figure 12.17.
The UCS icon is controlled by the UCSICON command.

Command: UCSICON
ON/OFF/All/Noorigin/ORigin‹current state›:

ON/OFF Enables/disables the UCS icon in the current active viewport.
All All is always used in conjunction with one of the other options. Thus All followed by ON will switch on the UCS icon in all the current viewports.
Noorigin Positions the UCS icon at the bottom left hand corner of the screen regardless of the 0,0,0 position.
Origin Places the icon at the user-defined origin of the current UCS. If the icon cannot be fitted at this position without being clipped by the viewport borders it will be placed in the lower left-hand corner of the screen.

12.2.3 Definition of a UCS

There are four principles by which a new UCS may be defined relative to the active coordinate system:

1. By specifying a new origin, a new Z-axis or a new $X–Y$ plane.
2. By aligning with the orientation of an existing object.

3. By aligning with the current view.
4. By rotation about the *X*-, *Y*-, or *Z*-axis.

> *Note:* It should always be remembered that, when defining a new UCS, it is done relative to the current (active) UCS.

Command: UCS

**Origin/ZAxis/3point/Entity/View/X/Y/Z/Prev/Restore/Save/Del/?/
‹World›:**

Origin **Origin point ‹0,0,0›:**

Allows the definition of a new UCS origin relative to the current UCS, leaving the orientation of the axes unchanged. This can be achieved either by pointing or by the numerical input of the new origin point from the keyboard (Figure 12.18).

ZAxis **Origin point ‹0,0,0›:**
       Point on positive portion of the Z axis ‹default›:

Allows the definition of a new UCS origin relative to the current UCS but with the *Z*-axis direction redefined. (AutoCAD specifies the directions of the *X*- and *Y*- axes for you.) See Figure 12.19.

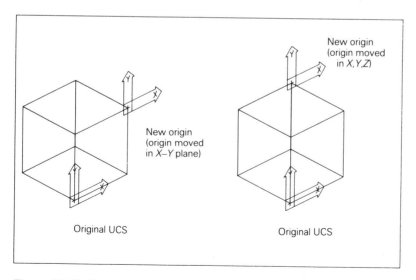

Figure 12.18 New UCS origin

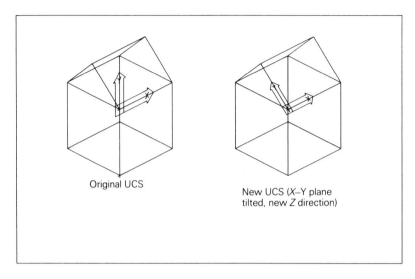

Figure 12.19 New UCS Z direction

3point   Origin point ‹0,0,0›:
Point on positive portion of the X axis ‹default›:
Point on positive Y portion of the UCS X-Y plane ‹default›:

Allows the definition of a new UCS origin relative to the current UCS by specifying the origin, the direction of the new positive *X*-axis and

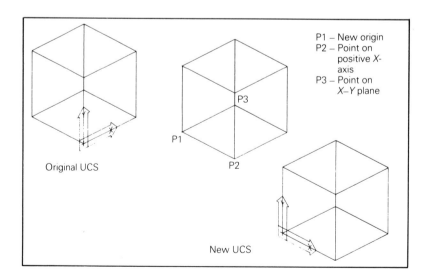

Figure 12.20 New UCS by three-point selection

the inclination of the *X–Y* plane. This is the most versatile method but does take a little practice (Figure 12.20).

Entity   Select object to align UCS:

Allows the definition of a new UCS origin relative to the current UCS by selection of a particular entity. The new *Z*-axis will be aligned with the extrusion direction (positive *Z*) of the chosen entity (Figure 12.21). The origin and the *X*- direction are derived by reference to the following set of rules:

- Arc. Origin=centre point: *X*-axis passes through end point of arc.
- Circle. Origin=centre point: *X*-axis passes through the pick point (radius or diameter).
- Dim. Origin=centre point of dimension text: *X*- axis is parallel to the *X*-axis of the dimension.
- Line. Origin=endpoint (the nearest endpoint to the picked point will be adopted): *X*-axis lies along the line and the *X–Y* plane remains unchanged.
- Point. Origin=point location: *X*-axis is in an arbitrary direction!
- 2D pline. Origin=start point: *X*-axis is in the direction of the next vertex.
- Solid. Origin=first definition point: *X*-axis lies along the line joining the first two points.
- 3D face. Origin=first definition point: *X*-axis lies along the line joining the

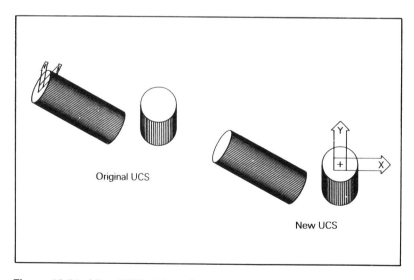

Original UCS

New UCS

Figure 12.21 Align UCS with entity

first two points: the *Y*-axis lies along the line joining the first and fourth points.

- Shape. Text. Block. Attribute. Origin=insertion point: *X*-axis follows the line of rotation specified when the entity was inserted.

View   In this option the origin remains unchanged. The *X–Y* plane is rotated so that it is perpendicular to the current view direction, i.e. if a new view is selected which lies at a particular angle with respect to the original view, then the *X–Y* plane will be rotated through the same angle.

X/Y/Z   **Rotation angle about the X** (or Y or Z) **axis‹0.0›:**

In this option the origin remains unchanged. If *X* is selected the *X*-axis remains unchanged and the *Y*- and *Z*-axes are rotated through the specified angle. The direction of this rotation is governed by AutoCAD's right-hand rule. This states that if you grip the selected axis and point your thumb in the positive direction then your curled fingers will indicate the positive direction of rotation. See Figures 12.22 and 12.23.

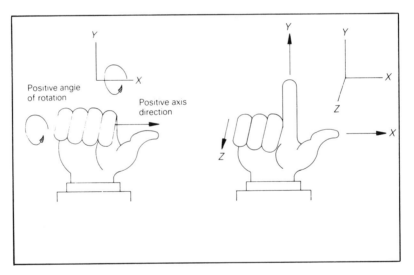

Figure 12.22 The right-hand rule to define coordinate systems

Prev   Returns you to the previously used UCS. AutoCAD allows you to step back through the last 10 UCS definitions.

Restore   Allows you to return to a previously saved UCS.

Save   Allows you to name (31 characters maximum) and save the current active UCS.

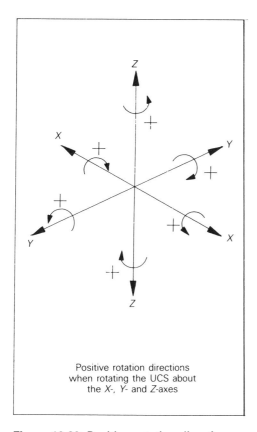

Positive rotation directions
when rotating the UCS about
the X-, Y- and Z-axes

Figure 12.23 Positive rotation directions

Del   Deletes a previously saved UCS. Wild card characters (? and *) can be
    used to delete more than one UCS.
?   Returns a list of all the previously saved UCS definitions.
World   Returns you to the world coordinate system (WCS).

12.2.4 The UCS Dialogue Box

As with all the dialogue boxes this can be accessed from either the pull down
menu (under **Settings**) or from the command line by typing DDUCS. All the
above described options for defining and saving a UCS are also available through
this dialogue box (Figures 12.24 and 12.25).

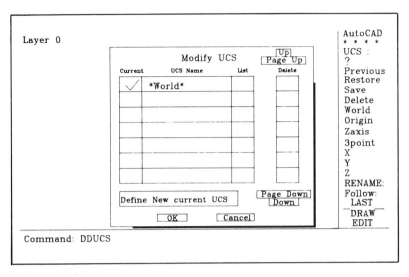

Figure 12.24 UCS dialogue box

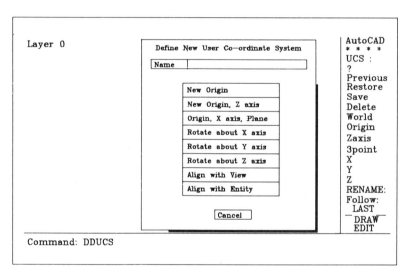

Figure 12.25 UCS definition dialogue box

12.2.5 The UCS Options Icon Menu

This additional icon menu may be used to define a limited number (6) of standard UCS options. It also allows you to define a new UCS as with the View option of the UCS command (Figure 12.26).

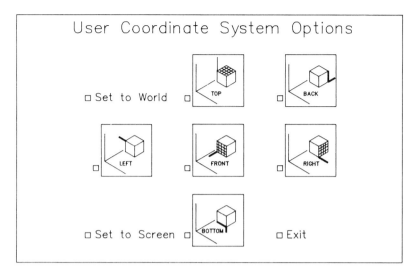

Figure 12.26 UCS options dialogue box

12.2.6 PLAN

When changing from one UCS to another, the viewing direction remains unaltered. The PLAN command has been introduced as an easy way to change the viewpoint automatically to the plan view (viewpoint=0,0,1) each time the UCS is changed (Figure 12.27).

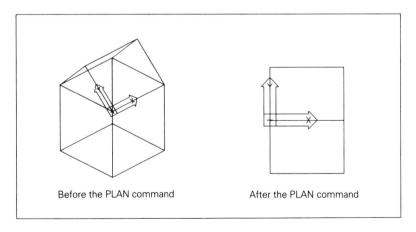

Figure 12.27 Use of the PLAN command

Command: PLAN
‹current UCS›/Ucs/World:

The Ucs option allows you to generate a plan view of a previously saved UCS *while remaining in the current UCS*. Similarly, the World option gives a plan view of the WCS.

12.2.7 The UCSfollow System Variable

If the UCSFOLLOW system variable is set to 1 then, on changing from one UCS to another, the plan view of the new UCS is automatically invoked. UCSFOLLOW may be set from screen menu under UCS or by using the SETVAR command. UCSFOLLOW may be set individually for each viewport.

12.3 Advanced Three-dimensional Drawing

The standard technique for constructing 3D drawings is to set the relevant UCS and then proceed to use the familiar 2D entity commands such as circle, arc, ellipse etc. Although this allows complex drawings to be constructed it is sometimes more efficient to be able to position 3D entities in 3D space by specifying their X-, Y- and Z-coordinates.

> *Note:* This may be applied to any 2D entity *BUT* the entity will normally only be drawn parallel to the X–Y plane of the active UCS. The exception to this rule is the LINE command which has been given the properties of the old 3DLINE command which allows a line to be positioned at any orientation in space relative to the active UCS.

Other commands specific to 3D construction are 3DPOLY and 3DFACE.

12.3.1 LINE in three dimensions

In standard 2D construction the Z-coordinate is omitted and is assumed to be zero (unless the ELEVation has been set to some other value).

Any point in space can now be specified by supplying the absolute (relative to the current UCS) X-, Y- and Z-coordinate points:

Command: LINE   **From point**   100,120,50
To point: 50,20,150

See Figure 12.28.

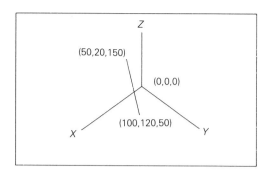

Figure 12.28 LINE in 3D

Convenient alternatives to this rather laborious process are to use either point filters (Section 12.4.1) or Object snap (Section 12.4.2).

Relative and polar coordinates may also be used and can greatly simplify the construction of 3D drawings. The basic rules are exactly equivalent to those outlined in Section 3.1.1.

In the case of relative coordinates, the Z-displacement is now required in addition to the X- and Y-displacements. As with absolute coordinates this allows the line to be positioned anywhere in 3D space. This is not the case with polar coordinates as the angle is always taken to lie in the X–Y plane of the active UCS.

Relative and polar coordinates can if required both be referred to the WCS whilst remaining in the active UCS. This is achieved by introducing an asterisk (*) after the @ symbol and before the displacement(s).

12.3.2 3DPOLY

The 3DPOLY command is very similar to the 2D PLINE command but it has reduced capabilities – only straight line segments can be drawn, it is not possible to change the width and the editing facilities supplied by PEDIT are greatly curtailed.

Command: 3DPOLY
From point:
Close/Undo/‹Endpoint of line›:

If a 3DPOLYline is selected when in the PEDIT command the following limited options are available:

Close/Edit vertex/Spline curve/Decurve/Undo/eXit‹X›:

These options work in the same way as for the editing of 2D polylines

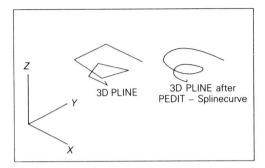

Figure 12.29 Editing a 3D polyline

(Section 4.3) apart from the Spline curve option which produces a 3D curve as in Figure 12.29.

12.3.3 3DFACE

If lines or 3Dpolylines are used to construct a 3D object the result is always a wire-frame model and the HIDE command will have no effect. It is for this reason that AutoCAD introduced the 3DFACE command (Figure 12.30). 3DFACE is now treated as the basic building block for the majority of 3D solid constructions and forms the basis of all the 3D polygon meshes.

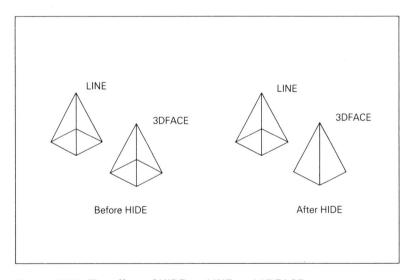

Figure 12.30 The effect of HIDE on LINE and 3DFACE

Command: 3DFACE
First point:
Second point:
Third point:
Fourth point:
(If this is coincident with the first point a triangle results; if it is a separate point an automatic close will be executed to produce a closed 4-sided face.)

Third point:
(This prompts for the third point of the next face, and assumes that the first two points have already been specified as points 3 and 4 of the previous face.) See Figure 12.31.

Fourth point: (See above.)
Third point: (See above.)
Fourth point: (See above.)
    ⋮

One of the major problems associated with realistic 3D construction is that of representing a solid face containing an aperture e.g. a house wall with a window. Although it is possible to 'represent' this using simple line construction techniques it is not possible to make the wall appear solid by use of the HIDE command. This may be overcome by the use of 3DFACEs to make up the solid walls surrounding a hole (the window). This in turn creates the problem that the edges of the 3DFACEs are visible and tend to destroy the effect (Figure 12.32). One of the extra features of 3DFACE is specifically designed to overcome this problem – each edge as it is defined can be made *invisible*. See Figure 12.33.

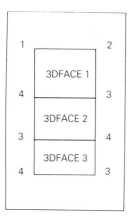

Figure 12.31 Definition points for 3DFACE

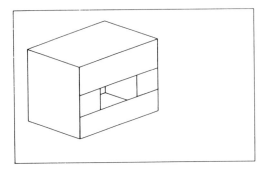

Figure 12.32 Window constructed with visible 3DFACEs

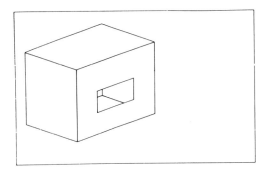

Figure 12.33 Window constructed with invisible 3DFACEs

To understand how the invisible feature may be used it is necessary to remember that the first point represents the first 3Dface edge, the second point the second edge etc. Therefore, if you require the first edge to be invisible this must be specified when you are prompted for the first point by entering an I at the prompt followed by the coordinates of the point (Figure 12.34).

Command: 3DFACE
First point: I
Second point:
Third point:
Fourth point:

The visibility of 3DFACE invisible edges is controlled by the SPLFRAME system variable; if SPLFRAME is set to any non-zero value then previously invisible edges will be displayed. This can also be achieved by picking Showedge from the 3DFACE screen menu followed by a REGEN. This can be useful when locating phantom 3DFACEs which have been created with all edges invisible.

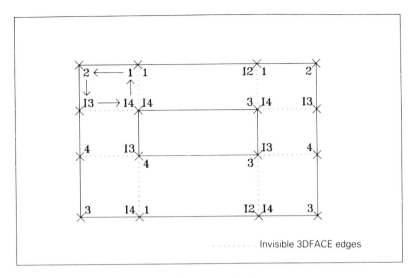

Figure 12.34 Invisible 3DFACE edge definition

12.4 Aids to Three-dimensional Construction

A common fault when constructing 3D drawings is to place entities by pointing to what appears to be the correct position on the screen. This will almost invariably cause the object to be incorrectly positioned because of the ambiguity inherent in presenting a 3D image on a two-dimensional screen. This problem may be reduced by presenting alternative views simultaneously in two or more viewports. However, it is still advisable wherever possible to use point filters and/or object snap to ensure the accurate location of all 3D coordinates.

12.4.1 Point Filters

If you wish to specify a 3D point using both the mouse (for pointing) and the keyboard (for coordinate entry) then you *must* use *X/Y/Z* point filtering. By choosing the appropriate filter it is possible to input, say, the *X*-component by pointing and the *Y,Z* components from the keyboard. Alternatively two coordinate components may be input by pointing leaving the remaining component to be supplied from the keyboard. The pointing component(s) must always be given first. Any combination of *X* followed by *Y,Z*; *X,Y* followed by *Z*; *Y* followed by *X,Z* etc. can be used.

There are three ways to choose the appropriate filter combination: by selecting filters from the **Tools** pull down menu, by selecting LINE, 3DPOLY or 3DFACE from the screen menu, or from the keyboard by typing .X, .Y, .Z, .XY, .XZ or .YZ at the point prompt of the above three commands.

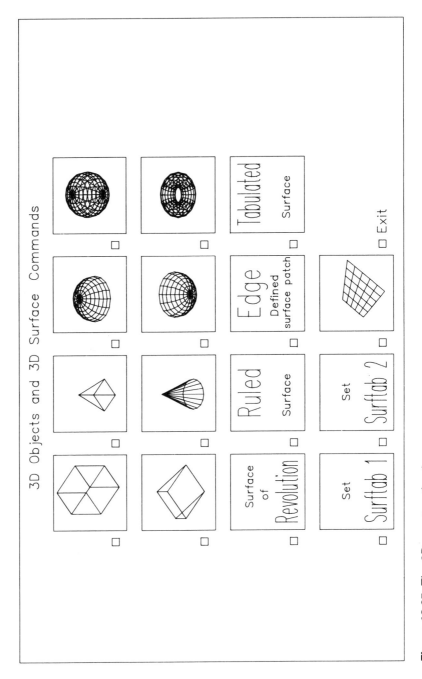

Figure 12.35 The 3D construction icon

Command: LINE
From point: .XY **of** (Point with mouse to *X,Y* position.)
(need Z) (Supply *Z* coordinate from the keyboard.)

12.4.2 Object snap in 3D

If simple pointing is attempted the *X–Y* position will be accepted but the *Z*-coordinate will always default to the current value of the elevation. This may be altered to the required value during pointing using the transparent command 'SETVAR but the process is again rather cumbersome.

A better approach is to use object snap. If object snap is used to snap a 3D line to, say, the end of an existing line on a drawing the *Z*-coordinate of the endpoint will also be taken into account and therefore the line will automatically start or finish at the correct elevation.

12.4.3 Basic 3D Objects

As a further aid to 3D construction, AutoCAD supplies a number of basic 3D shapes which may be accessed from the Draw pull down menu under 3D construction (Figure 12.35). These include boxes, wedges, pyramids, cones, spheres, hemispheres and toroids which are not resident in the AutoCAD main program but which are defined by an AutoLISP program called 3D (loaded automatically when the required object is selected from the icon menu). Alternatively, the AutoLISP program may be run directly from the keyboard (see Appendix 3).

12.5 Three-dimensional Polygon Meshes

One of the main features of AutoCAD Release 10 is the ability to represent complex 3D shapes by the use of polygon meshes consisting of columns and rows of 3DFACE elements in an *M* by *N* matrix (Figure 12.36). The command 3DMESH allows the construction of a 3D mesh by specifying each individual element of the mesh through numerical input of each vertex position in 3D space. This process is extremely laborious and in practice is usually employed only within a LISP program.

The resolution of the 3D mesh is controlled by two system variables SURFTAB1 and SURFTAB2.

AutoCAD provides four methods for the automatic generation of 3D meshes which avoid the pitfalls inherent in the 3DMESH command.

> *Note:* The further examples given in Appendix 6 demonstrate the versatility of these polygon mesh commands.

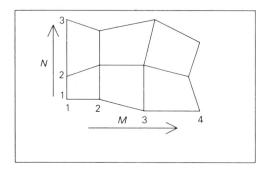

Figure 12.36 3DMESH M=4, N=3

12.5.1 RULESURF

RULESURF constructs a simple set of ruled lines between two specified objects. This is not a true mesh because it is made up of only two columns of N rows, N being controlled by the value of SURFTAB1.

> **Command:** RULESURF
> **Select first defining curve:**
> **Select second defining curve:**

A 'defining curve' may be a line, point, arc, circle or polyline. If the first defining curve is closed (e.g. a circle or closed polyline) then the second defining curve must also be closed. A point is a special entity as it is treated as either open or closed (Figure 12.37).

When selecting the defining curves the choice of selection point will affect the final shape of the ruled surface (Figure 12.38).

12.5.2 TABSURF

TABSURF allows the construction of a 3D parallel mesh by the specification of a path curve (an open or closed single entity constructed from a line, arc, circle or polyline) and a direction vector (derived from a line or polyline). Again, as in the case of RULESURF, this produces a 2 by N mesh, N being controlled by the value of SURFTAB1. See Figure 12.39.

> **Command:** TABSURF
> **Select path curve:**
> **Select direction vector:**

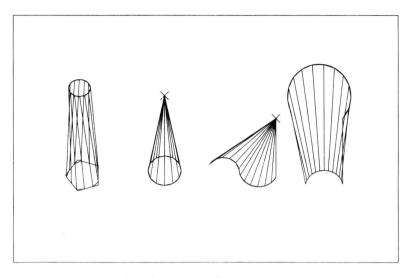

Figure 12.37 Examples of open and closed ruled surfaces

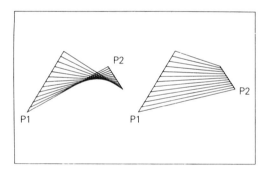

Figure 12.38 The effect of choosing different selection points when using RULESURF

The length of the direction vector controls the length of extrusion and the position of the selection point (i.e. which end of the line it is closest to) controls the direction of extrusion (Figure 12.40).

12.5.3 REVSURF

A surface of revolution is represented by a true M by N mesh constructed from a specified path curve and an axis of rotation. The path curve may be an open or closed line, arc, circle or polyline while the axis is derived from a line or open

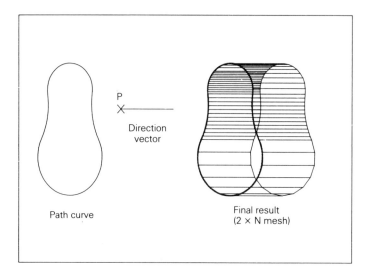

Figure 12.39 Use of TABSURF

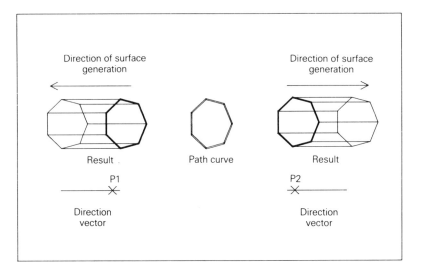

Figure 12.40 TABSURF generation direction

polyline. The axis of revolution determines the *M*-direction of the mesh; the mesh density is controlled by both SURFTAB1 and SURFTAB2.

Command: REVSURF
Select path curve:
Select axis of rotation:
Start angle ‹0›:

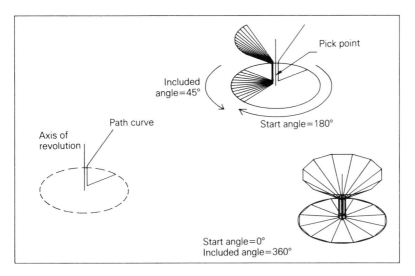

Figure 12.41 Use of REVSURF

If non-zero this specifies an initial offset from the path curve.

Included angle (+=CCW,−=CW)‹Full circle›:

The angle through which the path curve is rotated.

See Figure 12.41.

12.5.4 EDGESURF

This produces a true *M* by *N* mesh bounded by four adjoining edges made up from lines, arcs or separate open polylines, their endpoints touching to form a closed quadrilateral. Again, the mesh density is controlled by SURFTAB1 and SURFTAB2.

Command: EDGESURF
Select edge 1:
Select edge 2:
Select edge 3:
Select edge 4:

The four edges may be selected in any order but the first selected edge defines the *M*-direction (Figure 12.42).

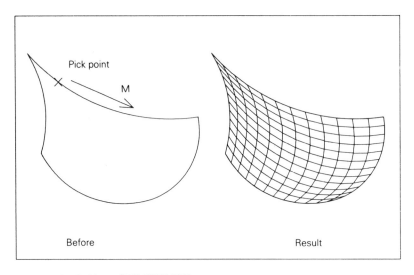

Figure 12.42 Use of EDGESURF

If the endpoints of the component edges do not touch then AutoCAD will respond with:

Edge x does not touch another edge

A 3D mesh constructed using one of the above commands is treated as a single entity. Most of the standard editing commands may be used to modify the 3Dface component of a mesh but it should be remembered that the mesh *must* be EXPLODEd first.

All the above mesh construction commands can be accessed either directly from the keyboard, under 3D Construction on the **Draw** pull down menu or from the screen menu.

12.5.5 Editing 3D Polygon Meshes with PEDIT

The PEDIT sub-commands available for editing 3D polygon meshes are closely related to those used for editing 3D polylines and, before you attempt to edit 3D meshes it is strongly recommended that you familiarise yourself with polyline editing.

Command: PEDIT
Select polyline: (Choose a 3D mesh.)
Edit vertex/Smooth surface/Desmooth/Mclose/Nclose/Undo/eXit‹X›:

Edit   Vertex(m, n). Next/Previous/Left/Right/Up/Down/Move/ REgen/eXit‹N›:

A cross appears on the first vertex of the mesh. As in the case of Polyline editing, this indicates the vertex which may be edited and may be moved through the mesh by use of the commands Next, Previous, Left, Right, Up and Down. Next, Previous, Left and Right allow the cross to be moved in the *N*-direction. Up and Down move it in the *M*-direction. The **Vertex(m, n)** indicator shows the current coordinates of the cross within the mesh. When the cross has been positioned at the required vertex the Move command allows you to distort the mesh by re-positioning the marked vertex (Figure 12.43).

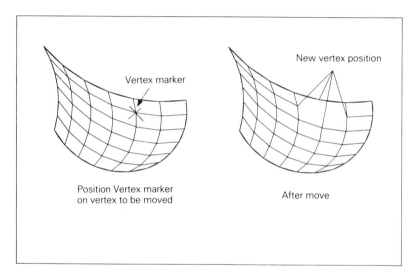

Figure 12.43 Vertex editing using PEDIT

Smooth surface   This corresponds to the Spline sub-command in polyline editing. There are three smoothing functions available – the quadratic B-spline, the cubic B-spline and the Bezier function. See Figure 12.44. The system variable SURFTYPE is used to select the required smoothing function – SURFTYPE may be set to 5 (quadratic), 6 (cubic) or 8 (Bezier) and the smoothing effect increases in the same order. There are limitations on which smoothing may be used – a quadratic may be used on meshes of 3 × 3 or more, a cubic on 4 × 4 or more and a Bezier requires more than 11 vertices in either the *M*- or *N*-direction. The density of the mesh is controlled by the two system variables SURFU and SURFV. SURFU controls the mesh density in the *M*-direction while SURFV controls it in the *N*-direction.

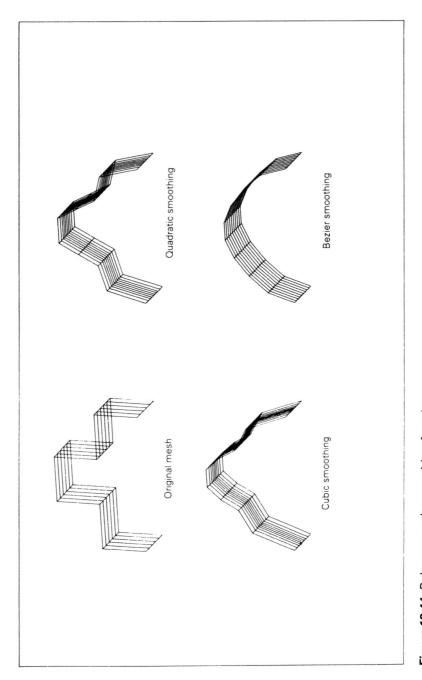

Figure 12.44 Polygon mesh smoothing functions

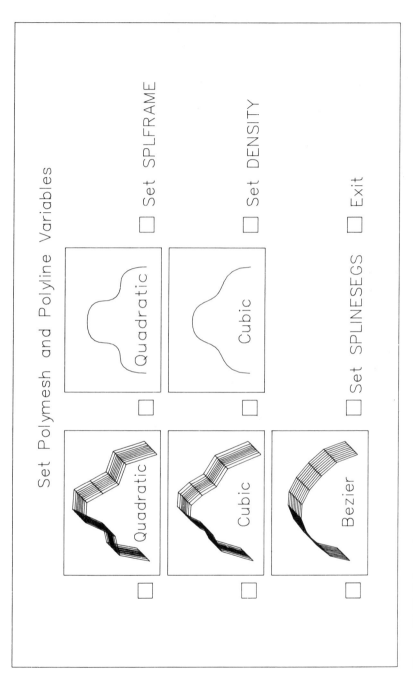

Figure 12.45 Polymesh and polyline variables

The choice of smoothing function and the values of mesh density variables may be set by selecting PolyVars from the PEDIT screen menu. This invokes an icon menu (Figure 12.45) which gives easy access to these variables and also to SPLFRAME and SPLSEGS.

Desmooth   Restores the original polygon mesh after smoothing.

Mclose   Closes the polygon mesh in the *M*-direction if open. If the polygon mesh is already closed Mclose is replaced in the menu with Mopen.

Nclose   Closes the polygon mesh in the *N*-direction if open. If the polygon mesh is already closed Nclose is replaced in the menu with Nopen.

Undo   Progressively reverses the actions of the PEDIT command.

eXit   Exits PEDIT and returns you to the command line.

12.6 Perspective Projection using the DVIEW Command

AutoCAD, like most other CAD packages, makes use of parallel projection for viewing 3D objects. This, although satisfactory, does not always give a true visualisation of the objects. The DVIEW command allows a perspective projection to be constructed by specifying a target point and a camera (observer) position, i.e. a viewing vector (Figure 12.46). The default positions of the camera and target are initially set by AutoCAD.

DVIEW incorporates a clipping function which allows 'cut-away' sections to be produced. A cutting plane is specified and the visibility of objects on either side of this plane can be controlled to give a 'clipped' view, i.e. a section through a 3D drawing (Figure 12.47).

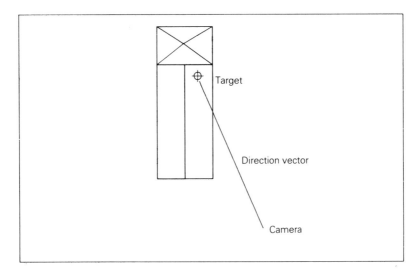

Figure 12.46 Plan view of target and camera positions

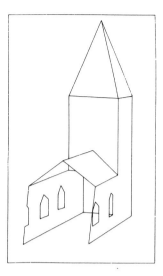

Figure 12.47 A section produced by the clipping function

DVIEW makes use of *slider bars* which appear whenever a scale factor or angle is requested. As the cursor is moved along the slider bar (Figure 12.48) the drawing is dynamically dragged to show automatically the effect of the new scale or angle.

Command: DVIEW
Select objects:

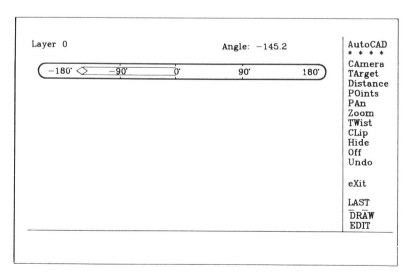

Figure 12.48 DVIEW slider bar (camera angle)

Carefully select a number of objects which will give a good representation of the complete drawing (Figure 12.49). AutoCAD will use these objects to give a perspective preview. If too many objects are chosen then generation of the perspective preview is slow and sometimes frustrating. When exiting the DVIEW command the complete drawing is regenerated based on the preview settings.

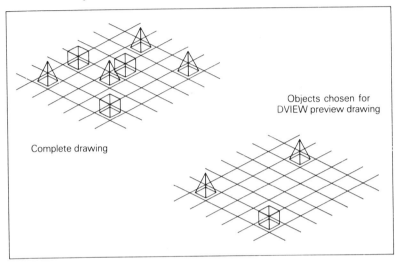

Figure 12.49 Selected representative objects

CAmera/TArget/Distance/POints/PAn/Zoom/TWist/CLip/Hide/Off/ Undo/‹eXit›:

CAmera Allows rotation of the camera about the target point, firstly in the Z-direction ($-90°$ = looking straight down, $0°$ = looking along the

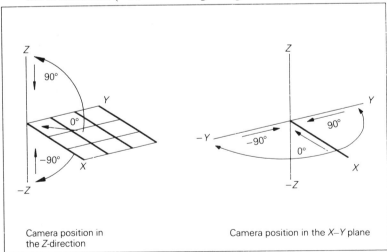

Camera position in the Z-direction

Camera position in the X–Y plane

Figure 12.50 Rotating camera position

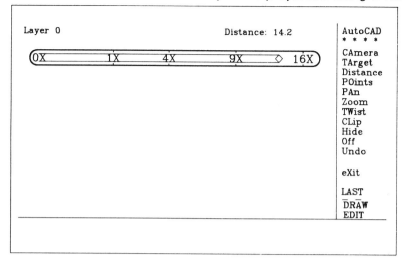

Figure 12.51 DVIEW slider bar (distance)

X–Y plane, +90° = looking straight up) and secondly in the *X–Y* plane (0° = looking straight along the *X*-axis, 90° = looking along the *Y*-axis). See Figure 12.50.

TArget   Allows the rotation of the target point about the camera point. The angle specification is the same as for CAmera.

Distance   This option allows the distance between the camera and target to be adjusted. A slider bar allows scaling of the viewing distance from 0× to 16× where 1× represents the current distance (Figure 12.51). *Perspective viewing is turned on only when this option is taken (Figure 12.52).*

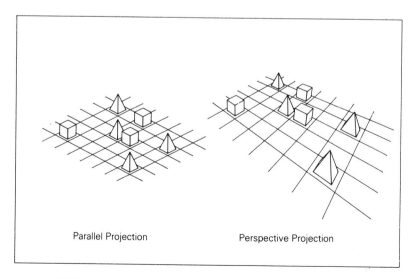

Parallel Projection   Perspective Projection

Figure 12.52 Two types of projection

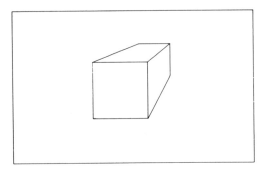

Figure 12.53 Perspective icon

The perspective icon (Figure 12.53) is displayed in the bottom left-hand corner of the screen when perspective viewing mode is on.

POints   The positions of the target and camera can be specified by input of their *X*-, *Y*- and *Z*-coordinates; point filters and object snap can be used. The target point is specified first followed by the camera position which is connected to the target point by means of an elastic band (the view direction) to help place the camera.

PAn   This is the same as the command PAN and moves the image without changing the magnification.

Zoom   The way in which zoom works depends on whether perspective is on or not. If perspective is off then AutoCAD performs a ZOOM Centre and presents a slider bar to allow the setting of the zoom scale factor. If perspective is on then zoom allows the changing of the camera 'lens', the default being 50 mm. A 35 mm lens would allow a wider field of view to be seen, whereas a 200 mm lens would act as a telephoto lens narrowing the field of view.

TWist   Allows tilting of the objects about the view direction.

CLip   This option allows the positioning of front or back clipping planes. AutoCAD temporarily 'erases' portions of the drawing which are behind a back clipping plane or in front of a front clipping plane. Clipping can be performed on both parallel and perspective projections. AutoCAD prompts: **Back/Front/‹Off›**:

Back   ON/OFF/‹Distance from target›:
   A positive distance places the clipping plane between the target point and the camera whereas a negative distance places the clipping plane beyond the target point. If the slider bar is used then the clipping plane is dynamically dragged through the objects (Figure 12.54).

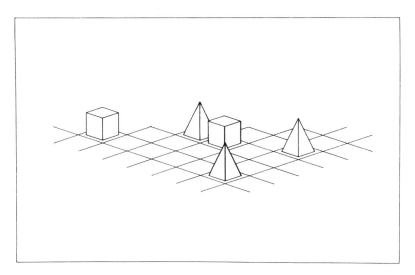

Figure 12.54 Back clipping

Front   Eye/ON/OFF/‹Distance from target›:
This option works in same way as Back except for the Eye feature which allows the clipping plane to be placed at the camera (its default position). See Figure 12.55.

Off   Turns clipping off.

Hide   Operates in the same way as the command HIDE and removes hidden lines from the preview drawing.

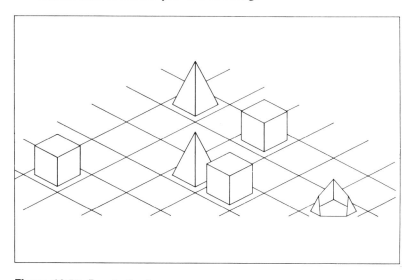

Figure 12.55 Front clipping

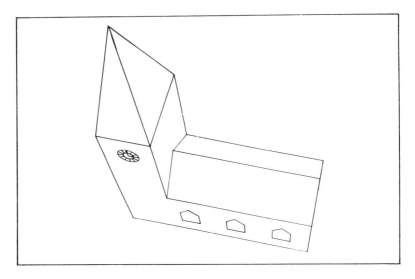

Figure 12.56 A hidden perspective view

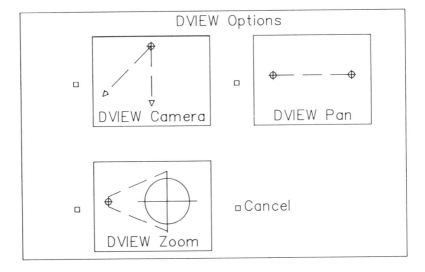

Figure 12.57 DVIEW options icon

Off   Disables perspective mode and returns to parallel projection.

Undo   Undoes the last DVIEW sub-command. By repeating this command you are allowed to step back through the DVIEW sub-commands.

eXit   Ends DVIEW and causes a regeneration of the whole drawing to match the preview drawing. An example of a hidden perspective view is shown in Figure 12.56.

When the final perspective view has been invoked from the preview drawing then certain Dview Options may easily be selected using the Dview Opt icon found under the **Display** pull down, which avoids the necessity of returning to the DVIEW command (Figure 12.57). These options include changing the camera angle, the zoom lens and drawing position on screen using DVIEW Pan.

13 · Customised lines, hatchings and shapes

13.1 Creating Text Files

When creating your own linetypes, hatch patterns, shapes, menus etc., as described in this section, you will need to be able to create text files to be saved within AutoCAD's system directory. AutoCAD provides a facility to do this:

> **Command:** EDIT
> **File to edit:–**

This makes use of a simple text editor called Edlin. Although Edlin is capable of producing the relatively simple text files required by AutoCAD, many people find it unfriendly and difficult to use. In this case it is probably worthwhile using a word processor to write these files. In some respects this is 'overkill' because you will not make use of many of the more sophisticated features of the word processor package. However, a word processor is usually easy to work with and, particularly when you come to write longer text files such as menus, life can be much easier with a word processor than with a simple text editor.

However, there is one problem. Word processors produce text documents within which are embedded a large number of control characters. These characters are used to indicate text features such as underlined words, emboldened words, paragraph indentations, etc. Such characters can only be recognised by the particular word processor package on which the text was written. They cannot be understood by AutoCAD and will cause trouble if they are included in the text files. Almost all word processor packages will allow you to save the text with these characters removed – such text files are usually known as DOS text files and it is essential that you always save your AutoCAD text files in DOS text format.

13.1.1 Accessing your Word Processor Directly from AutoCAD

It can be rather a laborious process to switch between AutoCAD and the word processor. If you are working on a drawing you must save it, exit AutoCAD, enter the word processor, write your text file, save it in AutoCAD's system directory, exit the word processor, enter AutoCAD, reload the drawing and then continue.

AutoCAD has a mechanism for calling up an external software package without leaving the drawing editor. A ProGram Parameters file called ACAD.PGP is supplied with AutoCAD. This is a text file which controls the external software accessible from the drawing editor. When supplied it probably looks like the following:

```
CATALOG,DIR /W,27000,*Files: ,0
DEL,DEL,27000,File to delete: ,0
DIR,DIR,27000,File specification: ,0
EDIT,EDLIN,42000,File to edit: ,0
SH,,27000,*DOS Command: ,0
SHELL,,127000,*DOS Command: ,0
TYPE,TYPE,27000,File to list: ,0
```

It is important to understand the structure of this file. Each line consists of five fields, separated by commas. The fields are:

- *Command name.* The first field gives the command which will be recognised as a valid AutoCAD command. This must not duplicate an existing AutoCAD command.
- *File command.* The second field gives the command which AutoCAD will issue as a result. The command name and the file command may be the same or they may differ. The file command must be a valid command which you would use to call up the external software at the DOS prompt. As in DOS, the command may include paths and parameters.
- *Memory reserve.* When AutoCAD boots up it normally 'grabs' all the available RAM memory for its own use. If you wish to run external software AutoCAD must be made to give up some of this memory for the external software's own use. This may be an area of conflict and you should aim to minimise the memory reserve to avoid hampering AutoCAD's operation. You should allow a minimum of 24 000 bytes and at least 4 000 bytes in excess of the size of the external software itself. This can end up as a process of trial and error to find a suitable number.
- *Prompt.* This is an optional prompt which appears in addition to any prompt generated by the external software itself. If not needed this field can be left blank.
- *Return Code.* Each Command in ACAD.PGP switches the display to text mode. The usual function of the final field dictates whether, on returning to AutoCAD's drawing editor, you remain in text mode (field set to 0) or switch back to graphics mode(field set to 4).

This all seems very complicated but is actually quite easy to use. A glance at the above ACAD.PGP file will show that AutoCAD is able to respond to the DOS commands DIR, DEL and TYPE and can call up Edlin. It can also return to DOS, either for a single DOS command or, if you respond to the SHELL or SH prompt with a Return, you can remain in DOS indefinitely until you type the command EXIT.

Once you understand the purpose of the ACAD.PGP file then you can experiment with some modifications. For example, the TYPE command will list out a text file on the screen, but if the file is longer than can be shown on a single screen it will scroll without giving you the chance to read it all. The DOS command MORE allows you to type the file on screen but will pause after each full screen to allow you time to read the information. Pressing Return will give you the next full screen, and so on. If you wish to incorporate this feature into your system, start up your word processor and load in theACAD.PGP file as a DOS text file. Then modify the line:

    TYPE,TYPE,27000,File to list: ,0

to:

    TYPE,MORE<,27000,File to list: ,0

Save this modified file in DOS text format as ACAD.PGP to replace the original file. Whenever you subsequently give the command TYPE from the AutoCAD command line, the new version including the MORE feature will be executed.

> *Note*: The location of any external software (such as MORE.COM) to be accessed through the ACAD.PGP file *must* be included in the DOS PATH set up *before* entering AutoCAD.

The really useful thing about ACAD.PGP is that you can add to it.

EXAMPLE

For example, you can add a line which will allow you to call up your word processor from the drawing editor. Thus, if your word processor is normally started with the command WP, and takes up 200 000 bytes, you could add the line:

    WORDPRO,WP,205000,,4

and again save this modified file in DOS Text format as ACAD.PGP

This effectively adds the new command WORDPRO to your AutoCAD package. When you type this command AutoCAD will issue the file command WP. You must be sure that the word processor directory is mentioned in the DOS path (See Appendix 1) so that the WP file can be found. When you have finished word processing you exit the package in the usual way and you will be returned immediately to your original AutoCAD drawing.

13.2 Multiple Configuration

When you use the AutoCAD package for the first time you will be told that the system must first be configured. You must then embark on the configuration routine, which is a lengthy ritual informing the package about the display cards and monitors, the mouse and/or digitiser and the plotter and/or printer which are to be used. Once this has been done there is usually no need to repeat it. However, if the package is run with several different sets of equipment the configurator would normally have to be run each time a change was made. This can be avoided if the configuration data files are separately retained.

The configuration data are normally stored in a file called ACAD.CFG. This is looked for in a separate directory called the configuration directory. In most cases this directory does not have a separate existence but is the same as the system directory – the directory in which the AutoCAD program files are located.

It is, of course, not possible to have two files called ACAD.CFG in the same directory, but it is possible to create them and keep them in two different directories. If AutoCAD is first told which of these directories is to be considered as the configuration directory, it becomes easy to switch between the different configuration files.

The name of the configuration directory may be set from DOS *before* AutoCAD is booted. This is done by using the DOS command SET to set a special environment variable called ACADCFG.

Thus, suppose that you wish to keep the first configuration file in a configuration directory called, say, MYCONF. Before starting up AutoCAD, you must issue the DOS command

SET ACADCFG=C:\ACAD\MYCONF
(or whatever is the correct path for your system)

On boot up, AutoCAD will be unable to find an ACAD.CFG file anywhere (you should have removed any old versions of ACAD.CFG before you start) and so will enter the configurator as normal. As a result of the information which you supply, the configurator will then write an ACAD.CFG file into the configuration directory, in this case MYCONF.

If you now exit AutoCAD and repeat the whole process with a second configuration directory called, say, HISCONF, you can create a second ACAD.CFG file (Figure 13.1). This may be repeated for as many different configurations as you require.

At any future time, before booting AutoCAD, you simply SET the

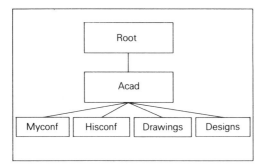

Figure 13.1 Multiple configuration directories

configuration directory to MYCONF, HISCONF, etc. and AutoCAD will then search the specified directory during its boot up routine and will configure the package accordingly.

13.2.1 Changing the Configuration from a Batch File

This setting of the configuration directory may conveniently be performed within a batch file and will then become automatic. This file may also be used to set any selected directory as the default. It is often convenient to create separate directories to accommodate all the drawings and associated files belonging, say, to one user or covering one topic etc.

Suppose that you wish to keep all your drawing files in a sub-directory called MYFILES. You should first create this directory – usually as a sub-directory of the AutoCAD system directory.

You must then write a batch file – this will usually be located in the root directory. The tasks of the batch file are

- To set MYFILES to be the default directory.
- To set MYCONF to be the configuration directory.
- To start up AutoCAD.
- To default to the root directory when AutoCAD has finished.

In order for the machine to be able to find the ACAD system files you should also include the AutoCAD system directory in the Path. This may also be done from the batch file.

EXAMPLE
The batch file example referred to in Section 2.2.1 may thus be modified:

PATH=C:\ACAD;\MYFILES;\
CD\ACAD\MYFILES

```
SET ACADFREERAM=28
SET LISPHEAP=42000
SET LISPSTACK=2500
SET ACADCFG=C:\ACAD\MYCONF
SET ACAD=C:\ACAD\SUPPORT
ACAD
CD\
```

If this batch file is saved on the root directory as MYDRAW.BAT then to start AutoCAD with your personal configuration and your personal drawing directory you need only type MYDRAW.

13.3 Customised Linetypes

AutoCAD contains a library of various linetypes which can be called at any time during the drawing execution. The standard AutoCAD linetypes are kept in a library file called ACAD.LIN. It is relatively simple to create your own linetypes (containing only dots and dashes) and add them to the supplied library file (ACAD.LIN) or create your own library file (which must have the .LIN extension).

Linetypes can be modified or created in two ways; by using an external text editor or by using the Create option from within the LINETYPE command. Both methods produce linetypes which are stored in a library file which must then be loaded into the drawing file for subsequent use.

13.3.1 Linetypes Created from Within AutoCAD

Command: LINETYPE
?/Create/Load/Set: C

Name of linetype to create: EXAMPLE
File for storage of linetype ‹ACAD›:

Enter the linetype name and the name of the library file where the linetype is to be stored. AutoCAD will then request a description of the new or modified linetype. This should preferably be a representation made up of dots and dashes e.g.

Descriptive text: ‒ ‒ ‒ . . . ‒ ‒ ‒ . . . ‒ ‒ ‒ . . . ‒ ‒ ‒ . . . ‒ ‒ ‒

AutoCAD will now require the pattern to be entered:

Enter pattern (on next line):
A,

The **A** represents the 'alignment' field which deals with the way in which lines, arcs and circles join or end, always with a dash. As there is only one alignment definition supported by AutoCAD it can be ignored. The line pattern is made up of 'pen down' and 'pen up' segments, each of a certain length. Positive values represent 'pen down' whilst negative values represent 'pen up'. A zero represents a dot.

EXAMPLE

$$A,40,-20,0,-4,0,-4,0,-20$$

would represent a dash of length of 40 drawing units, followed by a space of 20 drawing units, followed by a dot, followed by a space of 4 drawing units etc.

12 dash length specifications can be entered per linetype providing they fit on one 80-character line.

13.3.2 Linetype Creation using an External Text Editor

Linetypes can be formulated using an external text editor or word processor.

EXAMPLE

The following example will create a linetype identical to the example above.

```
*EXAMPLE,- - - . . . - - - . . . - - - . . . - - - . . . - - - . . . - - -
A,40,-20,0,-4,0,-4,0,-20
```

> *Note:* Do *not* forget the * or the A.

If this is now saved as a DOS text file with the file extension .LIN it will act as a library file in which AutoCAD can be directed to search when looking for the linetype. Any number of other linetype definitions may be contained within the same file.

13.4 Customised Hatch Patterns

In addition to being able to create very simple patterns for one-time use from within the HATCH command, it is also possible to create your own hatch patterns and store them for future use. You will need an external text editor and a lot of patience.

The new hatch pattern can be stored in the hatch library file ACAD.PAT or in an individual hatch pattern file having a file name which must be the same as the hatch pattern name and which must have the extension .PAT. It is not possible to compile your own hatch pattern library files.

The format specified by AutoCAD for writing the file containing the new hatch pattern is:

*pattern name[,description]

where **[,description]** is optional. It is used to describe in words the pattern to be generated. *Do not forget the comma!*

angle,‹space›x-origin,y-origin,‹space›delta-x,delta-y‹space›[,dash-1, dash-2, . . .]

Each pattern consists of one or more sets of parallel lines (no limit) specified by the above format (Figure 13.2). Therefore a hatch pattern is made up of one or more families of parallel lines.

- *Angle.* The angle parameter denotes the angle *and also the vector starting direction* at which the hatch pattern will be drawn. Angles are measured in an anticlockwise direction with 3 o'clock = 0°, 12 o'clock = 90°, 9 o'clock = 180°, and 6 o'clock = 270°.

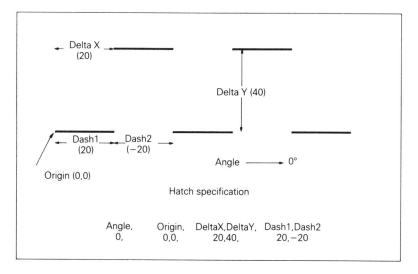

Figure 13.2 Hatch pattern specification

- *X-origin.* This is an arbitrary *X*-origin representing the beginning of a hatch line. All lines then relate to this origin.
- *Y-origin.* This is an arbitrary *Y*-origin representing the beginning of a hatch line. All lines then relate to this origin.
- *delta-X.* This is the displacement of the line in the *X*-direction. When AutoCAD hatches a designated area the specified hatch line will be regenerated a number of times until the area is filled. The delta-*X* parameter denotes the offset (in drawing units) in the *X*-direction of the line each time it is generated with respect to the previously drawn line. *The X-direction is always the direction in which the line is drawn.*
- *delta-Y.* This represents the corresponding displacement of the line in the *Y*-direction, i.e. the spacing between the generated lines, in drawing units.
- *dash-1,dash-2. . .* The dash-1,dash-2. . . parameters represent the line specification. The same rules apply as for drawing customised lines, i.e. a positive value represents pen down, a negative value represents a space/pen up, while a zero represents a dot.

Note: When designing your own hatch lines it is essential to include all the required spaces and commas.

EXAMPLE
Examples of simple hatch pattern definitions are as follows:

1.   *LINE1,straight line horizontal hatching
      0, 0,0, 0,20

    angle = 0, *X*-origin = 0, *Y*-origin = 0, delta-*X* = 0, delta-*Y* = 20

    The hatch pattern called LINE1 will be a horizontal straight line pattern with a line spacing of 20 drawing units. As there are no dash parameters AutoCAD will assume a single straight line.

2.   *LINE45,straight line at 45° to the horizontal
      45, 0,0, 0,20

    angle = 45, *X*-origin = 0, *Y*-origin = 0, delta-*X* = 0, delta-*Y* = 20

    This will produce an identical pattern to the above but it will be drawn at 45° to the horizontal.

3.   *DASHED,horizontal dashed line drawn beneath each other
      0, 0,0, 0,40, 20,-20

    angle = 0, *X*-origin = 0, *Y*-origin = 0, delta-*X* = 0, delta-*Y* = 40,
    dash1 = 20, dash2 = −20

This will produce a hatch pattern consisting of dashed lines, each dash being 20 drawing units long separated by 20 drawing units. Each hatch line will be 40 drawing units apart and drawn directly beneath each other.

4.   *DASHED1,horizontal dashed lines offset by 20 drawing units
          0, 0,0, 20,40, 20,−20

angle = 0, X-origin = 0, Y-origin = 0, delta-X = 20, delta-Y = 40, dash1 = 20, dash2 = −20

This will produce a hatch pattern consisting of dashed lines, each dash being 20 drawing units long separated by 20 drawing units. Each hatch line will be 40 drawing units apart and drawn with an offset of 20 drawing units with respect to the previous line.

5.   *T,lines of Ts drawn with a 20 offset
          0, 0,0, 20,20, 20,−20
          270, 10,0, 20,20, 20,−20

angle = 0, X-origin = 0, Y-origin = 0, delta-X = 20, delta-Y = 20, dash1 = 20, dash2 = −20

angle = 270, X-origin = 10, Y-origin = 0, delta-X = 20, delta-Y = 20, dash1 = 20, dash2 = −20

This is a hatch pattern made up of two lines. Both are dashed lines but the second is rotated by 270° and has a starting point of 10 drawing units from the X-origin. Each line of Ts is offset by 20 drawing units from the previous line.

These examples are illustrated in Figure 13.3.

13.5 Shapes

Shapes are special entities made up of lines, circles and arcs which have been defined numerically. They can be inserted into any drawing at any required scale and rotation angle. The desired shape must first be loaded from a special shape library file (which has the extension .SHX) into the current drawing file. Once loaded the shape can be generated any number of times. Shapes are superficially similar to blocks. While blocks are more versatile and easier to define, AutoCAD uses shapes more efficiently with considerable savings in memory.

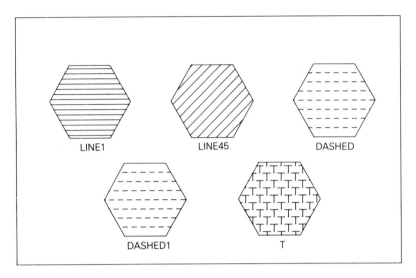

Figure 13.3 HATCH examples

13.5.1 Load

Before a shape can be used the file in which it is stored must first be loaded into the current drawing.

> **Command:** LOAD
> **Name of shape file to load (or ?):**

The ? input gives a list of the *currently loaded shape files*.

13.5.2 Shape

Once the shape definition file has been loaded into the current drawing shapes from within this file can be positioned in the drawing by using the SHAPE command.

> **Command:** SHAPE **Shape name (or ?)‹default›:**
> **Starting point:**
> **Height‹1.0›:**
> **Rotation angle‹0.0›:**

The shape can be dynamically dragged to its starting point and dragged to the required height and rotation angle.

? will give a list of the *currently loaded shapes*.

13.5.3 Compiling Shape Files

To compile a shape file it must first be written using a text editor and saved with the extension .SHP. The .SHP file is then compiled using Task 7 from the main AutoCAD menu. If there are no syntax errors in the text file the compilation is declared to be successful and the compiled file is given the extension .SHX. It is then ready to be loaded into your drawing using the LOAD command. A shape file may contain many shape definitions, all of which become available once the file has been loaded.

13.5.4 Preparing a Shape Text File

Shape files are written using an external text editor. This file acts as a library of shapes (maximum number of shapes 255) which must be loaded into a drawing before the shapes can be used.

The first line of each shape definition must follow the following syntax exactly:

*shapenumber,defbytes,shapename

shapenumber   Each shape definition saved in a shape file is given its own unique number between 1 and 255.
defbytes   The number of data bytes used in the subsequent shape definition (maximum of 2000). This number has to be supplied *after* the shape definition has been written.
shapename   The name assigned to the shape. This name must be written *IN UPPER CASE*.

13.5.5 Defining simple straight line shapes

The simplest shapes can be defined by using basic line elements orientated along one of the 16 predefined directions – each direction has its own specific code number/letter (Figure 13.4).

Each shape definition byte contains information about vector length and direction. The maximum length of any line is 15 units. For convenience, a diagonal of a unit sided box is considered to be also of unit length (but it will be drawn as its true length of 1.414), e.g. if a vector is defined 014 then it will be one drawing unit long in the vertical (4) direction but if it is defined 016 it will be stretched to 1.414 units long in the (6) direction.

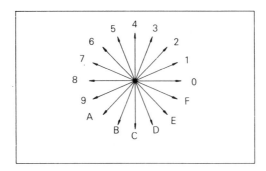

Figure 13.4 Sixteen pre-defined vector directions

13.5.6 Special Codes for defining complex shapes

Apart from the standard vector definition there are various special codes to assist in the definition of more complex shapes:

000	End of shape definition.
001	Activates draw mode (pen down).
002	Deactivates draw mode (pen up).
003	Divide vector lengths by next byte.
004	Multiply vector lengths by next byte.
005	Push (save) current location onto stack.
006	Pop (restore) current location from stack.
007	Draw subshape number given by next byte.
008	X–Y displacement given by next two bytes.
009	Multiple X–Y displacements, terminated by (0,0).
00A(10)	Octant arc defined by next two bytes.
00B(11)	Fractional arc defined by next five bytes.
00C(12)	Arc defined by X–Y displacement and bulge.
00D(13)	Multiple bulge-specified arcs.
00E(14)	Process next command only if text style is vertical

- *Code 0: End of shape.* Marks the end of a shape definition.

- *Codes 1 and 2: Draw mode.* This corresponds to 'pen up' and 'pen down'. Draw is On at the start of each shape and therefore any specified vectors will be drawn. If draw mode is set Off (code 002) then the move to the next specified location is made without drawing. Issuing the code 001 reactivates the draw mode.

- *Codes 3 and 4: Size control.* These set the relative size of each vector. When the SHAPE command is invoked and the height specified, it is assumed by

AutoCAD that this height is the orthogonal vector i.e. directions 0, 4, 8 or C. The byte following the code 3 or 4 contains the new scale factor (initial height multiplied by new scale), e.g. 4,5 would multiply the current scale by 5. Scale factors are cumulative and therefore you must be careful to reset the scale when necessary: AutoCAD does not automatically reset the scale for you.

- *Codes 5 and 6: Location save/restore.* Codes 5 and 6 are used to save and restore the current position within the shape so that it can be returned to at a later stage in the shape definition. Any location saved must later be restored. The stack is only four deep and if the stack overflows the following message will appear:

    Position stack overflow in shape nnn

    Similarly if you try to restore more locations than have been saved the following will appear.

    Position stack underflow in shape nnn

    You must remember that locations are restored from the stack in the reverse order to that in which they were saved – last on, first off.

- *Code 7: Subshape.* The vector following code 7 specifies the number of another shape which is saved in the same shape file. The shape with this number will be incorporated into the current shape.

    > *Note:* You should ensure that the draw mode is set ON before this code is issued.

- *Codes 8 and 9: X–Y displacement.* The existence of only 16 predefined directions can be very limiting. To overcome this, codes 8 and 9 can be used to specify *X–Y* displacements.

    Code 8 is used to specify a single *X–Y* displacement and must be followed by two bytes in the following format:

    8,X-displacement,Y-displacement

    X–Y displacements can be in the range −128 to 127.

    e.g. 8,(5,8) would result in a vector being drawn 5 units to the right and 8 units up.

    +ve up and right,−-ve down and left

> *Note:* The brackets are an optional aid to clarity and are not recognised by AutoCAD.

Code 9 is used where a *sequence* of non-standard vectors is required:

e.g. 9,(5,−6),(3,2),(−4,1),(0,0)

> *The sequence must be terminated with (0,0)*

● *Codes 00A (10): Octantarc.* Octants are arcs which span one or more 45° angle, starting and ending on an octant boundary. Octants are numbered counterclockwise from the 3 o'clock position and are specified as follows:

    10,radius,(–)0SC

The radius can be any value between 1 and 255.

S represents the number of the starting octant, 0 to 7.

C represents the number of octants to be drawn, 0 to 7, 0 representing a full circle.

   A negative sign represents an octant being drawn in the clockwise direction while a positive sign (or no sign) represents an octant drawn in the anticlockwise direction.

See Figure 13.5.

● *Code 00B (11): Fractional arc.* This is used to draw arcs which do not finish on an octant boundary and are defined as follows:

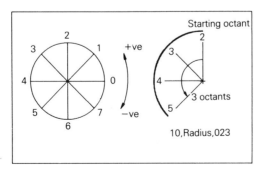

Figure 13.5 Octant arc definition

11,start-offset,end-offset,high-radius,low-radius,(–)0SC

The start and end offsets represent the amount that the arc is displaced from the octant boundary. The high radius is zero unless the radius is greater than 255. The low radius is any radius below 255. S and C are the same as for octants.

To calculate the start-offset, find the difference between the starting octant boundary and the start of the arc, multiply this by 256 and divide the answer by 45. If the arc ends on an octant boundary then the end-offset will be zero.

- *Codes 00C and 00D (12 and 13): Bulge-specified arcs.* These codes are similar to codes 8 and 9 but have the added facility of a 'bulge' factor which is applied to the displacement vector. Code 00C (12) draws one arc segment while code 00D (13) draws multiple arc segments (which must be ended with 0,0).

The format for code 12 or 00C is:

12,X-displacement,Y-displacement,bulge

The *X*- and *Y*-displacements are defined in the same way as for codes 8 and 9, and may be in the range −127 to 127. The bulge is the curvature of the arc and may be in the range −127 to 127. It is calculated by taking the distance *D* between the two arc ends, the perpendicular height *H* from the midpoint of this line to the arc, dividing *H* by *D*, multiplying the answer by 254 i.e. bulge = $(H/D)*254$ (Figure 13.6). This is negative if the direction of the arc is clockwise.

A bulge of 127 or −127 represents a semicircle, whereas a bulge of zero represents a straight line.

The format for 00D (13) is the same as for 00C (12) but multiple *X*-, *Y*- and bulge specifications are defined, terminated with (0,0).

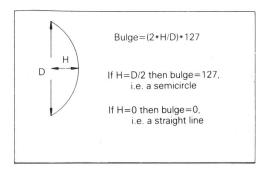

Figure 13.6 Bulge definition

EXAMPLE

Examples of simple shape definitions are as follows:

1. A triangle could be defined as follows:

   *165,4,TRIANGLE
   014,01E,018,0

   The final zero in the shape definition marks the end of the shape. This shape may now be saved within a file with extension .SHP, and compiled into an .SHX file using Task 7 from the main menu.

2. The following will draw a circle with two diametric lines at right angles to each other (north-south and east-west):

   *101,11,WOTSIT
   3,5,10,1,000,028,002,012,001,02C,0

   The constituent parts are:

3	represents 'divide vector by next byte'.
5	the division factor.
10	octant arc defined by next two bytes.
1	octant arc radius of 1.
000	draw a circle.
028	draw a line 2 units long in the 8 direction
002	pen up – deactivate draw mode
012	move 1 unit in the 2 direction
001	pen down – activate draw mode
02C	draw a line 2 units in the 'C' direction
0	end shape definition

3. To draw an arc from 65° to 100° with a 3 unit radius:

   11,(114,57,0,3,012)

11	Fractional arcs.
114	Start-offset = ((65−45)*256/45).
57	End-offset = ((100−90)*256/45).
0	High radius.
3	Low radius of 3 units
012	The 1 is the starting octant S, the 2 is the octant count C.

4. To draw a crude letter S:

   13,(0,5,127),(0,5,−127),(0,0),0

13	multiple bulge specification.
0,5,127	semicircle with a displacement of 0 in the X-direction and 5 in the Y direction, drawn anticlockwise.

0,5,−127 semicircle with a displacement of 0 in the *X*-direction and 5 in the *Y*-direction, drawn clockwise.

These examples are illustrated in Figure 13.7.

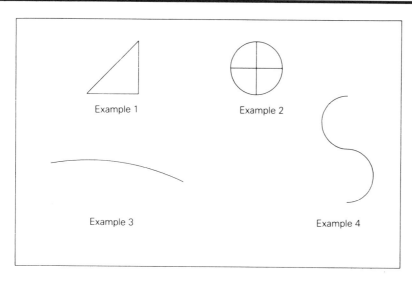

Example 1

Example 2

Example 3

Example 4

Figure 13.7 SHAPE examples

13.5.7 Using Shapes in Font Files

Text font files are used when text is to be added to a drawing. The text style used incorporates one of the font files, e.g. Simplex or Italic. These files are prepared in essentially the same way as are shape files.

Two fragments of the Simplex font file are shown below.

```
*0,4,Roman Simplex 1/20/86
21,7,2,0
*10,9,lf
2,8,(0,−36),14,8,(30,36),0
*32,9,spc
2,8,(19,0),14,8,(−19,−30),0
*33,38,kexc
2,14,8,(−1,−21),8,(1,21),1,02B,9,(1,−12),(1,12),(0,0),025,2,
02C,1,06C,2,0BC,1,01A,01E,012,016,2,8,(12,−2),14,8,(−12,−10),0
:
:

*65,27,uca
2,14,8,(−8,−21),1,8,(8,21),8,(8,−21),2,8,(−13,7),1,0A0,2,8,
```

```
(9,−7),14,8,(−14,−10),0
*66,46,ucb
2,14,8,(−7,−21),1,8,(0,21),090,8,(3,−1),01E,02D,02C,02B,01A,
8,(−3,−1),2,098,1,090,8,(3,−1),01E,02D,03C,02B,01A,8,(−3,−1),
098,2,8,(21,0),14,8,(−14,−10),0
```

This becomes a bit more comprehensible when you remember that

- lf stands for line feed and has an ASCII value of 10.
- spc stands for space and has an ASCII value of 32.
- uca stands for upper case A and has an ASCII value of 65 etc.

A font file must carry the special header:

```
*0,4,font name
above,below,mode,0
```

Where 'above' and 'below' refer respectively to the number of vector lengths that the upper case letters extend above the base line and to the number of vector lengths that the lower case letters extend below the base line. These effectively scale the font characters. Mode may be set to 0 for a horizontally oriented font or 2 for a dual orientation (horizontal or vertical font). The special command code 00E (14) is obeyed only when mode is set to 2.

The font characters are referenced by AutoCAD through their shape number only, never by name. The name should therefore always be written in *lower case* – this makes it visible to the reader but it is not recognised by AutoCAD. The shape number used for a text font character must always be the ASCII code (American Standard Code for Information Interchange) for that character. Within these restrictions, the font character is then defined exactly as any other shape.

It is possible to use standard shape definition techniques to add non-standard characters and symbols to an existing font. You must assign them code numbers between 130 and 255 to avoid interference with the standard characters.

To use these extra characters within a TEXT or DTEXT command you must include the string

%%nnn

within the text, where nnn represents the three digits of the code number which you have assigned to the character. See Section 8.1.3.

14 · Slides and presentations

14.1 Preparing and Viewing Slides

The SLIDE command in effect takes a snapshot of the drawing as it appears on the screen and saves this for future viewing. The slide is not a drawing and can only be viewed; it can not be modified in any way.

A slide is created with the MSLIDE (MakeSLIDE) command when the required display is already on the screen.

Command: MSLIDE Slide file ‹current›:

The **Slide file** prompt will supply the current *drawing* name. If you do not wish to use this name for the slide file you may supply an alternative. The slide will be saved on the specified directory with an .SLD extension.

Slides can be viewed at any time while in the drawing editor by using the VSLIDE command. It does not matter if you already have a drawing on screen, the slide will replace it temporarily and the drawing will be restored when the slide is cancelled with a REDRAW.

Command: VSLIDE Slide file: (Name)

14.2 Slide Libraries

Slides may conveniently be collected together into slide libraries. A slide library is created using the SLIDELIB utility program from DOS. The best way to use this program is first to prepare a simple list of the slides you wish to include, using a word processor or text editor (see Section 13.1), consisting of one slide name per line. The SLIDELIB program then calls upon this slide file list when compiling the library.

EXAMPLE

For example, to compile a library called MYLIB containing three slides, a slide file list called, say, MYSLIDES.TXT is first prepared and would look like the following:

> SLIDE1 (you do not need the .SLD extension)
> SLIDE2
> SLIDE3

The SLIDELIB program is then called from DOS:

> C>SLIDELIB MYLIB ‹MYSLIDES.TXT

It is important not to forget the redirection character ‹ before the slide file list name, otherwise SLIDELIB thinks that you have supplied two library names and will crash.

The slide library so formed carries an .SLB extension. It is not a text file and may not be inspected or altered. If you wish to make any changes you should alter the slide file list before recompiling the library using SLIDELIB.

To view a particular slide from a slide library, the library name is specified (without the .SLB extension), and the slide name is included in round brackets:

> **Command:** VSLIDE MYLIB(SLIDE1)

14.3 SCRIPT Files

A script file acts rather as a batch file in DOS or as a macro in Lotus 1-2-3, in that a number of AutoCAD commands may be written into the file – these are then executed sequentially when the file is used. Script files are particularly effective when used with a series of slides to present an automated slide show. They may also be used for performing repetitive tasks such as setting up units, automatically setting up the plotter menu for different paper sizes etc.

A delay between operations may be introduced by incorporating a DELAY command, specifying the delay in milliseconds.

A typical script file, called SLDSHOW1.SCR (written on a text editor), to display a sequence of three slides could be as follows:

> VSLIDE SLIDE1
> DELAY 2000
> VSLIDE SLIDE2
> DELAY 2000
> VSLIDE SLIDE3
> DELAY 2000

To run this script file:

Command: SCRIPT
Name of Script file: SLDSHOW1

This script file will show each slide for a period of 2 seconds. The last slide will remain on the screen until a REDRAW command is given.

The sequence of commands in the file may be repeated indefinitely if terminated with RSCRIPT. The process may be interrupted by a Ctrl C.

When the script file is running, each DELAY 2000 instruction gives a delay of 2000 milliseconds or 2 seconds. There will also be an unwanted delay between slides as the new slide is loaded from the disk prior to display. This can be eliminated by loading the next slide while the present slide is being viewed. When the next VSLIDE command is encountered, the previously loaded slide is displayed. Preloading is achieved by adding a * to the slide name.

These modifications are shown in SLDSHOW2.SCR:

```
VSLIDE SLIDE1
VSLIDE *SLIDE2
DELAY 2000
VSLIDE
VSLIDE *SLIDE3
DELAY 2000
VSLIDE
DELAY 2000
RSCRIPT
```

Script files can even be used from DOS to enter AutoCAD and select tasks from the main menu. The following script file, called AUTOSHOW.SCR, enters AutoCAD, selects main menu Task 2 and then loads a particular drawing called MYDRAWNG. It then calls two slides with a display time of five seconds, redraws MYDRAWNG, quits the drawing editor, and finally exits AutoCAD with a main menu Task 0.

```
2
MYDRAWNG
VSLIDE SLIDE1
DELAY 5000
VSLIDE SLIDE2
DELAY 5000
REDRAW
QUIT Y
0
```

To run AUTOSHOW from DOS requires the command:

C⟩ACAD X AUTOSHOW

The **X** is a dummy default drawing name which is replaced by MYDRAWNG as soon as AUTOSHOW is run.

The above command assumes that you are already in the AutoCAD directory. The ultimate in showing off can be achieved by incorporating the command into a batch file (called SHOWOFF.BAT) which can be run from the root directory. It changes directory to the AutoCAD directory (ACAD), starts up AutoCAD, runs AUTOSHOW and finally returns you to the root.

C:
CD\ACAD
ACAD X AUTOSHOW
CD\

The entire sequence can thus be achieved by typing the single command:

C⟩SHOWOFF

Go on! Show off!

15 · Creating screen and tablet menus

Although AutoCAD may be driven exclusively from the keyboard the majority of users will be familiar with and will employ the screen, pull down and tablet menus. All these menus are set up within the package from a single menu file called ACAD.MNU. This is written as a text file and can be examined and modified using a word processor. The file used by the drawing editor is ACAD.MNX, which is a compiled version of ACAD.MNU. If ACAD.MNX is not available, or if the corresponding .MNU file is newer, the package will automatically compile ACAD.MNU and store the result as ACAD.MNX for future use.

When a new drawing is started it depends for its parameters on the values specified in the prototype drawing. It will also use the menu specified by the prototype drawing, which is usually the standard menu ACAD.MNX. Because of this, all drawings will usually be produced and saved with the standard menu.

However, it is possible to write alternative menu files for specific applications and these can be used with and attached to any drawing.

> *Note:* Whatever menu is associated with a drawing when it is saved will remain with the drawing when it is subsequently retrieved.

In order to be able to write specific menu files it is helpful to understand the structure of the ACAD.MNU file.

> *Note:* Although it is instructive to modify this file to observe the effect, you are strongly advised to retain an unmodified version in case of accidents!

15.1 Structure of the Standard Menu

The standard menu file actually contains eighteen menus – one for the screen, four for the four separate tablet areas of the digitiser, one for the buttons on the mouse, one for the buttons of an auxiliary function box and ten pull down menus and one icon menu.

Looking at the beginning of the file with a text editor you will see the following:

```
***BUTTONS
;
$P1=*
^C^C
^B
^O
^G
^D
^E
^T
***AUX1
;
$P1=*
^C^C
^B
^O
^G
^D
^E
^T

***POP1
[Tools]
[OSNAP]^C^C$P1= $P1=* OSNAP \
CENter
ENDpoint
INSert
[INTersection]INT
MIDpoint
NEArest
NODe
[PERpendicular]PER
QUAdrant
[QUICK,]QUICK,^Z $P1=*
TANgent
NONE
[~—]
[FILTERS. . . ]$P1=filters $P1=*
[Cancel]^C^C
```

```
[U]^C^CU
[Redo]^C^CREDO
[List]^C^CLIST
⋮
```

Further down the same menu you will find the screen menu section:

```
***SCREEN
**S
[AutoCAD]^C^C$S=X $S=S $P1=POP1 $P3=POP3
[* * * *]$S=OSNAPB
[Setup]^C^C^P(progn(prompt "Loading setup. . . ")(load "setup"))
^P$[=X $S=UNITS

[BLOCKS]$S=X $S=BL
[DIM:]$S=X $S=DIM ^C^CDIM
[DISPLAY]$S=X $S=DS
[DRAW]$S=X $S=DR
[EDIT]$S=X $S=ED
[INQUIRY]$S=X $S=INQ
[LAYER:]$S=X $S=LAYER ^C^CLAYER
[SETTINGS]$S=X $S=SET
[PLOT]$S=X $S=PLOT
[UCS:]$S=X $S=UCS1 ^C^CUCS
[UTILITY]$S=X $S=UT
```

This is at first sight pretty incomprehensible – and it is over fifty pages long! (This is where a good word processor is essential.) However, it is possible to split it up into more digestible portions.

The 18 menus are each identified by ***. Thus, on line 1, ***BUTTONS marks the start of the menu which defines the functions of the buttons on the mouse/puck. Similarly, on line 11, ***AUX1 denotes the auxiliary function box button menu and on line 22 is the first pull down menu ***POP1. The screen menu starts on page 9 with ***SCREEN. The first of the four tablet menus is much further down, on page 46, and the others are on pages 50, 52 and 55.

15.2 Writing Simple Screen Menus

A menu item may consist of a command, a parameter or a sequence of commands and parameters. Normally, each menu item resides on one line of the menu file.

Suppose we want a simple screen menu to give facilities for drawing lines or circles:

```
***SCREEN
LINE
CIRCLE
[BYE]quit
```

You can use either capitals or lower case letters for menu items but you may find it helpful to reserve capitals for titles and screen display items, leaving lower case letters for commands.

The first line, which identifies the screen menu, is not strictly necessary here because, in the absence of a *** label, AutoCAD assumes that the first menu item of the file is the screen menu.

The above menu is easy to understand. The words LINE and CIRCLE will appear in the screen menu position (on the right of the screen) and when picked will result in the execution of the simple LINE and CIRCLE commands. [BYE]quit shows how to put a label on the screen (identified by square brackets – maximum label length 8 characters) which, when picked, will cause the execution of the corresponding command specified in the menu – in this case QUIT.

> *Note:*   The label must not itself be a valid AutoCAD command.

The file can now be saved (in DOS text format) with any legal name of your choice, but it must carry the .MNU extension, e.g. MYMENU.MNU. Make sure that the new menu file is in either the system directory or the current working directory and then enter AutoCAD. Once in the drawing editor, the standard menu will appear on the screen as specified by the prototype drawing. You can now load the new menu:

Command: Menu
Menu file name or . for none: ‹default› MYMENU

The new menu will now replace the standard menu.

> *Note:*   A . response will replace the old menu with no menu at all.

15.2.1 Sub-Menus

The AutoCAD standard menu frequently employs sub-menus. In such cases, on picking a screen menu item, the original menu is replaced by a totally separate sub-menu.

A sub-menu is identified by ** followed by a name not exceeding thirty-one characters in length.

EXAMPLE

```
***SCREEN
LINE
[DRAWCIRC]$S=MYCIRCLES
[BYE]quit
**MYCIRCLES
[CIRCLE10]circle \10;
[CIRCLE20]circle \20;
[CIRCLE30]circle \30;

[MAINMENU]$s=SCREEN
```

With this menu in operation the screen menu display looks similar to the previous one. However, if you pick DRAWCIRC the menu is replaced by the sub-menu called MYCIRCLES. The sub-menu is specified by the $S= menu command immediately following the [DRAWCIRC] label. S here refers to the screen menu so that $S=MYCIRCLES has the effect of making the sub-menu MYCIRCLES replace the current menu on the screen.

This sub-menu provides circles with predetermined radii of 10, 20 or 30 drawing units without the need to supply these parameters from the keyboard. Supplying predetermined parameters to commands is one of the strengths of a well-designed menu.

15.2.2 Inputs within Menu Items

The back slash \ after the circle command in the above MYCIRCLES sub-menu is prompting for an input from the pointer or the keyboard; in this case it is prompting for the centre point of the circle. When this has been received the command proceeds with the radius parameter provided by the menu.

The final semicolons are important – they act as the Returns which are needed to execute the commands. In some menu lines you can make the command work without the semicolon because the fact that AutoCAD has reached the end of the menu line is sufficient to execute the command, but this is not a reliable technique. You are far less likely to get into difficulties if you acquire the habit of *always* using a semicolon where a Return would be the normal response if you were executing the same command from the keyboard. Try writing the menu line:

```
[LINES]line 100,50;150,20;200,30;;
```

and observe the effect of missing out the various semicolons.

When writing such menu items you must make yourself completely familiar with the sequence in which the command expects its parameters!

> *Note:* This sequence, including any Returns, must be reproduced exactly in the corresponding line of the menu, otherwise AutoCAD will not respond as you might expect.

Conversely, if you are trying to disentangle an existing menu item which contains many semicolons and control characters, run through the same command manually within AutoCAD and take careful note of all the spaces and Returns and other responses that you use.

15.2.3 Returning from the Sub-Menu

There remains the problem of returning from the sub-menu to the main menu. This is achieved in the last line of the sub-menu. Just as the sub-menu was entered with $S=MYCIRCLES, so $S=SCREEN always returns you to the start of the screen menu. In this command the $ sign signifies that the menu is to be changed and the S refers to the screen menu. Similarly:

B	refers to the button menu.
T	to tablet menus.
A	to the auxiliary box menu.
P	to the pull down menus.
I	to the icon menu.

Menus can be 'nested' one inside the other up to a maximum of 8. Thus a sub-menu can lead to a further sub-menu etc. When exiting a nested sub-menu, $S= will always return you to the previous menu. In the example the previous menu is the main screen menu but this would not necessarily be the case if further nesting levels had been used.

15.2.4 Menu Blanks

When one menu is replaced by another the new menu is simply written on top of the old – the old is not erased first. This would cause no problems if all menus were of the same length but a short menu written over a long one will leave the last few lines of the original menu still visible. You will find that MYMENU suffers from this problem – the label MAINMENU refuses to disappear after you have left the MYCIRCLES sub-menu.

The problem may be overcome by adding blank lines to 'pad out' a short menu to the full length. Alternatively, a special blanking menu consisting almost entirely of blank lines may be called up and then succeeded by the desired short menu. This approach is used in the ACAD menu, where the blanking menu (on page 9 of the menu) is called **X.

Do not be tempted to make your menus too long. A sub-menu may theoretically be of any length, but any items which will not fit on the screen will be completely inaccessible – use further sub-menus instead.

If a sub-menu title is accompanied by a number, e.g.

**MYCIRCLES 2

then the sub-menu, when activated, will start at the position of item 2 of the previous menu rather than at the top. This allows part of an old menu to be retained and used.

15.2.5 Control Characters

Control characters can be included in menus by the use of the ^ symbol. Thus Ctrl C (delete), Ctrl B (snap toggle), Ctrl O (ortho toggle) may be represented as ^C, ^B, ^O etc. Examples of this may be seen in the button menu of ACAD.MNU.

15.2.6 Long Menu Items

If a menu item is very complicated it may not be possible to fit it on to one line of the menu. If it were allowed to wrap over on to the following line AutoCAD would try to interpret it as two separate menu items – probably with undesired results. To overcome this a long line should be terminated with a + sign. The following line will then be considered as a continuation. This may be used to include as many lines as necessary. In practice, multi-line items are likely to be needed only if you are using AutoLISP to perform complex menu tasks.

15.3 Pull Down Menus

The pull down menus may be written in a manner similar to that of the screen menu. Up to 10 pull down menus can be accommodated under the headings ***POP1 to ***POP10. If a POP section is absent from the menu it will simply be omitted from the menu bar at the top of the screen.

The first item in square brackets on the pull down menu will be treated as the title and will appear on the menu bar. If this title is picked, the remaining items will be displayed in pull down form.

The title may be up to 14 characters long but, since most screen displays are only 80 characters wide and since up to 10 pull down menus may be used, it is usually advisable to restrict titles to 8 characters.

EXAMPLE

For example, we can incorporate the MYCIRCLES routine from the screen menu onto a pull down menu by 'stealing' the instructions from the MYCIRCLES Screen subroutine and including them in a POP section:

```
***POP1
[DRAWCIRC]
[CIRCLE10]circle \10;
[CIRCLE20]circle \20;
[CIRCLE30]circle \30;

***SCREEN
LINE
[CIRCLES]$S=MYCIRCLES
[BYE]QUIT

**MYCIRCLES
[CIRCLE10]circle \10;
[CIRCLE20]circle \20;
[CIRCLE30]circle \30;

[MAINMENU]$s=SCREEN
```

15.3.1 Pull Down Sub-menus

Sub-menus can be added to pull downs and are handled very much as screen sub-menus. It is possible for an item on one pull down sub-menu to be used to call another pull down sub-menu. This menu swapping is controlled by the $P command.

EXAMPLE

For example, suppose a pull down menu, say ***POP2, consisted of three sub-menus called P2A, P2B and P2C.

```
***POP2
**P2A
[DRAW]
```

[BIGCIRCLE]$P2=P2B $P2=*
[ELLIPSES]$P2=P2C $P2=*

**P2B
[BIGCIRCLE]
[CIRCLE50]circle \50;
[CIRCLE60]circle \60;
[CIRCLE70]circle \70;
[EXIT]$P2=P2A
**P2C
[ELLIPSES]
[ELLIP10]ellipse \\10;
[ELLIP20]ellipse \\20;
[ELLIP30]ellipse \\30;
[EXIT]$P2=P2A

In this case P2A, being the first sub-menu encountered, behaves as the main menu of POP2 and is pulled down when POP2 is called from the menu bar. DRAW, being the first item on the menu, becomes the menu bar title of POP2. On pull down, the items BIGCIRCLE and ELLIPSES are displayed.

If BIGCIRCLE is picked, then the menu commands $P2=P2B and $P2=* are executed.

$P2=P2B makes sub-menu P2B the main menu of POP2, and its first item, BIGCIRCLE, becomes the menu bar title.

$P2=* is a separate command which forces a pull down of this current POP2 menu without the need to pick the menu bar title. CIRCLE50, CIRCLE60, CIRCLE70 and EXIT are thus displayed.

If any of the CIRCLE items is picked its commands are executed as normal and the pull down menu subsequently disappears – but P2B remains in effect as the main menu so that the POP2 menu bar title remains as BIGCIRCLE.

If EXIT is picked the command $P2=P2A resets P2A as the main menu of POP2 and the menu bar title returns to DRAW.

A similar sequence of operations pertains to the ellipse sub-menu, P2C.

> *Note:* The EXIT items do not include the $P2=* command so that the POP2 menu is not pulled down until it is next picked from the menu bar.

15.4 Icon Menus

A powerful feature of AutoCAD is the use made of icon menus. A number of small pictorially descriptive icons may be displayed on the screen and selection is made by picking, as in a pull down menu. When an icon is picked the corresponding command in the icon menu is executed and the icon display is removed.

Icons are composed of slides which have previously been prepared from AutoCAD drawings and stored in an accessible directory. The slides may be individuals or may be stored in a single slide library – the latter approach is neater and quicker in operation (see Section 14.2).

EXAMPLE

An example of a typical icon menu for inclusion in MYMENU is the following:

```
***ICON
**MYSLIDES
[These are my slides]
[MYLIB(Fig1)]
[MYLIB(Fig2)]
[Fig3]
[ HIS SLIDES]$I=HISSLIDES $I=*
[ EXIT]^C^C

**HISSLIDES
[These are his slides]
[HISLIB(Fig5)]
[HISLIB(Fig6)]
[Fig7]
[ MY SLIDES]$I=MYSLIDES $I=*
[ EXIT]^C^C$I=MYSLIDES
```

This menu contains two sub-menus to permit the display of two sets of slides – MYSLIDES and HISSLIDES. The mechanism for displaying the icon menus closely follows that of the pull down menus. Thus, MYSLIDES, being the first sub-menu, is the one normally displayed when picked. The first text item (in this case **These are my slides**) forms the title and is printed at the top of the icon display.

Subsequent items are the names of the slides which form the individual icons. In the case of MYSLIDES there are three icons (Fig1, Fig2 and Fig3). The first two are contained in a slide file library called MYLIB. The third is a separate slide which is not in a library. Both the library and the free slide should be resident in the current directory.

The icons are automatically displayed on the screen at a position and magnification commensurate with the number of icons in the menu. The maximum is 16 icons, which are displayed in 4 columns of 4 rows.

The final items in the sub-menu are the words HIS SLIDES and EXIT. Text items like this may be displayed instead of icons if the first character of the text is a space. EXIT simply cancels all actions and removes the icon menu from the screen. HIS SLIDES, when picked, performs a menu swap to the HISSLIDES sub-menu followed by a forced display ($I=*) of that icon menu.

> *Note:* Both these sub-menus are incomplete because, with the exception of EXIT and HIS SLIDES, there is no command issued when an item is picked.

To call up this icon menu a call line must appear in a pull down, a screen or a tablet menu. A typical pull down entry would be:

```
***POP3
[SLIDES]
[MY SLIDES]$I=MYSLIDES $I=*
[HIS SLIDES]$I=HISSLIDES $I=*
```

This allows direct access to either the MYSLIDES or HISSLIDES sub-menus. The $I= command sets the current menu and $I=* forces its display.

15.5 Tablet Menus

When using the standard menu, ACAD.MNU, you are in a position to make use of the tablet template (assuming that you are using a digitiser and not a mouse). However, you may not be aware of this, particularly if the digitiser is acting as a simple pointing device with the whole tablet area being used to point to different positions on the screen.

A tablet template (see Chapter 1) is supplied with AutoCAD for use with the standard tablet menu contained within ACAD.MNU.

> *Note:* To activate the tablet menu you must first configure the working areas of your digitiser.

Attach the template firmly to the digitiser tablet so that it will not slide around. It is sensible to position it to be as central and as square as possible, although AutoCAD will compensate for any misalignment.

Then invoke the configuration routine from the keyboard:

Command: TABLET
Option (ON/OFF/CAL/CFG): CFG
Enter number of tablet menus desired (0–4): 4
Do you want to re-align tablet menu areas?: Y

Digitize upper left corner of menu area 1:	(Point to indicated spot.)
Digitize lower left corner of menu area 1:	(Point to indicated spot.)
Digitize lower right corner of menu area 1:	(Point to indicated spot.)

This task is made easy when using the standard template because the requested corner points are clearly marked with small black circles (Figure 15.1).

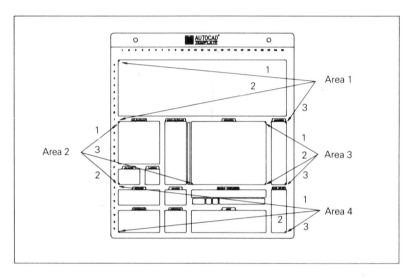

Figure 15.1 The four standard tablet menu areas

Enter the number of columns for menu area 1: 25
Enter the number of rows for menu area 1:   9

This ritual is repeated for the other three menu areas. To use the standard template you *must* respond to the questions about rows and columns as follows:

Menu area	*Columns*	*Rows*
1	25	9
2	11	9
3	9	13
4	25	7

Finally, the configuration routine asks you to specify the screen pointing area.

Do you want to respecify the screen pointing area?	Y
Digitize lower left corner of screen pointing area	(Point to spot.)
Digitize upper right corner of screen pointing area	(Point to spot.)

This is the end of the tablet configuration process.

This elaborate ritual may be shortened considerably if you enter configuration through the screen menu. Select the screen menu item SETTINGS followed by TABLET and finally config. The questions about rows and columns will then be answered for you. You will, however, still need to pick the corners of the menu areas on the tablet as before. For subsequent tablet configuration select re-cfg from the menu.

The tablet has now been divided up into invisible 'boxes'. The first 200 boxes are in tablet menu area 1, menu area 2 contains a block of 99 boxes, menu area 3 has 117, menu area 4 has 175 and the remainder of the tablet is allocated to the screen pointing area. The size of each box is determined by the physical size of each menu area divided by the number of rows and columns. The above procedure results in standard sized boxes for menus 1, 2 and 4 but smaller boxes for menu area 3.

At the end of the procedure you will find that the tablet is active but that the screen pointing area has been reduced from the whole tablet to a small area identified by the heading Monitor (on the template). If you now point to one of the marked areas on the template and press the pick button the corresponding command will be issued.

Menu area 1 is blank on the template and will not respond with any commands. If you examine the Tablet section of ACAD.MNU you will see:

```
***TABLET1
[A-1]
[A-2]
[A-3]
  :
  :
[A-24]
[A-25]
[B-1]
[B-2]
[B-3]
  :
  :
[H-22]
[H-23]
[H-24]
```

These items correspond to the 200 'boxes' of menu area 1. If you wish to use one of these boxes then you can delete the item in square brackets (which has no function) and replace it with the relevant command using the same syntax as discussed for the screen and pull down menus.

EXAMPLE

For example, suppose that you have designed 8 shapes, called SH1–SH8 and located in a file called MYSHAPES, using the techniques described in Chapter 13. These may be allocated to 8 boxes in tablet menu area 1 by modifying ACAD.MNU:

```
***TABLET1
load MYSHAPES;shape SH1 \1 0
load MYSHAPES;shape SH2 \1 0
load MYSHAPES;shape SH3 \5 0
load MYSHAPES;shape SH4 \1 0
load MYSHAPES;shape SH5 \1 0
load MYSHAPES;shape SH6 \1 45
load MYSHAPES;shape SH7 \1 0
load MYSHAPES;shape SH8 \1 0
[A-9]
[A-10]
:
```

Note that in this example shape SH3 will be inserted at a magnification of 5 and shape SH6 will be inserted with a rotation of 45°. All other shapes will take up the size and orientation specified in their design.

As an alternative to including the command to load the shape file in every box it is possible to allocate this command to a separate box of its own. This box must be picked before any of the shapes contained in the file may be used:

```
***TABLET1
load MYSHAPES
shape SH1 \1 0
shape SH2 \1 0
shape SH3 \5 0
shape SH4 \1 0
shape SH5 \1 0
shape SH6 \1 45
shape SH7 \1 0
shape SH8 \1 0
[A-10]
:
```

It is instructive to examine the menu items for areas 2, 3 and 4 and compare them with the layout of the standard template. You will see that the grey surrounds of the template (which are all within the defined menu areas) have the function Return and consequently contain semicolons as menu items. You will also see that the small boxes in menu area 3 are used in pairs – this gives an effective box size which is a compromise between the larger boxes of menu areas 1, 2 and 4 and the small individual boxes defined for menu area 3 by the configuration process.

If you always use the standard AutoCAD template you are restricted to the four menu areas and to the specified number of boxes in each area. If you wish to write your own tablet menus then of course you are free to define the menu areas to suit your requirements.

To return the tablet to a simple pointing device you must call TABLET CFG from the keyboard, specify the number of menus to be zero and then redefine the whole tablet as the screen pointing area.

16 · Extracting data from a drawing

16.1 Drawing Interchange (DXF) Files

The information contained in an AutoCAD drawing is stored in a form which is very difficult to interpret or alter. Within the AutoCAD system this does not matter but there are occasions when drawing data needs to be extracted and transferred to other software for analysis. In such cases AutoCAD can produce a drawing interchange file, which is a file in simple text format which can easily be read.

Such files are comprehensive. They contain every detail of a drawing so that if necessary the drawing may be reconstructed exactly within another system. Even a blank drawing contains a large amount of data – everything which is derived from the prototype drawing whenever a new drawing is initiated. As a result the DXF file can appear fearsomely complicated. In fact, because the data is presented in a rigid format with every type of entry identified by a code number, it is relatively easy to use a simple computer program – in BASIC for instance – to sift through the data and pick out only those bits which you require.

For instance, if you are interested in line elements, then the coordinates of the start and end points of all free lines within a drawing may be extracted. Similarly, any other entities may be picked out, or any blocks or shapes, or only those appearing on certain layers etc. The DXF file contains all the information you need – it is just a matter of identifying the right codes to extract the data.

16.1.1 DXFOUT – Writing a DXF File

To make a DXF file from the current drawing is very simple:

Command: DXFOUT
File name:

(The default name here is the current drawing name. The file will be given a .DXF extension.)

Enter decimal places of accuracy (0–16) (or Entities)‹6›:

(This sets the number of decimal places of the coordinates of any points specified in the file. If you select Entities you are prompted to select the required entities from the drawing; only those selected will be transferred to the DXF file.)

The file will then be assembled and written (on the default directory if no other directory was specified with the file name).

16.1.2 DXF File Structure

The DXF file is composed of four sections – header, tables, blocks, and entities. Of these the header section is the largest. It contains all the data held in the prototype drawing; approximately 100 items in all covering everything from the snap setting to the current polyline width.

The tables section covers the current line type, layer, text style and view data.

The blocks section gives full details of all blocks in the drawing including block attributes, whether constant or variable, and also full data on the entities of which the blocks are composed, e.g. lines, circles, polylines etc.

The entities section covers everything else. All entities not included in any blocks are detailed together with their coordinates in the drawing and the layer on which they appear. Also, when relevant, data is given on the entities' elevation, thickness, linetype and colour.

Figure 16.1 shows a simple diagram composed of three lines and a circle.

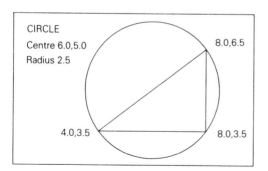

Figure 16.1 DXF extraction: example diagram

The entities section of the corresponding DXF file is shown below together with some added comments.

ENTITIES	(start of entities section)	—
0	(label preceding 1st entity – LINE 1)	
LINE	(entity type)	
8	(label preceding layer name)	E
GEOMETRY	(layer name)	N
10	(label preceding X primary coordinate)	T
4.0	(X primary coordinate – start of line 1)	I
20	(label preceding Y primary coordinate)	T
3.5	(Y primary coordinate – start of line 1)	Y
11	(label preceding X secondary coordinate)	
8.0	(X secondary coordinate – end of line 1)	1
21	(label preceding Y secondary coordinate)	
3.5	(Y secondary coordinate – end of line 1)	—
0	(NEXT ENTITY – LINE 2)	
LINE		
8		E
GEOMETRY	(layer name)	N
10		T
8.0	(Primary X)	I
20		T
3.5	(primary Y)	Y
11		
8.0	(secondary X)	2
21		
6.5	(secondary Y)	—
0	(NEXT ENTITY – LINE 3)	
LINE		
8		E
GEOMETRY	(layer name)	N
10		T
8.0	(primary X)	I
20		T
6.5	(primary Y)	Y
11		
4.0	(secondary X)	3
21		
3.5	(secondary Y)	—
0	(NEXT ENTITY – CIRCLE)	
CIRCLE		E
8		N
GEOMETRY	(layer name)	T
10		I
6.0	(primary X – centre of circle)	T
20		Y

5.0	(primary *Y* – centre of circle)	
40	(label preceding radius)	4
2.5	(radius)	—
0		
ENDSEC	(end of entities section)	
0		
EOF	(end of DXF file)	

At first sight this is confusing but a little study soon reveals the file structure.

The entity name, LINE or CIRCLE in this case, is always preceded by a zero which acts as a label. The 8 in the next line is another label and announces the layer title, GEOMETRY. The labels 10 and 20 precede the *X* and *Y* primary coordinates; here the start point of the lines and the centre of the circle. Similarly, labels 11 and 21 precede any secondary coordinates – the endpoints of the lines. The circle does not have an endpoint but it does have a radius, and this is given in the file after the identifying label 40. ENDSEC indicates the end of the entities section and EOF denotes the end of file.

The point to bear in mind about DXF files is that they define the drawing *totally* – so whatever information you want to extract from a drawing *must* be represented in the DXF file.

16.1.3 DXFIN – Loading a Drawing from a DXF File

It follows from the above that a DXF file can be used to reconstruct an entire drawing. This, like DXFOUT, is a simple operation:

Command: DXFIN
File name: (Enter the name of the DXF file to be loaded.)

If you wish to load a complete DXF file, including all the sections of header, tables, blocks and entities, this can only be done with a *new* drawing – i.e. one which has just been started from option 1 of the main menu. If this is not the case then only the entities section of the DXF file will be loaded.

> *Note:* If AutoCAD insists that the drawing is not a new one when you know that it is, then take a look at your prototype drawing to see if it has had any entities incorporated into it.

If you wish to load only entities then there is no need to use a complete DXF file. A file containing only the required entities set out in DXF format together with the end of file marker will be accepted. The resultant drawing will simply incorporate the header data derived from the prototype drawing.

A drawing loaded through DXFIN can be edited and saved just as a drawing created with the drawing editor.

16.1.4 DXF File Code Numbers

The identifying codes used within a DXF file are given below:

Code	Function
0	The start of an entity, table entry or file separator
1	The primary text value for an entity
2	A name; attribute tag, block name etc.
3–5	Other textual name values
6	Line type name (fixed)
7	Text style name (fixed)
8	Layer name (fixed)
9	Variable name identifier (used only in Header section)
10	Primary X-coordinate (e.g. start of line, Centre of circle)
11–18	Other X-coordinates
20	Primary Y coordinate (immediately following primary X-coordinate)
21–28	Other Y-coordinates
30	Primary Z-coordinate (immediately following X and Y-coordinates)
31–36	Other Z-coordinates
38	This entities elevation if non-zero (fixed)
39	This entities thickness if non-zero (fixed)
40–48	Numerical floating point (radii, text height, scale factors, . . .)
49	Repeated value
50–58	Angles
62	Colour number (fixed)
66	'Entities follow' flag (fixed)
70–78	Integer values (repeat counts, flag bits, modes etc)
210,220	
230	X-, Y-, Z-coordinates of extrusion direction
999	Remarks

Note: An X-coordinate value 10, 11, 12 . . . will normally be accompanied by the corresponding Y-coordinate 20, 21, 22 . . . which will immediately follow the X-coordinate in the file. Similarly, Z coordinates 30, 31, 32 . . . will, where appropriate, immediately follow the X- and Y-groups.

16.1.5 Programs to Extract Data from DXF Files

Because of the rigidly defined structure of a DXF file it is relatively easy to write programs to extract selected data.

A simple program written in BASIC to extract the start and end coordinates of all line entities in the file is given in the AutoCAD manual. A modified version which will additionally extract the centre points and radii of any circles in the DXF file is shown below:

```
500   CLS
1000 REM
1010 REM Extract lines from DXF file
1020 REM
1030 LINE INPUT "DXF file name: ";A$
1040 A$=A$+".dxf"
1050 OPEN "i",1,A$
1060 REM
1070 REM Ignore until section start encountered
1080 REM
1090 GOSUB 1320
1100 IF G% <> 0 THEN 1090
1110 IF S$ <> "SECTION" THEN 1090
1120 GOSUB 1320
1130 REM
1140 REM Skip unless ENTITIES section
1150 REM
1160 IF S$ <> "ENTITIES" THEN 1090
1170 REM
1180 REM Scan until end of section processing LINEs
1190 REM
1200 GOSUB 1320
1210 IF G% = 0 AND S$="ENDSEC" THEN END
1220 IF G%=0 AND S$="LINE" THEN GOSUB 1270:GOTO 1210
1225 IF G%=0 AND S$="CIRCLE" THEN GOSUB 1570:GOTO 1210
1230 GOTO 1200
1240 REM
1250 REM Line coordinates extract
1260 REM
1270 GOSUB 1320
1280 IF G%=10 THEN X1=X: Y1=Y
1290 IF G%=11 THEN X2=X: Y2=Y
1300 IF G%=0 THEN PRINT"LINE from (";X1;",";Y1;") to
      (";X2;",";Y2")":RETURN
1310 GOTO 1270
1320 REM
1330 REM Read group code and following value
1340 REM
1350 INPUT #1, G%
1360 IF G%<10 THEN LINE INPUT #1, S$ :RETURN
1370 IF G%>= 30 AND G%<= 49 THEN INPUT #1, V :RETURN
1380 IF G%>= 50 AND G%<= 59 THEN INPUT #1, A :RETURN
1390 IF G%>= 60 AND G%<= 69 THEN INPUT #1, P% :RETURN
1400 IF G%>= 70 AND G%<= 79 THEN INPUT #1, F% :RETURN
```

```
1410 IF G%>= 20 THEN PRINT"Invalid group code ";G% :STOP
1420 INPUT #1,X
1430 INPUT #1,G1%
1440 IF G1% <> (G%+10) THEN PRINT"Invalid coord code ";G1%
     :STOP
1450 INPUT #1,Y
1460 RETURN
1550 REM
1560 REM Extra extract routine for circles
1565 REM
1570 GOSUB 1320
1580 IF G%=10 THEN X1=X: Y1=Y
1590 IF G%=40 THEN R=V
1600 IF G%=0 THEN PRINT"CIRCLE   (Centre ";X1",";Y1;" Radius
     ";R;")":RETURN
1610 GOTO 1570
```

Corresponding flow diagrams are shown in Figures 16.2 and 16.3. A study of these in conjunction with the above table of code numbers shows that the extraction technique is very simple.

Once this technique is mastered it should be possible to perform virtually any extract required. It is always useful to make a test drawing containing the entities, blocks etc. to be extracted and then to study the format of the corresponding DXF file before starting to write the extraction program.

16.2 Transferring Data to dBASE III+ – Attribute Extraction

The key to extracting data from an AutoCAD drawing and transferring it to another package such as dBASE III+ is in the use of blocks. Attributes contained within the blocks of a drawing may be extracted and transferred to dBASE III+ where they can be manipulated and analysed. The basis for this is a *extract file*. This file is written by AutoCAD and read by dBASE III+. The attributes to be transferred are selected by their tag names. Attributes with a selected tag occupy a field in dBASE III+, although the field name does not have to be the same as that of the tag.

16.2.1 Template Files

The tags of the attributes to be transferred are specified in a separate file called a *template file*. This file must be written, using a text editor or a word processor, before you initiate the transfer (Figure 16.4).

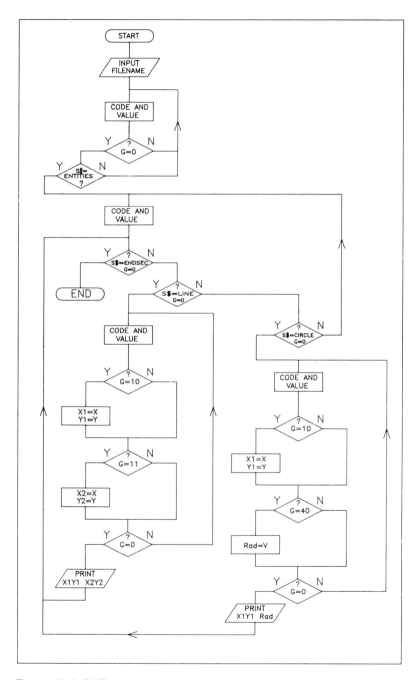

Figure 16.2 DXF entity coordinate extraction for lines and circles

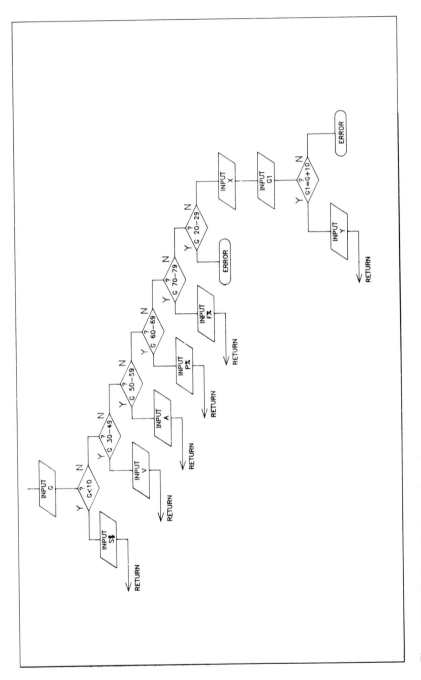

Figure 16.3 Code and value subroutine

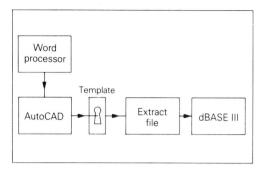

Figure 16.4 Use of a template file

In its simplest form the template file lists the tag names of the attributes to be transferred. For each tag name listed the template file must also specify:

- The corresponding database field type, i.e. a *character* field or a *numeric* field.
- The field width.
- In cases where the field is numeric, the number of places after the decimal point.

Suppose that some of the blocks in your drawing contained attributes with tag names ITEM and COSTWHSL, the first containing a descriptive name and the second the numerical wholesale cost of the item. A template file written to extract only these two attributes could look like:

```
ITEM         C012000
COSTWHSL     N010002
```

> *Note:* Do not use TABS when writing this file. To separate the columns (for improved readability) use only space characters.

The first non-space character after the tag name ITEM is a C indicating that the corresponding database field is a character field. This is followed by 012 to give a field width of 12 characters. The final 3 digits refer to the number of decimal places and are always zeros for a character field. Similarly, COSTWHSL is to be transferred into a Numeric field with 10 places before the decimal point and 2 after it.

> *Note:* If a numeric field is specified but the attribute contains non-numeric characters, then errors will occur. A warning message will be displayed when such an error is detected.

When AutoCAD uses this template file to extract the attributes it will apply the template to each block. Those blocks which contain one or both of the nominated tag names will have their corresponding attribute *values* written into the extract file. If a block contains one, but not both, of the tag names, the values for the absent one will be filled in with blanks (if character) or zeros (if numeric). Blocks containing neither of these tag names will be ignored.

A template file must obviously contain at least one attribute tag name but it can also contain optional special names which will result in more detailed data being extracted from blocks containing a nominated tag name.

These special names may occur in any order but they *must* be written in this exact form:

BL:NAME	Cwww000	(Block name)
BL:LEVEL	NwwwOOO	(Block nesting level)
BL:X	Nwwwddd	(*X*-coordinate of block)
BL:Y	Nwwwddd	(*Y*-coordinate of block)
BL:LAYER	C:www000	(Block insertion layer name)
BL:ORIENT	Nwwwddd	(Block rotation angle)
BL:XSCALE	Nwwwddd	(*X*-scale factor of block)
BL:YSCALE	Nwwwddd	(*Y*-scale factor of block)

where www and ddd represent the field width and decimal place data respectively.

When completed, the template file must be saved with a .TXT extension, e.g. MYTEMPL.TXT.

16.2.2 Extraction

To extract data from a drawing:

Command: ATTEXT
CDF, SDF or DXF Attribute extract (or Entities)?

The prompt refers to the format to be adopted in the extract file. CDF stands for Comma Delimited Format – the file contains fields separated by delimiters (commas by default) and character fields are enclosed in single quotes. SDF stands for Space Delimited Format – the fields are of fixed width and so no delimiter characters are needed. DXF stands for a variant of AutoCAD's normal Drawing Interchange File format, which contains only block reference, attribute and end of sequence entities. dBASE III+ can read extract files in either CDF or SDF format.

The entities prompt is used if you do not wish to extract attributes from every block in the drawing – it allows you to prepare a selection set of those blocks whose attributes you wish to extract. Once you have done so the CDF, SDF or DXF prompt reappears.

AutoCAD next prompts for the name of the template file to be used and also for a name to be given to the extract file which is about to be generated:

Template file: MYTEMPL
Extract file name: MYEXTRAC
(If you reply with a simple Return the extract file name will default to that of the drawing, but it will be given a .TXT extension)

The extract file MYEXTRAC.TXT will then be written on the default directory. Because this file is to be used by the dBASE package you may prefer to direct it to some other directory by specifying the appropriate path.

EXAMPLE

Extract file name: C:\DBASE\MYEXTRACT

By using a number of different template files it is possible to derive multiple extract files from a single drawing.

It will be found that CDF is the most flexible format for the extract files but it does result in all character fields being enclosed in single quotes 'like this'. This can be annoying. The single quote can be replaced by another character, e.g a " symbol, by including

C:QUOTE   "

in the template file, but this is not likely to be any more acceptable.

SDF format does not suffer from this problem but you must be certain to match the dBASE field widths and decimals *exactly* with those of the template file. If you fail to get this right the dBASE records will be hopelessly jumbled and impossible to use.

A typical CDF format extract file is shown below:

'Desk','Mr Jones','Mahogany'
'Desk','Mr Brown','Teak'
'Desk','Mr Green','Plywood'
'Chair','Mr Jones','Leather'
'Chair','Mr Brown','Plastic'
'Chair','Mr Green','Wood'
'Telephone','Mr Jones','Radio'
'Telephone','Mr Brown','Digital'
'Telephone','Mr Green','Standard'

The same file in SDF format would be:

Desk	Mr Jones	Mahogany
Desk	Mr Brown	Teak
Desk	Mr Green	Plywood
Chair	Mr Jones	Leather
Chair	Mr Brown	Plastic
Chair	Mr Green	Wood
Telephone	Mr Jones	Radio
Telephone	Mr Brown	Digital
Telephone	Mr Green	Standard

The order in which the attribute values are written in the extract file follows the order in which the tag names are specified in the template, *not* the order in which the tag names are written in the block definition. Similarly, the order of tag names in the template file must follow the order of the fields in the database.

16.2.3 Reading an Extract File into dBASE III+

A database file must first be created with the desired field structure. Field widths must be large enough to accept the corresponding data from the drawing and field types must be specified which are suitable for the data which they will contain and for the analysis which is later to be performed. It is not necessary for the dBASE field names to match the AutoCAD attribute tag names – the tag names are not transmitted by the extract file and are unknown to dBASE III+.

> *Note:* If SDF format is to be used in the extract file it is essential that the field widths specified in the database and in the template file match exactly.

The transfer of data from the extract file into the database is controlled from the dBASE III+ package. For a database called MYDBASE the commands would be as follows:

    .USE MYDBASE

If CDF format is to be used the transfer command is as follows:

    .APPEND FROM MYEXTRAC.TXT DELIMITED

If SDF format is to be used the command is as follows:

    .APPEND FROM MYEXTRAC.TXT SDF

Data from the extract file will immediately be appended to the dBASE file and from then on can be treated and analysed by the full range of dBASE III+ commands.

> *Note:* If you wish to repeat the transfer, say as a consequence of making some changes to the drawing, you must remember that the transfer is an APPEND process and so you must clear the original data using DELETE and PACK before the new data is transferred.

See Appendix 7 for an introduction to dBASE III+ and Appendix 8 for an example describing the transfer of attributes from an AutoCAD drawing into a dBASE III+ database.

Appendix 1
An introduction to DOS

DOS stands for Disk Operating System. Using DOS allows communication between the computer, disk drives, printer, etc.

When 'booting up' a computer i.e. switching on from cold, the user needs a SYSTEM or DOS disk to load the computer operating system instructions into the machines memory. These files are interpreters that take written English commands and turn them into machine code. There are three operating system files, which are retained in the computer's memory for as long as it is switched on. Two of these files are known as 'hidden files' and do not appear on any file directories or listings, and the third is called the COMMAND.COM, file.

In the general formats listed in this section, items in [ ] (square brackets) are optional.

The following symbols are used:

d: represents the disk drive to be used. – A:, B:, C:, . . .

Filename   represents the name of the file to be used.

.ext   represents the filename extension – a part of the filename which may be used to label a group of files collectively. For example, all program files written in the BASIC language are given the extension .BAS.

DOS commands such as COPY, ERASE, RENAME, can be entered in any combination of upper case or lower case letters.

Filenames and extensions may incorporate or be replaced by 'global characters' or 'wild cards'. The symbols used are ? and *.

?   replaces any single character.

*   replaces any number of characters up to the end of the filename or extension.

Note: The * should be used with care – particularly with the DEL command!

A1.1 Changing the Default Drive

The default drive is the disk drive (A, B, C, etc.) which the system will use in the absence of a particular drive being specified. The current default drive can be identified by the prompt symbol, e.g. C⟩ ,which appears at the left-hand edge of the screen when DOS is operating.

To change the default drive simply type the new drive letter followed by a colon, e.g.

    A⟩C: Changes the default drive from A to C with the result that the new prompt is now C⟩.

A1.2 Some Common DOS Commands

DIRectory: Lists the files resident on a disk. The syntax is

    DIR [d:][filename][.ext][/P][/W]

where the suffix /P means 'list the files a page at a time with a pause between pages' and the suffix /W means 'list the files by width', i.e. print their names across the screen instead of in a single column. This takes up less screen space but some information about the files is suppressed.
e.g.

    C⟩ DIR   DIRectory of default drive (C)
    A⟩ DIR C:/P   DIRectory of drive C by page
    C⟩ DIR A:*.COM   DIRectory of the files on drive A with
                                extension .COM
    A⟩DIR/W   DIRectory of drive A by width
    C⟩DIR *.   Lists all the directories on drive C

RENAME: Used to rename files. Can be used to change the filename, the extension or both. The syntax is

    RENAME [d:]Filename.ext Newname.ext

e.g.

    C⟩RENAME A:FILES.123 FILES1.LOT
                             Changes the filename FILES to FILES1
                             and the extension 123 to LOT.

FORMAT: Before a new disk can be used it has to be configured to the computer's particular format.

> *Warning: Formatting a disk whether new or used erases any information resident on that disk! Therefore great care must be taken when using this command. This is particularly important to users of hard/fixed disk machines where it is possible to wipe out 30 Megabytes of data with this single command.*

The syntax is:

FORMAT [d:][/S][/V]

where d: means disk drive; e.g. A,B or C.

/S means format disk with system files. This allows the disk to be used to 'boot up' the system from cold.

/V means volume name. This can be changed at a later date (if necessary) by using the LABEL command.

e.g.

A› FORMAT A:	Format disk in default drive A
A› FORMAT C:	Format disk in drive C,

Do not execute this command unless absolutely sure – all information stored on the hard disk will be erased!

C› FORMAT A:/S	Format disk in drive A with system files (hidden files) + COMMAND.COM
A› FORMAT A:/S/V	Format disk in drive A with both system files and volume name.

> *Note:* The system files are put onto floppy disks which are to be used to boot up the computer. They tend to be unnecessary when a hard disk machine is being used as the computer will normally be booted up from the hard disk where the system files are resident.

COPY: Copies one or more files from one disk to another. The syntax is

COPY [d:]filename.ext [d:][filename.ext]

e.g.

C› COPY A:ANYFILE.COM C:	Copy the file named ANYFILE.COM from drive A to drive C

C› COPY C:ANYFILE.COM A: Copy same file from C to A
C› COPY A:*.* C: Copy *all* files on drive A to C
C› COPY C:*.BAS A: Copy all file names with extension .BAS
                           from C to A

Note: Filenames and extensions can be changed when copying from one disk
to another.

C› COPY A:ANYFILE.COM C:MYPROG.RPS
                           Copy file ANYFILE.COM from A to C
                           changing name to MYPROG.RPS

DISKCOPY: Copies the total contents of one disk to another. This is generally
used to make disk back-ups on twin floppy machines – it is very rarely used with
hard disk machines. The syntax is

    DISKCOPY [d:][d:]

e.g.

    A› DISKCOPY A: B: Copy all files from A to B, formatting B
                            while copying

DELete or ERASE: This command is used to delete files from the disk. The
syntax is

    DEL [d:]filename.ext

e.g.

    C› DEL A:FILENAME.COM   DELetes the file Filename.COM from
                              drive A
    C› DEL A:FILENAME.*   DELetes all files with filename Filename
                              from drive A
    C› DEL A:*.*   DELetes all files from drive A

    A› DEL FILENAME.COM   DELetes file Filename.COM from default
                              drive A

TIME/DATE: Displays current time or date settings (in American format) on
the screen, and allows either to be reset. Useful, as both are stored when a file is
saved to disk. The syntax is

TIME   This is followed by a prompt for you to
                                supply the date. Don't forget the colons (:)
                                but you can ignore the seconds if you wish.

or

DATE   Again, you will be prompted to supply the
                                date (in American format – month first).
                                Don't forget the hyphens (-).

TYPE: Displays the contents of a file on the screen. Used mainly to check the
contents of batch and text files. The syntax is

    TYPE [d:]filename.ext

e.g.

    C›TYPE A:AUTOEXEC.BAT   Lists the contents of the file Autoexec.bat

A1.3 Batch Files

A batch file allows a number of commands or programs to be run automatically.
The batch filename always contains the extension BAT. There is a special file
called AUTOEXEC.BAT which is automatically executed when the computer is
switched on. All other batch files have to be executed manually.
    To create a batch file use the following syntax:

    COPY CON ‹filename›.BAT
    (enter desired batch of commands followed by F6 RETURN)

e.g.

    C›COPY CON AUTOEXEC.BAT
    cd basic   call directory basic
    keybuk   run keybuk
    cd\   go back to root dir.
    ˆZ   terminate batch file (this symbol results
                             from pressing the F6 key which terminates
                             the file)

Whenever a batch filename is used the batch of commands contained within the
file will be executed.

Batch files may also be created using a word processor or text editor instead of the COPY CON command shown above.

A useful application within an AutoCAD framework is to use batch files on floppy disk to start up the system. Each individual user would have his own drawings on a floppy disk together with a start-up batch file giving access to a working directory on the hard disk. The batch file could be used to set up the relevant path (see Section A1.5), set his directory to be default, copy his drawing files from the floppy disk into his directory, and start up AutoCAD. At the end of the AutoCAD session the *same* batch file could copy his files back to the floppy, clear his directory to conserve memory, and return to the **A>** prompt ready for the next user. Such a batch file would look something like:

```
C:
PATH=C:\ACAD;\FILES;\
CD\ACAD\FILES
COPY A:*.DWG
ACAD
COPY *.DWG A:
DEL *.DWG
CD\
A:
```

See Sections 2.2.1 and 13.2.1 for further uses of batch files with AutoCAD.

A1.4 Directories

When a hard or floppy disk is formatted, a single *ROOT* directory is created. *Sub-directories* can be created branching out from the root directory, and any of these can branch out to further directories, and so on. Therefore access is always gained to all sub-directories from the ROOT.

The following commands are used in association with sub-directories:

Make Directory: This allows the setting up of a new sub-directory either in the ROOT or any other sub-directory. Directory names obey similar rules to the eight letter filenames. The syntax is

   MD [d:]dirname

e.g.

   C>MD C:WORDPERF   Creates a new sub-directory called WORDPERF. Shown on ROOT directory as WORDPERF ‹DIR›

Change Directory: Used to change from the directory in use to a new directory. The syntax is:

CD [d:]dirname1[\dirname2][\] . . .

e.g.

C›CD C:WORDPERF	Changes from current directory to new directory called WORDPERF.
C›CD C:WORDPERF\FILES	Changes from current directory through directory WORDPERF to directory FILES.
C›CD	\ (backslash) is a special command used to return to the ROOT directory.
C›CD. .	The . . is used to return to the directory immediately above the current directory.

Remove Directory: Used to delete an *empty* directory. All files within the directory must be deleted before the directory can be deleted. The syntax is

RD [d:]dirname

e.g.

C›RD C:WORDPERF	Removes the directory WORDPERF from the disk (assuming that it contains no files or sub-directories).

A1.5 PATHways

Pathways are used to permit the operator to call files from different sub-directories without the need to leave the ROOT directory. Pathways are usually opened in the AUTOEXEC.BAT. file to save opening them each time the computer is switched on. The syntax is

PATH [d:]\dirname1;\dirname2;\ . . .

e.g.

C>PATH C:\WORDPERF; FILES;

> Allows direct access to the files in both the WORDPERF directory and the FILES directory at the same time.

A1.6 The System Environment and the SET Command

Approximately 200 bytes of memory is allocated to what is known as the system environment; this memory is checked by AutoCAD and other applications packages during initialisation for information regarding environment variables.

Many packages require the setting of environment variables before the package will run efficiently; it is therefore good practice to include them within a batch file.

The SET command is used to enter an environment variable into the system environment. The syntax is

SET variable name=value

Note: Do not leave spaces either side of the = sign.

A1.7 Shipdisk, Dpark, etc.

It is important to check the manufacturer's instructions with regard to the moving of your computer. The hard disk and disk reading head can be damaged if the head is not properly 'parked'. Some computer systems supply a program called 'SHIPDISK' or 'DPARK' which 'parks' the disk reading head; this must be run before the computer is moved.

A1.8 Glossary of DOS Commands

Back-up floppy disks	DISKCOPY
Change date	DATE
Change directory	CD
Change disk drive	d:
Change time	TIME
Copy disks	DISKCOPY or COPY
Copy files	COPY
Delete directory	RD

Delete files   DEL or ERASE
Display contents of file   TYPE
Display date   DATE
Display files on disk   DIR
Display time   TIME
Enter an environment variable   SET
Format new disks   FORMAT
Make new directory   MD
Move files   COPY
Rename files   RENAME

Appendix 2
AutoCAD environment variables

There are a number of environment variables which AutoCAD will inspect during initialisation. If the variables have not been set, then AutoCAD will assign default values but will not run at its most efficient.

The variables fall into two groups; those which control memory allocation and those which tell AutoCAD where to find support and configuration files.

The environment variables must all be set from DOS before AutoCAD is run and should therefore be included in a batch file.

A2.1 Environment Variable ACADFREERAM

The ACADFREERAM variable controls the amount of memory (in kilobytes) available to AutoCAD for workspace. The default value is 24 and the maximum is 30. ACADFREERAM may be set to any value between 5 and 30 but if you set it too small there is a danger that AutoCAD will give a **FATAL ERROR** message and return you to DOS.

Commands which require a high ACADFREERAM value include HIDE, TRIM and OFFSET.

    C>SET ACADFREERAM=28

A2.2 Environment Variables ACADXMEM and ACADLIMEM

These variables control the amount of extended and expanded memory which may be used by AutoCAD. Refer to your DOS and hardware manuals for full details relevant to your computer installation.

If ACADXMEM is not set, then AutoCAD will use *all available* extended memory.

The following SET options are available:

C›SET ACADXMEM=‹start› specifies the starting memory location
C›SET ACADXMEM=‹start, specifies the starting location and the size
size›   of reserved memory
C›SET ACADXMEM=‹size›   specifies the size of reserved memory
C›SET ACADXMEM=NONE
C›SET ACADLIMEM=‹value›

e.g.

To set aside 128 kilobytes of extended memory starting at 1664k:

C›SET ACADXMEM=1664k,128k

To limit the available expanded memory to 20 pages (320 kilobytes):

C›SET ACADLIMEM=20

A2.3 AutoLISP Environment Variables LISPHEAP and LISPSTACK

AutoLISP requires two independent areas of memory to be allocated for its use. The first stores all functions and variables and is called the heap while the second, called the stack, is the working memory.

The maximum total allocation for the heap and stack must not exceed 45,000 bytes. The default settings are:

Heap=40000
Stack= 3000

The two environment variables are called LISPHEAP and LISPSTACK respectively.

If insufficient memory is allocated to the heap the error message

Insufficient Node Space or **Insufficient String Space**

will be displayed.

If insufficient memory is allocated to the stack the error message

Lispstack overflow

will be displayed, e.g.

C›SET LISPHEAP=41000
C›SET LISPSTACK=3500

A2.4 Environment Variable ACAD

This variable specifies one directory containing support files such as text fonts, menus etc. which are not resident in the AutoCAD system directory. AutoCAD will first search for such files in its system directory. If they are not found, then only if the ACAD environment variable has been correctly set will AutoCAD search for them in the nominated directory. For example,

> If the support files are resident in a directory called SUPPORT, a sub-directory of the ACAD system directory, then the Acad environment variable may be set as follows:

> C›SET ACAD=C:\ACAD\SUPPORT

A2.5 Environment Variable ACADCFG

AutoCAD's hardware configuration data are stored in a file called ACAD.CFG. This is assumed to be in a separate directory called the configuration directory. If this directory is not specified by the environment variable ACADCFG then AutoCAD will search for the ACAD.CFG file in the system directory.

By specifying a separate configuration directory it is possible to maintain multiple configuration files for use as required (see Section 13.2). For example,

> To nominate a directory called MYCONF, a sub-directory of the ACAD system directory, as the configuration directory:

> C›SET ACADCFG=C:\ACAD\MYCONF

Appendix 3
Loading and running AutoLISP programs

A3.1 A Brief Introduction to AutoLISP

AutoLISP is a simple programming language developed by AutoCAD from the artificial intelligence language LISP. There are many features associated with AutoLISP but the most important is the ability to write simple programs which can fully customise the AutoCAD package to individual needs. This can include the customisation of commands and entity creation and also control of the AutoCAD system variables.

There are several specialist books already published covering AutoLISP programming which is beyond the scope of this book.

Before AutoLISP programs can successfully be executed, the two environment variables, LISPHEAP and LISPSTACK, must be set to suitable values (Appendix 2).

A3.2 Loading and Unloading an AutoLISP Program

Many AutoLISP programs are run automatically by AutoCAD; for example the shapes which may be selected from the 3D Objects icon accessed from the **Draw** pull down menu. Other AutoLISP programs may be loaded from the **Command** prompt.

EXAMPLE

To load and run a program called 3D:

Command: (LOAD'3D')
Command: 3D
Box/Cone/DIsh/DOme/Mesh/Pyramid/Sphere/Torus/Wedge:

Each time an AutoLISP program is loaded it remains memory-resident and therefore occupies valuable node space (heap memory). Because node space is limited it is advisable to remove or unload programs which are no longer required. To unload the above program, use the following syntax:

Command: (setq 3D nil)

A3.3 Automatic loading of AutoLISP programs

If you have some AutoLISP programs which are always required you can ensure that they are loaded automatically each time the drawing editor is entered. The program(s) must be included in a file called ACAD.LSP which may be located in the system directory. ACAD.LSP is in effect AutoLISP's version of an AUTOEXEC.BAT file.

Appendix 4
AutoCAD system variables

NAME	READ ONLY	FUNCTION
ACADPREFIX	R	Directory and path set by environment variable ACAD
ACADVER	R	AutoCAD version number
AFLAGS		Attribute type
ANGBASE		Direction of zero angle
ANGDIR		Positive angles clockwise or counterclockwise
APERTURE		Object Snap target box size
AREA	R	Computed area
ATTDIA		Calls attribute dialogue box
ATTMODE		Attribute display visibility
ATTREQ		Control of attribute prompts
AUNITS		Units of angular measurement
AUPREC		Number of decimal places (angles)
AXISMODE		Axis control (ON/OFF)
AXISUNIT		Axis marker spacing
BACKZ	R	Position of back clipping plane
BLIPMODE		Construction blips control (ON/OFF)
CBPORT		Active viewport identification number
CDATE	R	Current date and time
CECOLOUR	R	Current entity colour
CELLTYPE	R	Current linetype
CHAMFERA		First chamfer length
CHAMFERB		Second chamfer length
CLAYER	R	Current layer
CMDECHO		AutoLISP function display control
COORDS		Coordinate display presentation
DATE	R	Current date and time (in days and fractions of days)
DIMxxx		Dimension variables (see Section 8.2.8)
DISTANCE		Computed distance between digitised points
DRAGMODE		Drag feature ON/OFF
DRAGP1		Resolution of drag display
DRAGP2		Resolution of fast drag display
DWGNAME	R	Drawing name

DWGPREFIX	R	Full path of current drawing
ELEVATION		Elevation value (current UCS)
EXPERT		Controls 'safety net' prompts
EXTMAX	R	Upper right drawing extents
EXTMIN	R	Lower left drawing extents
FILLETRAD		Current fillet radius
FILLMODE		Fill ON/OFF
FLATLAND		Temporary variable controlling certain 3D functions
FRONTZ	R	Position of front clipping plane
GRIDMODE		Grid ON/OFF
GRIDUNIT		Current grid spacing
HANDLES	R	Handles feature ON/OFF
HIGHLIGHT		Selected entities identified ON/OFF
INSBASE		Insertion basepoint
LASTANGLE	R	Final angle of last drawn arc
LASTPOINT		Coordinates of last entered point
LASTPT3D		Coordinates of last entered point
LENSLENGTH	R	Perspective viewing zoom lens focal length
LIMCHECK		Allows drawing to transgress limits
LIMMAX		Upper right drawing limits
LIMMIN		Lower left drawing limits
LTSCALE		Linetype scale
LUNITS		Units of linear measurement
LUPREC		Number of decimal place (linear)
MENUECHO		Menu command echo control
MENUNAME	R	Active menu name
MIRRTEXT		Controls presentation of mirrored text
ORTHOMODE		Ortho ON/OFF
OSMODE		Current object snap mode
PDMODE		Representation of point entities
PDSIZE		Size of point entities
PERIMETER	R	Computed perimeter
PICKBOX		Selection box size
POPUPS	R	Pull down and icon menus and dialogue boxes ON/OFF
QTEXTMODE		Quick text feature ON/OFF
REGENMODE		Automatic regeneration ON/OFF
SCREENSIZE	R	Size of active viewport
SKETCHINC		Sketch resolution
SKPOLY		Defines sketch elements as lines of polylines
SNAPANG		Angle of snap and grid relative to current UCS
SNAPBASE		Origin of snap and grid relative to current UCS
SNAPISOPAIR		Current isometric plane
SNAPMODE		Snap ON/OFF
SNAPSTYL		Standard or isometric snap
SNAPUNIT		Current snap resolution
SPLFRAME		Controls visibility of polyline after smoothing
SPLINETYPE		Quadratic or cubic smoothing function (pline)
SPLSEGS		Resolution of smoothed polyline
SURFTAB1		Mesh density in M-direction
SURFTAB2		Mesh density in N-direction
SURFTYPE		Quadratic, cubic or Bezier smoothing function (mesh)

SURFU		Surface density in *M*-direction
SURFV		Surface density in *N*-direction
TARGET	R	Dynamic view target point coordinates
TDCREATE	R	Start time and date of current drawing
TDINDWG	R	Total time spent on current drawing
TDUPDATE	R	Time and date of last update
TDUSRTIMER	R	Time currently spent in drawing editor
TEMPPREFIX	R	Path and name of directory for temporary files
TEXTEVAL		Identifies a '(' or a '!' as initiating an AutoLISP command
TEXTSIZE		Current text height
TEXTSTYLE		Current text style
THICKNESS		Current 3D thickness
TRACEWID		Current trace width
UCSFOLLOW		Controls automatic execution of plan(UCS) command
UCSICON		Controls display and positioning of UCS icon
UCSNAME	R	Name of active UCS
UCSORG	R	Coordinates of active UCS origin relative to WCS
UCSXDIR	R	Positive *X*-direction of current UCS
UCSYDIR	R	Positive *Y*-direction of current UCS
USERI1-5		Five unused integer variables for package development
USERR1-5		Five unused real variables for package development
VIEWCTR	R	Coordinates of centre point of active viewport
VIEWDIR	R	Vector direction between camera and target (Dview)
VIEWMODE	R	Code number defining scene (clipped, perspective etc.)
VIEWSIZE	R	Height of current viewport in drawing units
VIEWTWIST	R	Dynamic view twist angle
VPOINTX	R	*X*-coordinate (WCS) of VIEWDIR
VPOINTY	R	*Y*-coordinate (WCS) of VIEWDIR
VPOINTZ	R	*Z*-coordinate (WCS) of VIEWDIR
VSMAX	R	Coordinates of upper right of virtual screen
VSMIN	R	Coordinates of lower left of virtual screen
WORLDUCS	R	Indicates active UCS same as WCS
WORLDVIEW		Changes operation of Dview and Vports from active UCS to WCS

Note: In the case of ON/OFF variables AutoCAD uses the convention that 0=OFF and 1=ON

Appendix 5
Simple two-dimensional construction tutorial

Figure A5.1 shows a simple drawing of a kitchen. To recreate this drawing you will need to employ virtually all of the commands outlined in Chapter 3. There are numerous ways in which the drawing may be constructed but the following suggestions are designed to minimise needless repetition and to familiarise you with basic CAD drawing concepts.

No dimensions are specified but you should aim to preserve the appearance of the original drawing.

A5.1 Walls, door, window and work surfaces

1. Set the Snap resolution to a suitable value and turn Snap On. Use parallel lines to draw the walls of the kitchen, leaving spaces for the door and window. You may prefer to use Ortho for this operation but with Snap On it is not really necessary.

2. Draw one pillar of the door frame and COPY this to form the other pillar. To produce the door, draw a LINE between the two pillars, enter the ROTATE command, select the line and choose the left-hand end of the line as the base point of rotation. ROTATE the line through a suitable angle. Using the ARC command in Center,Start,End mode select the previous base point of rotation as the centre point, the middle of the inner face of the right-hand door pillar as the Start point and finally a suitable End point.

3. Construct the two window frame pillars. Draw in two more parallel lines to form the window.

4. The work surfaces are constructed with LINEs and ARCs. Draw in one of the work surface edges using LINE, enter the ARC command (Continue mode) and draw in an arc of a suitable radius. Resume the LINE command and at the first prompt (**From point:**) respond with a Return, complete the rest of the work surface.

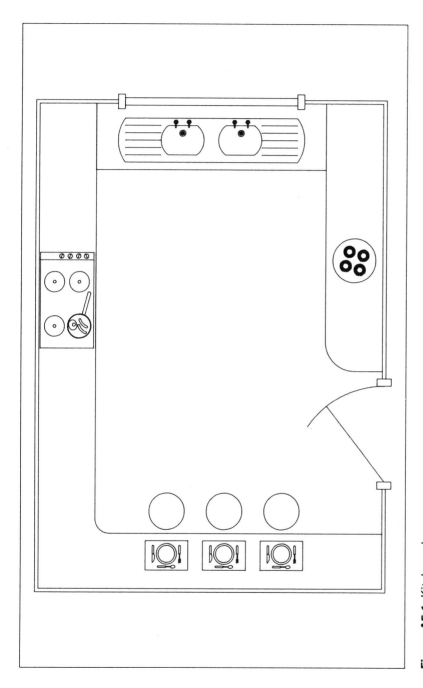

Figure A5.1 Kitchen plan

A5.2 The cooker

1. Construct the outline of the cooker shown in Figure A5.2 and use ZOOM Window to give a magnified view on screen. Draw two CIRCLEs to represent one of the hotplates. Use COPY (Multiple) to give the other two hotplates. Draw one of the control knobs and again use COPY (Multiple) to draw in three other knobs. ROTATE one knob about its centre point to show that it is turned on.

2. Draw in the circular outline of the frying pan and add a handle using LINE and ARC and again use ZOOM to give a convenient view on screen. The egg consists of a CIRCLE within an ELLIPSE. A sausage is constructed from 4 ARCs – it may take some practice to create a good sausage! COPY this sausage as required.

3. Use ZOOM Extents to return to an overall view of the kitchen.

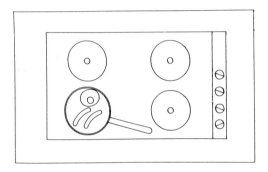

Figure A5.2 Detail of cooker

A5.3 Place settings

1. The detail of the place setting is shown in Figure A5.3. Draw the rectangular mat and use ZOOM Window to give a magnified view on screen. Add two concentric CIRCLEs for the plate.

2. The bowl of the spoon is an ELLIPSE. Use LINEs and an ARC to construct the body and handle of the spoon.

3. COPY the handle of the spoon and ROTATE it by $-90°$ to create the handle of the fork. Add the body and prongs of the fork using LINE.

4. COPY the fork handle to give the handle of the knife. The blade is constructed using a LINE and an ARC. Use ZOOM Extents to return to an overall view of the kitchen.

Figure A5.3 Detail of place setting

5. Add a circular seat and then COPY (Multiple) the complete place setting including the seat twice.

A5.4 The sink unit

The double sink unit (Figure A5.4) has a line of symmetry through its centre. Therefore it is only necessary to construct one half of the unit, the other half being obtained using the MIRROR command.

1. Using LINEs and ARC create the outline of one half of the sink unit. Use a suitable ZOOM command to give a working view.

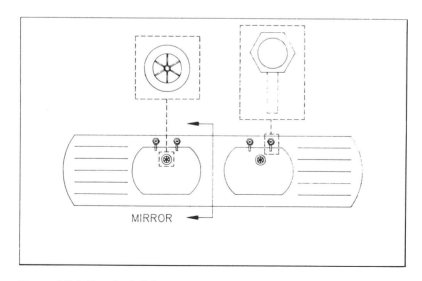

Figure A5.4 Detail of sink unit

2. Similarly, use LINEs and ARCs to construct the sink bowl. Add the five parallel LINEs.

3. Draw concentric CIRCLEs to represent the drain hole. Use ZOOM to give a magnified view. Add a small CIRCLE and radial LINEs to form the grill.

4. Using ZOOM Previous, return to the previous view and draw a hexagonal handle for the tap using the POLYGON command. ZOOM in on this, add a concentric CIRCLE and complete the tap using LINE. ZOOM Previous and COPY the tap to make the pair.

5. Use the MIRROR command to complete the other half of the sink.

6. Use ZOOM Extents to return to an overall view of the finished kitchen.

Appendix 6
Three-dimensional drawing tutorial

A6.1 3D coordinates and 3DFACEs

(a) Use the LINE command to construct the outline of a house using the absolute coordinates given in Figure A6.1.

Command: LINE
From point: 100,100,0
To point: 300,100,0
To point: 300,200,0
To point: 100,200,0
To point: 100,100,0
To point: 100,100,100

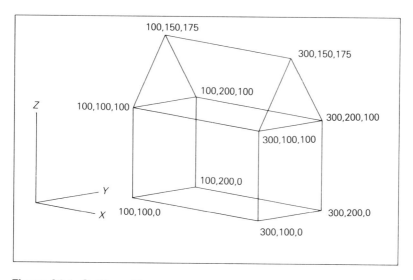

Figure A6.1 Outline of house

To point:	300,100,100
To point:	300,200,100
To point:	100,200,100
To point:	100,100,100
To point:	100,150,175
To point:	100,200,100
Command: LINE	
From point:	300,100,100
To point:	300,150,175
To point:	300,200,100
Command: LINE	
From point:	100,200,0
To point:	100,200,100
Command: LINE	
From point:	300,100,0
To point:	300,100,100
Command: LINE	
From point:	300,200,0
To point:	300,200,100
Command: LINE	
From point:	100,150,175
To point:	300,150,175

View the drawing from a suitable oblique angle using either the 3D icon or the VPOINT command. This drawing will be in wire frame form and HIDE will therefore have no effect.

This outline will form the basis of this example so it is advisable to save the drawing for later use. Make three copies of this outline (to be used in the following sections (b)–(e)).

(b) While retaining the same oblique view, use Object Snap (Endpoint mode) to add 3DFACEs to all four sides and the roof. Check, using HIDE, that this now gives a solid model (Figure A6.2).

(c) Use the LINE command to construct a doorway 45 units high and 30 units wide in the centre of the front wall and subsequently add 3DFACEs to produce the drawing shown in Figure A6.3. One possible way to achieve this is as follows.

Command:	ID
Point:	MID
of	(select base line of front wall)
Command:	LINE
From point:	@15,0,0
To point:	@0,0,45

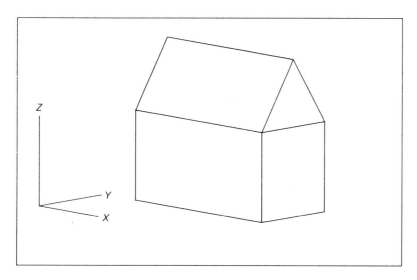

Figure A6.2 Solid house using 3DFACE

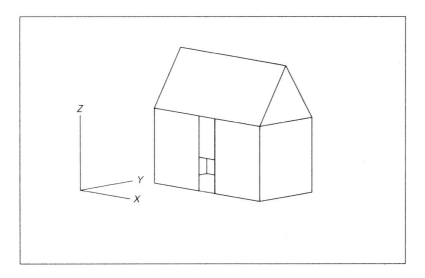

Figure A6.3 Doorway constructed using visible 3DFACEs

To point: @−30,0,0
To point: @0,0,−45
Command: 3DFACE
First point: END
of   (select upper left corner of front wall)
Second point: END
of   (select lower left corner of front wall)

Third point: END
of (select lower left corner of door)
Fourth point: PERP
to (select top line of front wall)

Repeat for the remaining two 3DFACEs. Use the HIDE command to demonstrate that the door forms a true opening in the wall.

(d) Repeat the previous exercise but using invisible 3DFACEs to give Figure A6.4.

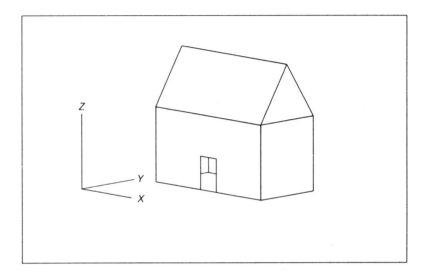

Figure A6.4 Doorway constructed using invisible 3DFACEs

.

.

.

.

Command: 3DFACE
First point: END
of (select upper left corner of front wall)
Second point: END
of (select lower left corner of front wall)
Third point: I
                   END
of (select lower left corner of door)
Fourth point: PERP
to (select top line of front wall)

Repeat for the remaining two 3DFACEs.

(e) Add a skylight centred on one face of the roof which is 60 units wide by 50 units high.

This section is included to show the difficulties encountered in versions of AutoCAD prior to Release 10 when constructing objects lying in planes which are not in line with or orthogonal to the axes of the original drawing. In practice the easiest way is to calculate the coordinates of the corners of the skylight using trigonometry.

Command: LINE
From point: 170,138.87,158.30
To point: 170,111.13,116.70
To point: 230,111.13,116.70
To point: 230,138.87,158.30
To point: C

Invisible 3DFACEs may now be added to produce Figure A6.5.

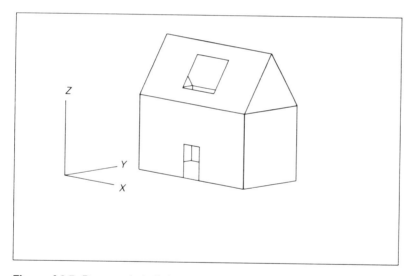

Figure A6.5 Door and skylight constructed using invisible 3DFACEs

A6.2 Mastering the User Coordinate System (UCS)

This example is a virtual repeat of Example 1 but uses the UCS facilities of the package. As a result it is possible to make quite complex additions to the basic drawing with ease.

(a) Using the house skeleton of Example 1, add a door and some windows to the front wall.

Start by using the UCSICON command to set the icon so that it is automatically located at the origin of each new UCS.

Command: UCSICON
ON/OFF/All/Noorigin/ORigin ‹ON›: OR

Create a new UCS with its origin at the lower left corner of the front wall and its plane in the plane of the wall (Figure A6.6).

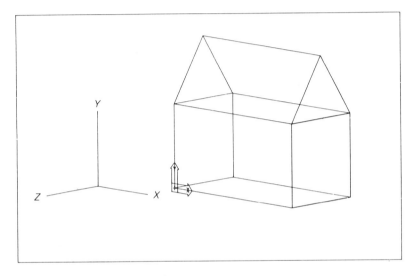

Figure A6.6 New UCS: FRONT

Command: DDUCS
(Define new current UCS and name it FRONT)
(Origin, *X*-axis, Plane)
Origin point‹0,0,0›: END
of (point to lower left corner of front wall)
Point on positive portion of Xaxis ‹1,0,0›: END
of (point to lower right corner of front wall)
Point on positive Y-portion of the UCS X–Y plane ‹0,1,0›: END
of (point to upper right corner of front wall)
Command: PLAN
‹Current UCS›/UCS/World: C

Note: An alternative to using the PLAN command is to set the system variable UCSFOLLOW to 1. This in effect automatically issues the PLAN command after a new UCS has been defined.

A door and windows may now be drawn in directly using standard 2D techniques (Figure A6.7). 3D faces may be added if required.

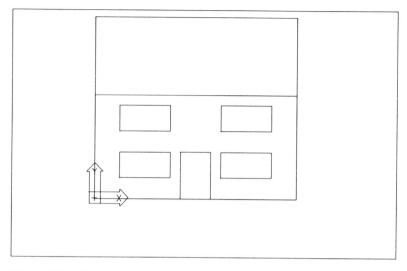

Figure A6.7 Door and windows constructed on new UCS FRONT

(b) Place a window in the right-hand end wall.

   Create the required new UCS in two stages. First create a temporary UCS with its origin at the lower right corner of the front wall and its plane in the plane of the wall and then rotate this UCS about the *Y*-axis (Figure A6.8).

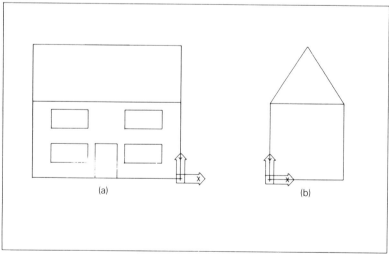

Figure A6.8(a) Temporary UCS
Figure A6.8(b) New UCS: SIDE1

Command: DDUCS
                (Define new current UCS)
                (New origin)
Origin point ‹0,0,0›:   END
of   (point to lower right corner of front wall)
Command: DDUCS
                (Define new current UCS and name it SIDE1)
                (Rotate about *Y* axis)
Rotation angle about Y axis ‹0.0›:   90
Command: PLAN
‹Current UCS›/UCS/World: C

A window may now be added (Figure A6.9).

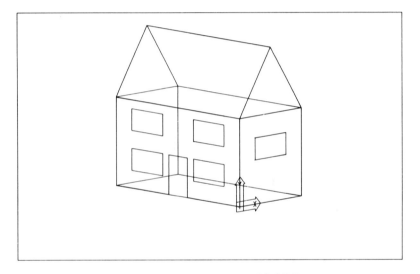

Figure A6.9 Window constructed on new UCS SIDE1

The above may be repeated to place other windows etc. in other walls.

Note: The reason that the SIDE1 UCS was defined in two steps was that only the plan view was available on screen and it would have been necessary to return to an oblique view to define SIDE1 in a single step (using Origin, *X*-axis and Plane as in section (a)). To overcome this problem, multiple viewports may be used to provide alternative views of the drawing.

(c) Place a skylight in the roof as required in Example 1(e).

Firstly, make two viewports – the left-hand one with an oblique view of the drawing (which will act as a reference view) and the right-hand one showing a plan view of the current UCS (UCSFOLLOW=1 in this viewport).

Command: VPORTS
Save/Restore/Delete/Join/SIngle/?/2/‹3›/4: 2
Horizontal/‹Vertical›: V   (Figure A6.10)

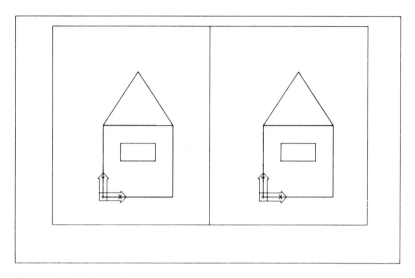

Figure A6.10 Two viewports

Take the cursor into the right-hand viewport and press the Pick button to make it the active viewport and set UCSFOLLOW to be 1 (using SETVAR or the UCS screen menu).

Make the left-hand viewport active, change the UCS to World and select a suitable oblique view of the drawing (Figure A6.11).

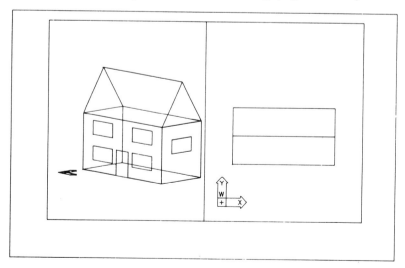

Figure A6.11 Oblique and plan world view

We now need to create a new UCS, called ROOF1, which has its origin at the bottom left-hand corner of the front face of the roof and which lies in the plane of this face. Using the oblique view in the left-hand viewport and with object snap set to Endpoint mode:

> **Command:** DDUCS
>   (Define new current UCS and name it ROOF1)
>   (Origin, *X*-axis, Plane)
> **Origin point‹0,0,0›:**   (point to lower left corner of roof)
> **Point on positive portion of *X*-axis ‹1,0,0›:**
> (point to lower right corner of roof)
>
> **Point on positive *Y*- portion of the UCS *X-Y* plane ‹0,1,0›:**
> (point to upper right corner of roof)

Note that the right-hand viewport has automatically changed to the plan view of the new UCS (Figure A6.12). Make this active and draw in the specified skylight using standard 2D techniques.

(d) Convert the skylight into a dormer window as shown in Figure A6.13.

Use the UCS Dialogue box to set the previously defined UCS, SIDE1, to be the current UCS. Then define a new UCS, called DORMER:

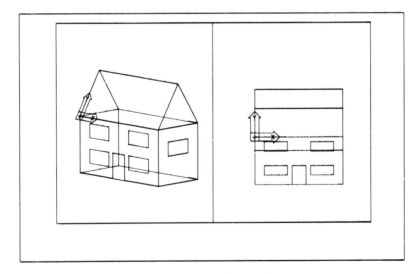

Figure A6.12 UCS ROOF: oblique and plan views

Figure A6.13 Dormer window

Command: DDUCS
(Define new current UCS)
(New origin)
Origin point ‹0,0,0›:   (point to bottom corner of the skylight)

Use the LINE command and work in both viewports to construct one side of the dormer window. COPY this to the opposite end of the skylight. Complete the construction by adding the dormer roof.

(e) Finally, add a chimney and chimney pot. There are many ways to achieve this but this is probably the simplest:

Set ROOF1 to be the active UCS and draw in the interface between the chimney and the roof as shown in Figure A6.14. Repeat this on the other face of the roof by setting SIDE1 to be the active UCS and using the MIRROR command. Erect four verticals representing the edges of the chimney stack from each corner to some suitable height (you will again need to work in both viewports – use the oblique view to locate these corner points and the view in the other viewport to set the height). Complete the stack by joining together the top ends of these lines. To add a chimney pot you must create a new UCS – called POT – using Origin, *X*-axis and Plane (Figure A6.15). Set Thickness to −20 (you will understand why this must be negative when you consider the right-hand rule as applied to this current UCS). Use the CIRCLE command to place the pot on the stack. 3DFACEs may be added as required to complete the drawing as shown in Figure A6.16.

Figure A6.14 Chimney–roof interface

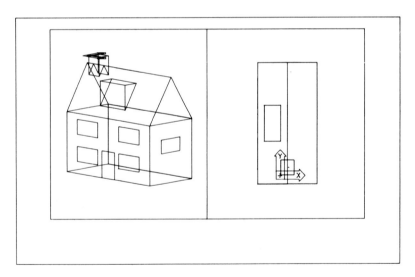

Figure A6.15 UCS POT

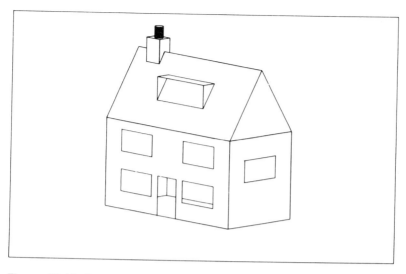

Figure A6.16 Completed house

A6.3 REVSURF and RULESURF

The dart shown in Figure A6.17 may be constructed using both REVSURF and RULESURF.

Set the UCSFOLLOW system variable to 1 – this will automatically generate the plan view on each change of UCS.

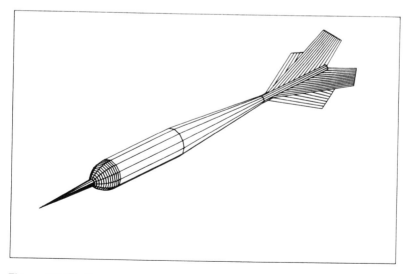

Figure A6.17 Dart

The first step is to use a 2D polyline to draw the profile of the dart and the axis of revolution. The profile will be used as the path curve for the REVSURF command (Figure A6.18).

Command: REVSURF
Select path curve:

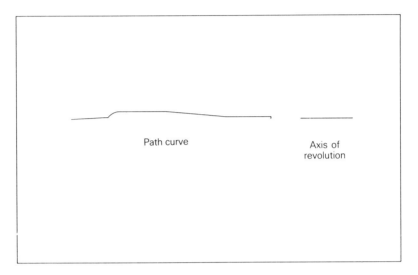

Path curve   Axis of
                              revolution

Figure A6.18 Profile and axis of revolution to be used by REVSURF

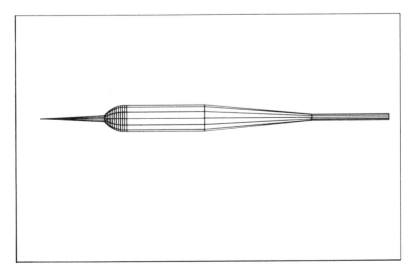

Figure A6.19 Body of dart produced by REVSURF

Select axis of revolution:
Start angle ‹0›:   0
Included angle (+=CCW,-=CW) ‹Full circle›: 360

This will produce the body of the dart as shown in Figure A6.19. Now erase the axis of revolution which is no longer required.

To construct the tail of the dart it is only necessary to draw one of the four fins. First use LINE to draw the two defining curves as shown in Figure A6.20. Then use RULESURF:

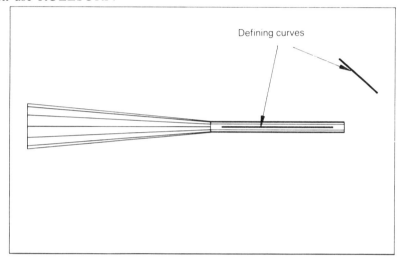

Defining curves

Figure A6.20 Two defining curves for use with RULESURF

Command: RULESURF
Select first defining curve:
Select second defining curve:

Figure A6.21 shows the result.

The remaining three fins may be produced using ARRAY but it is essential first to change to a suitable UCS orthogonal to the axis of the dart (Figure A6.22).

Command: DDUCS
               (Define new current UCS)
               (New origin)
Origin point ‹0,0,0›:   (position new origin on fin end of dart)

Command: DDUCS
               (Define new current UCS and name it END)
               (Rotate about Y axis)
Rotation angle about Y axis ‹0.0›:   90

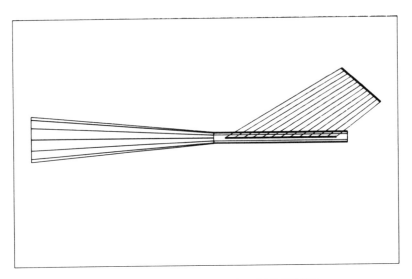

Figure A6.21 A single fin constructed using RULESURF

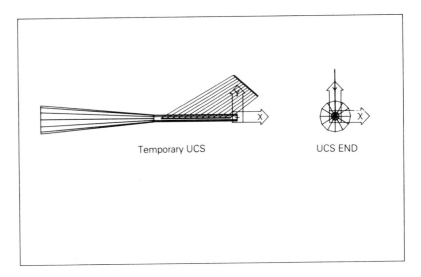

Figure A6.22 Defining new UCS END

Now use a Polar ARRAY, remembering to use a Crossing Window to select the components of the fin, to create the remaining fins and complete the drawing (Figure A6.23).

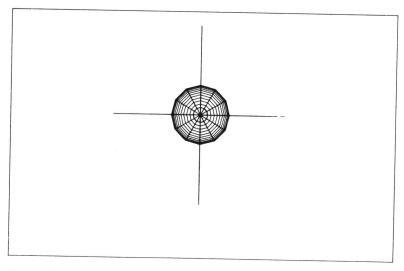

Figure A6.23 Rear view of completed dart

A6.4 REVSURF AND TABSURF

The links of the chain shown in Figure A6.24 are constructed using REVSURF and TABSURF. Each link is composed of four sections – two curved and two straight.

Set the UCSFOLLOW system variable to 1 – this will automatically

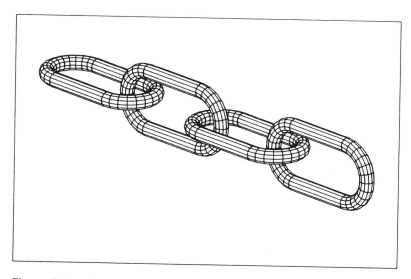

Figure A6.24 Chain

generate the plan view on each change of UCS.

One of the curved sections may be constructed as follows:

Draw a CIRCLE (representing the cross section through one arm of the link) and an axis of revolution.

> **Command:** REVSURF
> **Select path curve:** (select the circle)
> **Select axis of revolution:**
> **Start angle ‹0›:** 90
> **Included angle (+=CCW,-=CW) ‹Full circle›:** 180

This is shown in Figure A6.25. Erase the axis of revolution to complete this section.

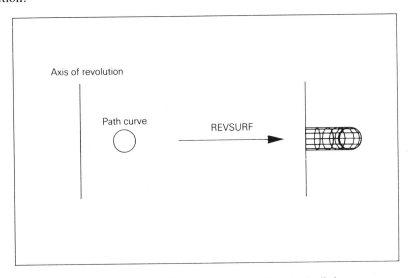

Figure A6.25 Construction of an end section of a single link

Use the MIRROR command to give a replica of this end section of the link. To complete the link the two straight sections need to be constructed using TABSURF, which in turn requires a circular path curve and a direction vector. Despite appearances, there is no circle at the ends of the previously drawn sections – the circular effect is due to an end-on view of the component 3D faces of the mesh. To place a CIRCLE on one of the ends it is necessary to create a new UCS in the plane of this end face.

> **Command:** DDUCS
> (Define new current UCS)
> (New origin)
> **Origin point ‹0,0,0›:** (position new origin on end of link)

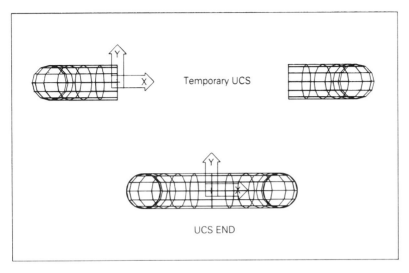

Figure A6.26 Defining new UCS END

Command: DDUCS
        (Define new current UCS and name it END)
        (Rotate about *Y*-axis)
Rotation angle about Y axis ‹0.0›: 90   (Figure A6.26)

Draw two circles – one on each end face – to the same radius as that of the original REVSURF path curve (Figure A6.27). Reset the UCS to World. Create a new UCS:

Command: DDUCS
        (Define new current UCS and name it SIDE)
        (Rotate about *X*-axis)
Rotation angle about X axis ‹0.0›: 90

Draw in a direction vector, the length of which is the distance between the two opposing faces of the end sections (Figure A6.28)

Command: TABSURF
Select path curve: (select one of the circles)
Select direction vector: (select the end nearest to the path curve)

Repeat for the other straight section and erase the direction vector (Figure A6.29) to finish one complete link of the chain.

    Subsequent links may now be derived. COPY the link and place the copy above the original. Change the UCS to END and ROTATE the copy through 90°. Change the UCS back to SIDE and MOVE the rotated link to couple with the original (Figure A6.30). Further extension of the chain may be achieved by simple copying of this pair of links.

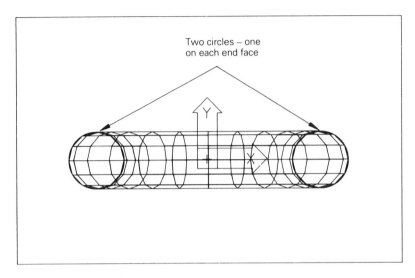

Figure A6.27 Creating end sections

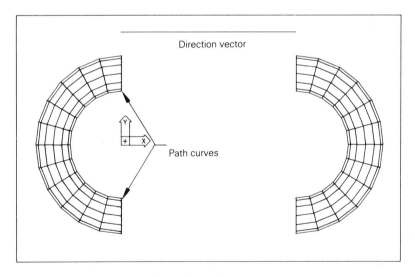

Figure A6.28 Two opposing end sections

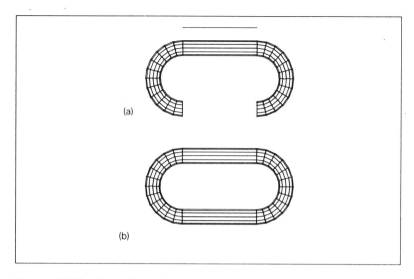

(a)

(b)

Figure A6.29a Straight section constructed using TABSURF

Figure A6.29b Completed single link

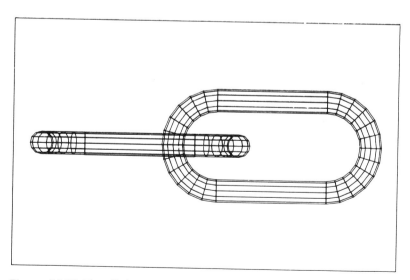

Figure A6.30 Two links of the chain

Appendix 7
An introduction to dBASE III+

A database is a collection of related information which is organised by the computer in such a way that comprehensive management operations can be performed. Such a system allows the user to store and selectively retrieve information when required. The data can be manipulated directly by typing instructions at the keyboard. However the dBASE package has a built-in programming language, which means that data manipulation can be customised and the system configured for easy operation by unskilled personnel.

A typical database structure is shown below.

	Field 1	*Field 2*	*Field 3*	*Field 4*
Field name	SURNAME	FIRSTNAME	ADDRESS	TOWN
Record 1	Adams	Andy	1 Green St	Bury
Record 2	Smith	Sandra	2 Grove St	Hull

A7.1 Terminology

A *database* is a group of records – the computer equivalent of a filing cabinet.

A *record* is a group of associated data such as **Adams,Andy,1 Green St,Bury** – the equivalent of a single card in the filing cabinet.

A *field* is an individual item of information such as a surname – **Adams** – or a place of residence – **Bury**.

A *fieldname* is the name given to a field – e.g. **SURNAME** – and is allocated by the user when the database is first created.

The *dBASE prompt* (corresponding to the word **Command:** in AutoCAD) is simply a dot '.'

A7.2 The ASSIST Menus

dBASE III+ has a built-in ASSIST facility with option menus which appear on the screen when the package is first loaded. To switch off the ASSIST menus press the Esc key: to switch back to assist type ASSIST from the dBASE prompt or press the F2 key. Considerable hands-on practice is required before the ASSIST facility can be fully appreciated and some people prefer to work without it.

A7.3 Creating a New Database

The design of the database structure is crucial to the subsequent data management, and usually requires careful planning.

CREATE   This is the command used to create a new database structure:

> .CREATE

(or use the ASSIST menus). The new database file must first be named and you are then requested to define the structure of the database one field at a time. There are several types of field, including Character, Numeric, Logical, Date and Memo, and a choice has to be made when establishing each individual field.

- A **Character** field is used for any data which is never going to be used in calculation. The data may contain alphabet letters, numerals or symbols and are generally known as *alphanumeric* data. Names, addresses and telephone numbers are typical examples. Up to 128 different character fields are allowed in a single database and fields may be up to 256 characters wide.
- A **Numeric** field contains true numeric data which may be used for calculations. A numeric field may be up to 19 digits wide with up to a further 15 digits after the decimal point.
- **Logical** fields are used to tie a logical label on to a record. They are only one digit wide and may contain only T or Y representing a True condition and F or N representing a False condition.

> *(Note:*   Even when Y and N are used the data are always stored as T and F.)

- The **Date** field is fixed at 8 characters wide and the date format can be set to British, American, Italian etc. The British format is dd/mm/yy.
- **Memo** fields, if used, can be up to 4000 characters wide. Memo fields are not commonly used and reference to the manual is recommended.

After the structure of the database has been defined, data can be entered, using APPEND or BROWSE. The command DISPLAY STRUCTURE gives the field information for the currently open database. The command MODIFY STRUCTURE allows the basic structure to be changed, automatically appending the data after modifications have been completed.

The following is a simple example of a database called MYDBASE

Field	Field Name	Type	Width	Dec
1	Surname	Character	15	
2	Firstname	Character	15	
3	Age	Numeric	3	0
4	Sex	Character	1	
5	Occupation	Character	15	
6	British	Logical	1	

After the creation of the structure, a blank Return shows that you have finished creating fields and a Y reply to the question

Input data records now (Y/N)   Y

allows the immediate input of data. This process may be terminated with a Return or an Esc.

A7.4 Using an Existing Database File

In order to use an existing database from the dBASE prompt:

.USE (database name)

or follow the assist screen menus.

You will now be able to check any existing records in the database (using LIST or DISPLAY), change data in existing records (using EDIT or BROWSE), add new records (using APPEND) and delete records (using DELETE and PACK).

A7.5 The HELP Facility

At any stage you may check the full syntax of a command by using the built-in help facility. For example, if you type HELP LIST from the dBASE prompt, a full description of the LIST command with all allowed variations will be shown.

A7.6 The Function Keys and Esc

A number of the more commonly used dBASE commands are available on the function keys F1 to F10. A list of the default functions can be obtained by typing LIST STATUS or by pressing key F6.

Programmable function keys:
F2   assist;
F3   list;
F4   dir;
F5   display structure;
F6   display status;
F7   display memory;
F8   display;
F9   append;
F10   edit.

The Esc key can usually be used to abort to the dBASE prompt. If you are using assist sub-menus an Esc will take you back to the previous level of menu.

A7.7 Shortened Commands

All dBASE commands can be shortened to the first four letters. For example, BROWSE can be typed BROW.

A7.8 The Record Pointer

The record pointer allows you to access any particular record in the database. It can be set manually from the dBASE prompt by simply typing the appropriate record number. This has several uses, one of which is to allow the user to insert a record at any particular point in the database using the INSERT command.

During listing the record pointer automatically increments to the last record listed. dBASE III+ gives the current value of the record pointer at the bottom of the screen.

A7.9 Extracting Selected Data from a Database using LIST

The LIST command can be used for more selective data extraction than simply listing the entire contents of the database. The full LIST syntax is:

LIST [OFF] [‹scope›] [‹fieldlist›] [FOR ‹condition›] [WHILE ‹condition›]
[TO PRINT]

Upper or lower case may be used when typing in an instruction unless a text condition has been specified in which case the exact text format is required.

The following example of the LIST syntax may be used with the MYDBASE database:

LIST OFF surname,age,occupation FOR age›25 .AND. age‹45 .AND. british

In this complex looking instruction, surname, age and occupation are three of the field names in the database. The › means greater than, ‹ means less than, the .AND. (typed with the full stops) links the three conditions together.

The full instruction will list on the screen the contents of the three fields called surname, age and occupation only for those records where the age falls between the limits specified and where the logical field British is True. The OFF instruction in the command switches off the record numbers which otherwise would be included in the listing.

Alternatively:

LIST NEXT 5 surname FOR .NOT. british

will LIST the NEXT five surnames in the database for which the logical field 'british' is False.

In the above examples note the syntax used to establish the logical conditions for logical fields.

A7.10 Other Ways to Extract Data

- DISPLAY This command is very similar to LIST – the standard format displays the contents of the current record. See the HELP facility to check the full syntax.
- ? ‹fieldname› Translates as 'What is ?' and can be used to display the contents of the designated field in the current record
- LOCATE FOR Searches for the record which satisfies the condition. For example:

  LOCATE FOR age›50

  LOCATE will find the *first* record which satisfies the condition.
- CONTINUE Continues the above search for further records.
- FIND ‹string› Can be used like LOCATE if the file has been indexed.
- SKIP {+ or − number} Moves forwards or backwards the specified number of records through the database.
- GOTO ‹number›, GO TOP, GO BOTTOM Moves to a specific record or to the first/last record in the database.

- COUNT [FOR expression] TO variable   Counts the number of records which meet the specified condition. It is possible to store the result of the count in a VARIABLE:

        COUNT FOR age‹25 TO young
        ? young

- SUM ‹fieldname› [FOR expression list] TO variable   This is used numerically to add the contents of an indicated numeric field for specified records.

The above list covers most of the frequently used commands which are available for interrogation. You should consult HELP and the manual for further information.

A7.11 Adding Further Records to the Database

APPEND is a command which allows additional records to be added to the end of the database. The BROWSE command can also be used for this purpose but is less flexible than APPEND because it can not easily be incorporated in a dBASE program.

If a record needs to be inserted in an intermediate position in the database then move the record pointer to the required position and use the INSERT command.

A7.12 Changing Information in the Database

There are several different ways of changing information stored in a database. The database structure can itself also be modified if required.

        EDIT   .USE ‹database filename›
                  .EDIT ‹record number›

        The specified record will be displayed and information in the
        different fields may be changed. The screen editor is available for
        moving the cursor, deleting, inserting etc. After making the
        modifications press the Ctrl and End keys to save the new record
        (Ctrl W is another way of saving the information). Pressing the
        Return key at the very end of a record moves the cursor to the
        next record in the database, allowing it to be edited in turn. This
        also has the effect of making permanent any changes made in
        previous records.

BROWSE   .USE ‹database file›
                .BROWSE

In this mode of operation the records below the current position of the record pointer are displayed on screen. Information can be changed and a screen editor is available. If a record is wider than the screen width a 'panning' function may be used. Ctrl → (right arrow key) pans to the right while Ctrl ← pans to the left.

Additional records may be added to the end of the database by pressing the Return key.

A screen assist table is normally displayed whilst in BROWSE mode.

The Esc key provides a convenient exit from the BROWSE mode to the dBASE prompt but any changes made to the current record will not be saved. The commands Ctrl End and Ctrl W can be used to exit the BROWSE mode and make any editing changes permanent.

DELETE, RECALL, PACK   Deleting records is a two-stage process, first the DELETE command is used to delete the chosen records, either single records controlled by the position of the record pointer or a range of records specified in the 'scope' part of the command. Also records satisfying a specified condition can be deleted. (See the HELP file for the full syntax.)

The DELETE command marks a record or range of records for deletion by inserting a * symbol in the first field.

After marking records for deletion it is possible to reverse the decision by using the RECALL command.

To complete the delete process it is necessary to use the PACK command.

```
.USE MYDBASE
.DELETE ALL FOR age›30
.LIST   (notice the marked records)
.RECALL ALL
.LIST
.DELETE ALL FOR age›25
.LIST
.PACK
```

REPLACE   This command is used to scan through the database, changing entries as required.

```
.USE MYDBASE
.REPLACE age WITH age+20
.LIST (To check change)
```

CHANGE   This command is very similar to EDIT. The fields to be changed may be specified but be careful to set the record pointer first.

> .USE MYDBASE
> .CHANGE FIELDS surname,occupation

In the above example only the fields 'surname' and 'occupation' will be displayed for editing purposes.

A7.13 SORTing and INDEXing

Data, which is very often entered in a random fashion, can be organised with the SORT and INDEX facilities.

SORT   This command creates a new database with information sorted in ascending (A) or descending (D) order for any field or fields which are specified. The syntax is:

> SORT TO filename ON fieldname [A/D], fieldname [A/D]

The new database is specified by the filename and the field names are chosen as required. The command defaults to A if this parameter is not specified.
>   With a large database this operation can be time consuming and it is preferable to INDEX the database against a key field for faster retrieval of data.

INDEX   The syntax is:

> INDEX ON fieldnames TO filename

If one or more index files have been created for a database then the command SET INDEX TO ‹filename› should be used in order to activate the index files.
>   Index files can be identified on the directory by the file name extension .NDX

A7.14 Producing a REPORT

A simple print out of lists of records can be achieved by directing output to the printer with the command:

SET PRINTER ON

If this command is given from the dBASE prompt then any information displayed on the screen will also be printed.

If single sheets of paper are being used then first type:

SET EJECT OFF

This command stops the printer 'paging' (automatically moving the print head to the top of the next page) at the end of each page.

More elaborate reports can be produced if required with the aid of the built-in REPORT facility.

REPORT   This is a command which initiates a series of questions relating to the data output and the format required. After establishing a report format a new file is created (with the file extension .RPT) This can be used at any time to produce printed output.

To print the report, include TO PRINT at the end of the REPORT command.

A7.15 Customized Data Entry Screens – Format Files

A customised screen format file can be produced for displaying fields in any desired order and position on the screen. The specified format can then be used for entering and editing records. This is particularly useful when the field names do not adequately describe the data or when not all the fields in the database are required.

In order to do this with dBASE III+ it is necessary to construct a dBASE file called a FORMAT file, with file extension .FMT. This file contains information, descriptions for the required fields, and field names. The format file can either be created directly through the MODIFY COMMAND procedure or with the aid of the ASSIST facility.

Screen locations are established by row and column numbers. dBASE III+ defines screen positions starting from the top left-hand corner (0,0). Lines are numbered from 0 to 23 and columns from 0 to 79.

The command SAY is used to position text on the screen and the command GET is used to input information from the keyboard into the record structure. Each line of a format file must start with the symbol @ followed by a space and then the screen position. For example:

@ 2,0 say "THIS IS SOME TEXT"

A7.16 dBASE III+ Programming

One of the major strengths of dBASE III+ is its built-in programming facility. This allows the user to 'automate' all the standard dBASE commands thus customising the package. People with no knowledge of the operation of a database can then use the package to perform specific functions such as costing, stock control, etc.

A full treatment of this extensive subject is beyond the scope of this book but some sample programs are included. These may be typed in from within dBASE using the MODIFY COMMAND procedure or by using an external word processor and saving the file with a .PRG extension. They may be activated from the dBASE prompt by use of the DO command:

.DO (program name)

Appendix 8
Attribute extraction and dBASE III+ programming tutorial

A8.1 Attribute Extraction

The central heating drawing shown in Figure A8.1 is constructed solely from lines and blocks. In this example the blocks have the following names :

COLDTANK
HOTTANK
RADIATOR
BOILER
PUMP
RADVALVE
PIPEVALV
ELBOW
TEE

and each of the blocks has the following five attributes :

Attribute Tag		Attribute Type
ITEM	(descriptive name of block)	Constant
COSTWHSL	(wholesale cost)	Preset
COSTRTL	(retail cost)	Preset
CODENO	(a 4-digit identification code)	Constant
LOCATION	(stores location of the item)	Variable

Selected attributes of all the blocks in the drawing may be extracted using the ATTEXT command.

A template file must first be created using a text editor or word processor.

The following template file, called MYTEMPL.TXT and saved into the current AutoCAD working directory, will enable every attribute to be extracted from the drawing.

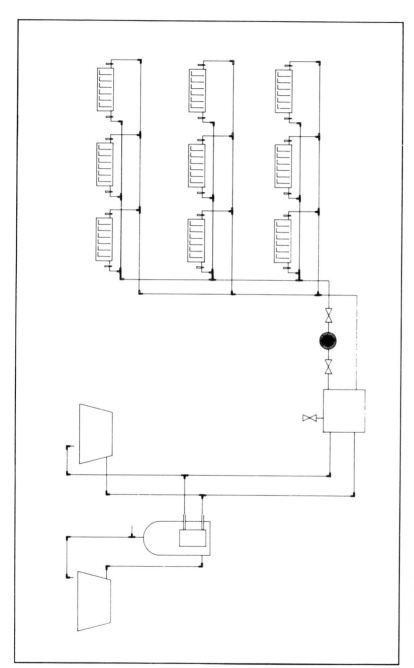

Figure A8.1 A domestic central heating system

ITEM	C012000
COSTWHSL	N010002
COSTRTL	N010002
CODENO	C006000
LOCATION	C012000

> *Note:* The attributes with tag names ITEM, CODENO and LOCATION are to be treated as Character fields in the database with field lengths of 12, 6 and 12 characters respectively. Similarly, COSTWHSL and COSTRTL will be treated as Numeric fields with a total 10 digits, including 2 decimal places.

The attribute extraction may now be performed by creating an extract file called MYEXTRAC and using SDF format. If the dBASE III+ software is resident in some other directory, called DBASE, say, then it is convenient if the extract file is written directly into this directory from AutoCAD.

Command: ATTEXT
CDF, SDF or DXF Attribute extract (or Entities)? S
Template file: MYTEMPL
Extract file name: C:\DBASE\MYEXTRAC

This will write an SDF (space delimited format) extract file called MYEXTRAC.TXT into the DBASE directory.

A fragment from a typical file would look like the following:

coldtank	15.00	20.008759	shed1
hottank	45.00	75.007699	shed2
coldtank	15.00	20.008759	shed1
boiler	150.00	225.003354	shed3
radiator	20.00	30.001020	shed1
pump	50.00	85.002298	shed1
pipevalve	8.00	10.009087	shed1
pipevalve	8.00	10.009087	shed1
radvalve	5.00	7.502341	shed1
radiator	20.00	30.001020	shed1
elbow	0.50	0.658897	shed4
tee	0.60	0.758899	shed4
elbow	0.50	0.658897	shed4
elbow	0.50	0.658897	shed4

|←——————→|←————→|←————→|←——→|←——————→|
| 12 | 10 | 10 | 6 | 12 |

> *Note:* Because Character fields are left justified and Numeric fields are right justified, fields 3 and 4 appear to be run together. This will not cause any problems as long as the database is created with a structure to match the template file.

The database may now be created within the DBASE directory. The structure should be as follows:

Structure for database: C:HEATING.DBF
Number of data records:
Date of last update:

Field	Fieldname	Type	Width	Dec
1	NAME	Character	12	
2	WHOLESALE	Numeric	10	2
3	RETAIL	Numeric	10	2
4	CODE	Character	6	
5	STORE	Character	12	
** Total **			51	

> *Note:* It is only the *structure* which must match the template file – there is no need for the field names to match the tag names of the attributes.

Transfer of data held in the extract file to the empty database may now be achieved from the dBASE prompt:

.APPEND FROM MYEXTRAC.TXT SDF

An excerpt from a typical dBASE III+ file derived from this drawing is shown below:

. list

Record#	NAME	WHOLESALE	RETAIL	CODE	LOCATION
1	coldtank	15.00	20.00	8759	shed1
2	hottank	45.00	75.00	7699	shed2
3	coldtank	15.00	20.00	8759	shed1
4	boiler	150.00	225.00	3354	shed3
5	radiator	20.00	30.00	1020	shed1
6	pump	50.00	85.00	2298	shed1
7	pipevalve	8.00	10.00	9087	shed1
8	pipevalve	8.00	10.00	9087	shed1
9	radvalve	5.00	7.50	2341	shed1
10	radiator	20.00	30.00	1020	shed1

11	elbow	0.50	0.65	8897	shed4
12	tee	0.60	0.75	8899	shed4
13	elbow	0.50	0.65	8897	shed4
14	elbow	0.50	0.65	8897	shed4

A8.2 dBASE Programs

The following suite of six programs may be typed in for use with the HEATING database just created.

A second database called STOCK giving the supposed levels of stock for the various components of the central heating system should be created separately and manually filled with nominal stock levels. The structure of the STOCK database is shown below:

```
Structure for database: C:STOCK.DBF
Number of data records:
Date of last update:
```

Field	Fieldname	Type	Width	Dec
1	NAME	Character	12	
2	NUMBER	Numeric	6	
3	REORD	Numeric	6	
4	BRITISH	Logical	1	
** Total **			26	

A8.2.1 dBASE III+ Program Listing – INVENT.PRG

This program provides the main menu for the suite and calls on the other programs – PARTS.PRG, STOCK.PRG, LIST.PRG, TOTALS.PRG and REORDER.PRG as required. The whole suite may be run by calling this program with the command .DO INVENT.

```
set safety off
set talk off
store 0 to choice
do while choice<5
    clear
    @2,5 say "Inventory System"
    @4,5 say "Make a selection from the following menu items:"
    @6,0
    TEXT
    ==================================
    1. COUNTING AND COSTING PARTS IN THE AUTOCAD
       DESIGN
```

2. UPDATE MAIN STOCK INVENTORY
3. LIST ITEMS BELOW THE REORDER LEVEL
4. TOTAL WHOLESALE & RETAIL VALUES FOR PARTS
5. EXIT THIS PROGRAM

```
     ===================================
     endtext
     input "Enter a number:" to choice
         if choice › 5
         clear
         @2,2 say "Please type a number from 1 to 5."
         @3,2
         input "Enter a number now:" to choice
     endif
     do case
         case choice = 1
         do parts
         case choice = 2
         do stock
         case choice = 3
         do reorder
         case choice = 4
         do totals
         case choice = 5
         return
     endcase choice
enddo
```

A8.2.2 dBASE III+ Program Listing – PARTS.PRG

```
use heating
set talk off
clear
text
  This demonstration dBASE III+ program is designed to be used
  with an AutoCAD design file called HEATING.DBF.
  The program evaluates the numbers and costs of items used in
  a typical central heating system layout.

endtext
wait to cont
accept "Do you wish to see the wholesale cost (y/n) "to
wcost ?
accept "Do you wish to print the results? (y/n) "to prin
store "y" to choice
```

```
store 0 to total
store 0 to total1
if prin = "y"
  set printer on
endif
do while choice = "y"
    clear
    ? "The items in the list are as follows:"
    ?
do list
    ?
    accept "Type in the name of the item "to item
    count for name = item to no
    ?
    ? "The total number of these items in the design "
    ?? " is "
    ? no
    ?? " --------- "
    ?? item
    if wcost = "y"
       sum wholesale for name = item to cost
       ?
       ? "The total wholesale cost of these items is "
       ? cost
       ?? " pounds."
       ?
       ? "The cost of a single "
       ?? item
       ?? " is"
       ? cost/no
       ?? " pounds"
       store cost + total to total
       ?
       ? "Wholesale cost to date:"
       ?? total
    endif
    if wcost = "y"
    sum retail for name = item to sale
    ?
    ? "The total retail cost of these items is "
    ? sale
    ?? " pounds."
    ?
    ? "The cost of a single "
```

```
    ?? item
    ?? " is"
    ? sale/no
    ?? " pounds"
    store sale + total1 to total1
    ?
    ? "Retail cost to date:"
    ?? total1
    endif
?
accept "Do you wish to have another count (y/n)" to choice
enddo
close all
set printer off
return
```

A8.2.3 dBASE III+ Program Listing – STOCK.PRG

```
clear
text
     Enter the name of the stock item you wish to update:
endtext
?
?"The stock items are as follows"
?
do list
?
select 1
use heating
select 2
use stock
store "y" to cont
do while cont="y"
   accept "enter the item name  " to stock
   select 1
   count for name=stock to no
   clear
   ? "The number of "
   ?? stock
   ?? "s in the AutoCAD design is "
   ?? no
   select 2
   sum number for name=stock to s2
```

```
        ?
        ?"The original number of "
        ?? stock
            ?? "s in stock is"
            ?? s2
            repl number with number-no for name=stock
            sum number for name=stock to ns
            ?
            ?"The number remaining in stock is "
            ?? ns
            sum reord for name=stock to re
            if ns‹re
                    ?
                    ? "The number of "
                    ?? stock
                    ?? "s in stock is LESS than the reorder level "
                    ?
        endif
        if ns›=re
                    ?
                    ? "The number of "
                    ?? stock
                    ?? " in stock is above the reorder level "
                    ?
        endif
        accept "Do you wish to do another stock item ? y/n " to cont
        ?
enddo
close all
return
```

A8.2.4 dBASE III+ Program Listing – LIST.PRG

```
close all
use stock
go top
do while .not. eof()
? name
skip
enddo
use heating
return
```

A8.2.5 dBASE III+ Program Listing – TOTALS.PRG

```
set exact on
select 1
use stock
select 2
use heating
select 1
store 0 to total
store 0 to total1
clear
? "NAME            WHOLESALE    RETAIL "
go top
?
do while .not. eof()
store name to n1
select 2
sum wholesale for name = n1 to cost1
sum retail for name = n1 to sale1
? n1
?? cost1
?? sale1
store cost1 + total to total
store sale1 + total1 to total1
select 1
skip
enddo
?
? "TOTALS:     "
?? total
?? total1
?
wait to cont
close all
return
```

A8.2.6 dBASE III+ Program Listing – REORDER.PRG

```
use stock
set talk off
clear
go top
? "Please REORDER the following"
```

```
?
? "NAME           NUMBER  REORDER "
?
do while .not. eof()
if reord>number
? name, number, reord
endif
skip
enddo
?
wait
set talk on
close all
return
```

The above programs have been written to provide a simple introduction to dBASE programming and may of course be improved. It is hoped that they have given some insight into what may be achieved by combining the two powerful packages, AutoCAD and dBASE III+.

Supplementary Disk

The supplementary disk described in the Preface is available at a cost of £20.00 (plus £1.50 to cover postage and packing, plus £2.00 per item for air mail) cheques should be made payable to:

Dr A. E. Hill and Dr R. D. Pilkington
c/o Department of Electronic and Electrical Engineering
University of Salford
Salford M5 4WT
UK

General Index

Index of Commands